TACHO'S STORY

Tacho's Story

Kitty Pride

paternoster
Lifestyle

Copyright © 2001 by Kitty Pride

First printed 2001 by Paternoster Lifestyle

07 06 05 04 03 02 01   7 6 5 4 3 2 1

Paternoster Lifestyle is an imprint of Paternoster Publishing,
PO Box 300, Carlisle, Cumbria CA3 0QS, UK
and Paternoster Publishing USA
Box 1047, Waynesboro, GA 30830–2047
www.paternoster-publishing.com

British Library Cataloguing in Publication Data

A catalogue record for this book is available from the British Library

ISBN 1–85078–402–7

Cover design by Campsie
Typeset by Waverley Typesetters, Galashiels
Printed in Great Britain by Omnia Books Ltd, Glasgow

Contents

Preface

When we first met our friend who is the model for Tacho, and when we heard the story of his conversion and the subsequent change in his whole family, we were awed and amazed at what God had done. We know the Chatino area well, and particularly the rural district that he came from in the mountains of south-west Mexico. We have seen and felt the fear that dominated that place. We have observed the terrible conflicts and almost despaired of ever seeing any change. What a privilege it is to be given the opportunity to see the Holy Spirit of God at work, causing radical change in people's attitudes as they are reborn and their lives renewed.

Almost all the names of people and places in this book have been changed for security reasons. Everything recorded here happened, but not everything attributed to Tacho happened to his prototype, and some other remarkable events in his life are not included. We have known the prototypes of Armando and Esteban for many years and marvel at what God has done in and through both of them. I would like to acknowledge the happy

viii   *Tacho's Story*

hours my husband and I have shared with these men and their families, and the personal encouragement that they have given us.

I also owe a great deal to the encouragement of my husband in writing this book, and to helpful comments from various fellow members of the Wycliffe Bible Translators and SIL International.

Kitty Pride

1

Home

Tacho sat grieving. Now what would happen? They had just completed the ten days' vigil after burying his mother, so his father, grandfather, uncles and older cousins were all drunk. Tacho's father was ugly drunk and looking for someone to blame for his wife's death. He searched in vain for his razor-sharp machete and his gun so that he could go out and punish the guilty person. His quick-witted, bird-like little old mother had foreseen this turn of events and hidden the weapons securely. Eventually her son stumbled out of the house bent on picking a quarrel and fist-fighting with anyone he could find who might be blameworthy. He took a last quick guzzle of mezcal and looked slowly round the yard at his friends and relatives who were mostly in the same sad state as himself. They returned his glazed stare with tentative, foolish smiles. Only the women quietly went about the work of clearing things up, cleaning borrowed pots used at the wake which now needed to be returned to their owners, and thinking ahead to the preparation of the next meal. One man was violently sick round the corner of the house, after which his pretty young wife persuaded him to come in and lie down. He wrapped a heavy arm round her slim shoulders and allowed himself to be guided indoors, where he fell onto a bed and was soon soundly asleep. Without a word Tacho's father lurched off the long porch and out through the gate, only to collapse senseless a hundred yards down the grassy street.

With his father gone, Tacho moved over to the kitchen where his grandmother gave him a bowl of coffee and assured him that a proper meal would follow shortly. Granny was making every effort to get back to the normal routine, even though everyone had been up all night with the wake.

'Your cousins Chila and Sana have gone to the village grinder with the corn so that we can make today's tortillas,' she said.

Soon the girls reappeared with large plastic bowls full of corn dough balanced on their heads. They and Tacho had been in the same class at primary school and all three had finished their fourth year there four years earlier. It was possible to do the fifth and sixth years of school in Tutula, the county town and commercial centre for the surrounding mountainous district, and so complete primary schooling and earn the coveted certificate. Tacho had longed to do this but their village of Mulaca was three hours' fast walk from the town and to get there they had to follow a precarious footpath that ran along the side of the mountain to wind its way up the valley. He had no relatives living in Tutula that he could stay with, so his father had refused: paying for lodgings would be too expensive. His mother had been confident that she would eventually find a friend in the town and so make his dream possible. But now she was gone the prospect was hopeless, thought Tacho, as he moodily sipped his coffee.

The girls set to work with their grandmother. One stirred up the fire under the clay griddle, while the other rinsed off the grinding stone and its stone rolling pin or 'hand'. Granny kneaded a little more water into a big ball of corn dough and started rhythmically to regrind it little by little with the stone rolling pin. When the fire was burning satisfactorily, Susana and Lucila, known locally as Sana and Chila, each took a good handful of the finely ground dough. They fashioned it into a flat round with the fingers of both hands, then patted it to and fro between the palms of their hands until it was about six inches in diameter. They laid this on the table on a piece of plastic the size of a dinner plate and continued to pat with the heel of one hand while turning the plastic with the other until a thin, even disc of dough was ready for the griddle. Picking up the plastic on one hand they dexterously slid the uncooked tortilla onto the outstretched other hand and then laid it on the lime-washed clay griddle. At the appropriate moment they spread a hand over the half-cooked tortilla and, starting one edge with a thumb, flipped it over in a single movement. 'A well-made tortilla should puff up in the middle with hot air,' thought Granny, watching from the corner of her eye as she continued her rhythmic grinding and the girls spread their newly patted products on the hot griddle. She gave a little nod of satisfaction as their first tortillas rose and cooked evenly. Soon these were transferred to their special cloth in the tortilla basket to keep warm. 'These girls have learned well,' she thought. 'They will not disgrace us when they marry and move in with their mothers-in-law. Their husbands will be well looked after. But at the moment they must think of their cousin Tacho.'

'Are the beans on the other fire done yet, Sana?' she asked. 'And how about the coffee pot, Chila? Is there still plenty?'

'The beans are soft now, Ma,' replied Sana.

'Good. Add the salt and those little bits of cooked pork and the crackling,' responded her grandmother.

'There's plenty of coffee and it is hot, Ma,' said Chila.

'Good, then you can make some chilli sauce – the chillies are beside you on the table with the tomatoes. Onions are hanging up in that rope bag in the corner, and there is some fresh coriander today over there in a jar on that shelf. We won't be many minutes now, Tacho.'

Soon he was settled at a corner of the table with a steaming bowl of pork-flavoured beans and a small bowl of chilli sauce in front of him. The beautifully woven cloth contained a pile of fresh, tasty tortillas and they were deliciously warm. He caught himself listening for his mother's step as she bustled into this familiar scene, and then he remembered that her calm, smiling presence and quiet efficiency would never grace that kitchen again. The food tasted good, but he had little appetite and was only eating to please his grandmother. Just as he finished two of his brothers rushed in.

'Tacho, come quick! Papa is coming to and he doesn't look angry any more.'

Granny had sent the younger boys to play in the street near where their father fell so that they could keep watch over him. Now Tacho jumped up from the table and all three dashed away together. They helped their father to get up, then guided him back to the house and put him, unresisting, to bed.

The next day the younger ones went back to school, but Tacho and his next brother Chico accompanied their father out to the cornfield. The rainy season had just begun and it was time to plant the maize seed corn that they had been preserving carefully in the smoky rafters of the kitchen house. Before breakfast they had taken those special cobs down and shucked off the grains of maize with great care into a particular, rather flat, flask-like gourd that they used at planting time. It had an oblong opening cut out of the top, just big enough for a man to put his hand in. This was for their 'small cornfield', a steep but fertile patch of mountainside not far from the edge of the village. They used fast-growing corn for this and would have a crop in less than two months. Later they would plant the main cornfield with long-lasting maize, but that took several months till harvest time.

They had cleared the land completely the previous month. The bushes and weeds had dried out quickly in the hot sun and then all the rubbish had been burnt off. Now the ground was thoroughly wet from a couple of heavy tropical rains and ready for planting. They each carried a long, specially hardened stick that had been sharpened to a point, but when they reached their mountain patch Tacho's father put his dibble stick aside under a bush, together with his machete and rope bag. He tied the cord attached to the seed-corn gourd round his waist so that the gourd hung in front like a pocket along with another seed gourd holding black beans, and then he followed Tacho and Chico. The side of the field was so steep that they climbed it as if they were going up a ladder. They could hardly ever stand up straight as they worked their way across the top of the field; one leg was always bent. Tacho and Chico went ahead, making holes with their dibble sticks, while their father followed close behind. He let five grains of corn and one bean fall into each hole, then kicked dirt over them, pressing down firmly with his heel. Here and there poles were still standing where small saplings had been trimmed off to a height of about five feet. When they came to one of these Tacho made a hole close to the pole and his father dropped in two beans but no corn kernels.

It was tedious and tiring work in the hot sun and they were glad to stop for a few minutes when they saw Sana and Chila approaching. Sana carried a rope bag with the traditional cloth in it full of freshly made tortillas, still warm, along with a little bag of salt, some toasted chillies and a piece of cheese. Chila had two small blue enamel pots, one containing sweetened coffee and the other black beans. Since they were not far from home, the pots were still hot and the men hastened to rinse off hands and faces in a nearby stream, before settling down in the shade to eat.

The girls had news. The priest had arrived, and as he passed their home he had stopped and offered his condolences on the death of Tacho's mother. He expressed sorrow that he had not been on hand for the funeral, and said he would like to speak to

Tacho's father that afternoon. The youngsters asked the older man excitedly what it could be about. But he had no idea, so they fell to animated conjecture among themselves, leaving him to eat in peace.

The men finished their meal and hastily returned to work. They wanted to complete the planting of the small field before the rain, threatened for the late afternoon, reached them. The girls collected up the pots, tortilla cloth and rope bag and made their way back home.

Granny was waiting for them with the family laundry in three large bundles. Tacho's youngest brother and sister, who were too small for school, were with her. The four-year-old had a small bucket with laundry soap in it plus a bar of hand soap, a couple of gourd dippers, a comb and a set of clean clothes for himself, while the two-year-old carried a traditional striped bag containing her clean clothes. Sana, who lived with her grandmother as she was an orphan, darted into their house to get another bucket and her own clean clothes, comb and mirror. Then she quickly picked a few ripe lemons from the tree in the yard to take with them to the river. Scrubbing the men's and boys' clothes on the rocks was hard work, but a bath in the river was always refreshing and there were usually other girls there to swap gossip. The lemons helped to bleach out any bad stains in the clothes and were very good for rinsing one's hair. There did not seem to be a spare egg available today, so she would just have to manage with the laundry soap as shampoo.

Granny spoke to Chila: 'I would like you to come too because there are a lot of dirty clothes today. Tell your mother, and ask her to keep an eye on my house and to be sure not to let the dog or the chickens into my kitchen!'

Chila dashed across the yard to her own home and quickly reappeared with more buckets, clean clothes and a small sister in tow. Her teenage sister Catalí followed with a small baby tied to her back in a *rebozo*, a traditional black shawl, and yet another bundle of laundry on her head. Then they all set off for the nearby river in a long line.

There were many convenient places for washing clothes with big, well-worn rocks dotted about and the shallow river eddying past bringing clean water all the time. There were also plenty of safe pools with sandy bottoms where the children could play. Chila and Catalí improvised a hammock for the baby by tying up the *rebozo* between two small trees in the shade. Catalí fed him and he contentedly dropped off to sleep in his hammock after being rocked for a moment, so his mother could join her grandmother and the others already in the river washing clothes. The three little ones were happily splashing about in a small rock pool. The women got the really dirty clothes thoroughly wet and well soaped, then left them in a pile to soak while they worked on the other garments. When they had rinsed them they spread these clothes out to dry on the warm rocks. Then they came back to the heavier things and 'Thwack! thwack!' resounded up and down the river as they slapped the soapy trousers on the rocks to loosen the dirt.

Catalí had bathed the baby at home earlier in warm water so she had a pile of baby things to cope with. Chila relieved the other three children of their dirty and now very wet clothes, which Sana then took to wash while Chila bathed the two little girls in their pool. The four-year-old solemnly soaped himself from head to toe and then rinsed himself off by pouring water over himself with a gourd. One of the little girls suddenly let out a shriek when she felt the soap getting into her eyes as Chila washed her hair, but she was soon happy again and the three eagerly returned naked to their water games. Finally, the women all had a bath and washed their own dirty clothes. Now it was time to dress the children in their clean clothes, comb out their wet hair, and gather up the almost dry clean clothes from the rocks. They took down the 'hammock' and loaded the baby onto his mother's back again. Although only slightly damp the clean clothes still made heavy bundles for the women to carry on their heads for the return trip.

When they got home the little ones were clamouring for a meal. The schoolchildren had arrived home and were ready for something to eat as well. Granny was glad that there were still plenty of beans in the pot and a good pile of tortillas left from breakfast to satisfy them all. The big clay pot of drinking water on its three-pronged stand provided cool drinks for everybody, so Granny and Sana were able to sit and eat with the young ones.

The clouds were really threatening now, so they hung up the clothes that were still wet on a line along the porch. This ran the whole length of the house and acted as an open-air, general-purpose family room. Suddenly there was a crash of thunder and the rain began like an enormous, gushing waterfall just as Tacho, Chico and their father dashed round the corner of the house and onto the porch.

Conversation was impossible as the rain drummed on the tile roof, but Granny set about reviving the fire and she and Sana quickly had a hot meal ready for the men.

By the time they had finished eating the rain had slackened off and Tacho's father was eager to hear more about Granny's encounter with the priest.

'He just said that he would like to see you this afternoon,' she told him. 'Your clean clothes are all ready for you in there on the bed.'

'Where are the soap and the gourd and the comb? I'll just go and have a quick dip first,' he said.

Sana handed them to him, and picking up their clean clothes the men in their turn, set off for the river, the rain having now stopped. Chila was sitting in a hammock strung up on the porch of her family's house on the other side of the yard, braiding her little sister's hair. Then she applied scented oil to her own waist-length black hair and quickly plaited it into a single, neat, shiny braid. Granny and Sana appeared on their own porch to perform the same operation for themselves and Tacho's little sister Rita. They were all dressed in full skirts, brightly coloured and adorned with lace or contrasting ribbon and topped with beautifully embroidered blouses in the traditional highland Chatino style.

From the river Tacho's father went directly to the priest's house beside the village church. After commiserating with him concerning the death of his wife, the priest said: 'Your oldest boy Tacho never did finish primary school, did he?'

'No, Padre. We have no relative in Tutula for him to stay with while he completes the last two years.'

'How about if I took him to Oaxaca City?' suggested the priest.* 'He could stay in the orphaned boys' home that we have there and go to the local school. If he does well and wants to continue to study he could then go on to the secondary school. Who knows? He might feel a calling to train as a priest later and continue on in our prepa. school† to get ready for the seminary.'

'Would he ever come back, Padre?' asked Tacho's father in surprise.

'Oh yes. There are the usual school holidays, and he can travel with me.'

'Well, I'll talk to my mother and the boy about it and let you know, Padre.'

'Good, but you must decide by tomorrow evening as I need to leave again the day after that. It would be best if the boy went with me then, so that he can get used to everything in the city before the next school year starts.'

Tacho's father walked home slowly, trying to think what was best for the family.

'Chico is already helping me with the field work and doesn't seem interested in further schooling,' he thought. 'We could probably manage with the younger ones helping out a bit in the holidays. If Tacho really wants to try this, perhaps we should let him go for the two years to finish primary at least. Perhaps his thirst for knowledge will be slaked by then and he will come back and follow our traditions. But I still owe that storekeeper some days

---

* Oaxaca: pronounced 'wa-*ha*-ka'.

† Three years of pre-university schooling.

of work to pay for all the mezcal that he supplied for my wife's funeral. I wonder how I am going to fit it all in with my own work? He is bound to want me just when my own fields need attention!'

It was dark when he reached home and everyone gathered round, eager to hear about the interview. It was not every day that the priest asked to see someone like that. Tacho became really excited when he heard the news. He could hardly believe his ears that perhaps he was to have this opportunity to continue at school. He eagerly responded when his father asked him: yes, he certainly wanted to go. Then he sat quietly listening as the discussion went on and on, knowing that his father and grandmother would make the final decision.

Next morning Tacho and Chico were sent off with the family donkey to get firewood while their father and grandmother brought other family members into the discussion.

'Tomorrow you will go to Oaxaca with the priest,' Tacho was told when he came back with the load of wood. 'You might as well get ready now.'

2

The county town

Next morning Tacho was up with his grandmother long before dawn. He rushed off to the river for a bath and dressed in his best clothes. When he got back, coffee was ready with some of the local sweet bread rolls that he always enjoyed. On the other side of their yard Catalí's mother had an adobe mud-brick oven, shaped like a beehive, and often made a batch of the sweet bread rolls. Chila would take a large, flat basket of them on her head to sell door to door to all the neighbours.

Granny and Sana were busy making tortillas again. First they produced some tostadas which they made in the same way but cooked more slowly so that they dried out like crisp-bread. Then they made another variation with mashed beans mixed into the maize dough. Every home kept tostadas on hand for emergencies, especially for long journeys, as they last for many months. Still, Granny wanted Tacho to have fresh ones to take with him: he might want a little snack along the way and who knew when he would get his next square meal?

Just as dawn was breaking Sana made a tasty dish of eggs, tomatoes, onions and chillies for Tacho and

his father. The bean pot was bubbling as usual, and
they ate an ample breakfast.

'Come on, it's time to go now,' said Tacho's father
as he finished eating.

Sana followed the men outside with a gourd of
water. She handed them a bar of soap and poured
water over their hands so that they could wash after
their meal. Then Granny handed Tacho a flour
sack with his other two sets of respectable clothes
inside. All were lovingly laundered and folded.
Earlier he himself had put in his one or two
cherished possessions. So, with his rope bag of
tostadas, a little bag of salt and a plastic cup, he
was ready for the road.

Outside the priest's small house at the side of the
church stood a man with a mule already saddled.
Several local church officers were there in attendance and the priest was on the porch bidding them
farewell. He looked up with a smile as Tacho and
his father approached, and then moved over to
mount the waiting animal. Tacho's father was
going to walk with them to Tutula, so he assured
the mule's owner that he would bring the animal
back later in the day. Then they set off.

They kept up a brisk pace as the mule carrying
the priest was fresh and Tacho and his father were
quite used to tramping the mountain trails. The
priest was lost in his own thoughts, but Tacho was
busy looking round one last time at all the well-
known foliage of his home environment and listening to the familiar sounds of the trail. Meanwhile,
his father was wondering yet again if this really was
the best and wisest course for his son. 'He won't get
another opportunity like this to continue at school,

and that seems to be what he wants most,' he comforted himself.

The three-hour hike passed swiftly in spite of the
many climbs, drops and curves as they worked their
way up the valley. It was mid-morning when they
splashed across the ford in the little river and
entered the hilly town of Tutula. Tacho had seldom
visited the town, so he was all eyes and ears as they
climbed the steep track to the church in the central
square. They made their way to the priest's house
round behind it. Tacho stopped in his tracks when
he saw the jeep that stood parked there.

'So this is a "carro"!' he exclaimed in amazement.
'But how does it work? How do you get inside?
Didn't they say that people ride inside?'

Then he realised that no one was listening or
ready to answer his questions: the priest had dis-
mounted and was moving towards the house
while his father was taking charge of the mule in
preparation for leaving again.

'I'm going home now, Tacho. You just let me
know how things are going when you can, and we
all look forward to seeing you and hearing all about
life in the city when you come home. The Padre said
that you could come with him during the school
holidays, so that won't be till Christmas, I suppose.
Just learn all you can.'

Then he was gone and Tacho turned to find
Tutula's resident priest had come out to welcome
them. Tacho's benefactor had some business here,
so they would stay the night and start their long
drive to the state capital the following day. Just then
the housekeeper appeared to announce that a meal
was ready for the priests. She showed Tacho where

he could leave his things, then served him dinner in the kitchen. He did not say much to the kindly woman as he was only too aware of his very elementary, school Spanish. It suddenly dawned on him that he would not see anyone else who spoke his own language for many months. Who would be his friends? How could he share his thoughts and feelings when his knowledge of Spanish was so inadequate? How would it all turn out?

His presence did not seem to be required so, after the meal, he set out to explore the town. He saw a reassuring number of his own people in the square. As he caught snatches of conversation, he could hear from their varying accents that they came from several different towns and villages in the surrounding mountains. Apparently all had special errands in the county town and took no notice of the lone teenager as he stared about him. Then he heard a loud hammering, and remembered a previous visit with his father to buy a new machete. He followed the sound and soon came to the forge where three men were working. One had tongs to hold the red-hot metal on an iron post, while the other two alternately hit it with heavy metal mallets. They worked very fast and with practised precision. Tacho watched in awe. Surely one of them would miss his swing in a minute? Or one would hit the hot metal awkwardly and knock it from the block? But no, the rapid clanging continued rhythmically, accurate every time. However, the metal cooled quickly and had to be reheated in the forge. Tacho was fascinated as the bellows were blown to raise the fire to tremendous heat, then the red-hot blade was pulled from the fire to be tempered again. It became the shape of a Tutula machete before Tacho's wondering gaze. He really admired these metal workers, but was not at all sure that he would enjoy such work himself, even though they must get a great amount of satisfaction from seeing the good machetes and knives that they produced.

He drifted over to a big workbench where there was a dazzling display of new machetes and knives of various sizes and shapes. There were even some with fancy engraving on the blades saying such things as 'Souvenir from Tutula'. They were decorated with leaves, flowers and other little twirls and squiggles. Then he noticed yet another man sitting on a stool in the corner carving and polishing horn handles to be fixed onto the new blades.

'Don't touch them now, lad, unless you want to buy one,' he cautioned Tacho. The boy was startled to realise that he was being watched as he admired the gleaming assortment of marvellous blades. He hastily stepped away from the display bench saying: 'Oh no, I was just admiring them.'

He was too embarrassed to watch any longer or ask questions, so he wandered on along the narrow, muddy street. He found himself passing a big shop. He was afraid to stop this time in case someone thought that he wanted to steal something, but as he slowly sauntered past he could not keep from staring goggle-eyed at the variety of goods for sale. There were enamel pots and pans and other kitchen utensils hanging from the rafters, along with varying thicknesses of wire, bunches of garlic and several different sizes of candles. Shelves from floor to ceiling were stuffed with all kinds of things that must be strange foods in packages, bags,

tins, boxes and bottles, along with medicines for
both people and animals. Sacks of beans, rice, maize
corn, sugar, coffee beans and flour, plus troughs of
onions and dried chillies, were on the floor, while
bottles of sweets, chewing gum, biscuits and pastas
stood on the counter. There were crates of beer and
bottled soft drinks too, while tiny glasses of potent
mezcal were being served from large bottles.
Other expensive, fancy bottles of strong drink
were on another shelf with various brands of
cigarettes and matches. Over to one side were
bolts of cloth, needles and different kinds of sewing
and embroidery thread, country sandals, a few
boxes of shoes and some ready-made clothes in
various sizes. Ball-pens, pencils, notebooks and
other school supplies were available, not to mention
special paper and ribbon for wrapping gifts. In spite
of his resolve, he stopped to stare; it was all so
fascinating and bewildering.

'Is there anything else in the whole world that
people might need or want?' Tacho wondered.
Many of the things he saw he did not yet recognise
and he shook his head in confusion at the idea that
anyone would know what to do with them all.

Across the street he caught sight of another open
workshop and soon draped himself round a corner
post to watch a carpenter and his assistant absorbed
in their craft. They were making the most beautifully
decorated table Tacho had ever seen. Then he spied
another workman in a corner carving out a wooden
pack-saddle. He watched excitedly. Perhaps this
was where his father had bought their own pack-
saddle for the donkey? He had come home with
it one day the year before, soon after buying the

donkey. That animal had certainly transformed the job of getting firewood, because it had been really hard work when they had to go out every single day and carry the load home on their backs. He and Chico would go out together, both riding the donkey like rich people, then chop and chop with their machetes till they had enough to make a good load for both sides of the donkey's pack-saddle and a small load for each of them to carry on their backs as well. This much firewood had lasted their mother two or three days so that neither she, their grandmother nor Sana needed to go wooding at all, unlike neighbouring families where the women were the main fuel-collectors. He remembered that in some families the mothers and older children spent most of their spare time wooding, but his mother and grandmother had time to visit friends and family, while Sana had time to do the beautiful embroidery that she enjoyed and still had time to spend with her own friends.

Goodness, however much time had passed? Had they missed him at the priest's house? Perhaps there was something he was expected to do there? He must return straight away because he did not want to give a bad impression to the priests. He was genuinely grateful for this chance to go on with his education and to live in the state capital. His imagination failed him as he tried to picture what a city would be like. Tutula itself seemed enormous to him, so full of houses, shops and workshops of every description with people everywhere.

He scuttled into the town square and then stopped, listening. There was a terrific noise coming nearer and nearer with much banging and clattering. Suddenly he blinked and backed up against a wall as a metal room moving along on wheels came snorting into the square. It was the daily bus from Oaxaca City, filled with people, and there were piles of baggage tied onto a big rack on the roof. As he watched, the bus stopped and its roar ceased. People poured out of its door and the first man nimbly climbed a ladder at the back and started to untie the ropes holding the cargo. Another young man climbed up to help and started throwing down the boxes, bags and bundles to the waiting owners.

'So people really *do* travel inside these metal vehicles,' Tacho thought. 'But what a terrible noise they make going along!'

Would the priest's jeep be as noisy as that? His head was full of unanswered questions as he ran back towards the priest's house.

3

Oaxaca, the state capital

By dawn next morning the jeep was loaded and ready to go. A friend of the priest was driving, and they were also taking a man who had been ill for several months to see a doctor. There was another young passenger, a boy a bit younger than Tacho, but he did not know if this was the sick man's son or perhaps another youngster who had been given the chance to go to school in Oaxaca like himself. Tacho was too unsure of his command of Spanish to venture any questions. This experience was all so new! Tacho had carefully copied the others as he got into the jeep, took a seat and found a place for his belongings. Now he settled down to enjoy the ride. He had not been on this road before and there were so many new things to see as they trundled smartly out of Tutula and on up the valley. Finally, it closed in to become a steep ravine and he saw that they had to ford the river in order to gain a steeply climbing shelf of rock, gouged out of the mountainside, that looked like the continuation of the road. He marvelled as his gaze followed signs of the shelf snaking higher and higher up the

precipitous mountain through a tough series of
hairpin bends.

The jeep easily churned through the water and
then the climb began. Tacho did not know that
they were climbing up to a pass over the southern
extension of the Sierra Madre del Pacifico mountains
or that they would cross two other mountain ranges
as they made their way inland to the state capital.
He had no idea that his home village of Mulaca, the
town of Tutula and various other communities were
all in this one fertile, wedge-shaped valley in the
Sierra Madre range. A long day's trudge in the
other direction over the mountain and down several
thousand feet would bring one to the vast Pacific
Ocean, but Tacho had never seen the sea either.

They climbed on and on, up through the forest of
huge ocote pines with little patches of scrub oak in
clearings interspersed here and there. There were
other trees that he did not recognise as they got up
higher than he had ever climbed before. Occasionally he caught glimpses of Tutula getting smaller
and smaller. Then they were through the pass and
the valley was gone as they wended their way along
the other side of the ridge, a little below the summit.
Soon they left the big trees behind and everything
seemed much drier and dustier. The mountains
were rockier, not like the verdant valley Tacho was
used to. At last they came to the junction with the
main road from the coast, and here they met another
amazing sight, a compound with several enormous
yellow road-building machines in it. Passing the
compound they started to go down. The main road
was a little wider, the hairpin bends not quite so
tight, but it was the same kind of shelf cut out of the

mountainside, only even more rocky and bumpy. There were just as many blind corners to be approached cautiously. Suddenly the big river came into view at the bottom of the mountain as the steep valley opened out, and the view was lush and green again across the valley. The priest said that this was the same river that ran through Oaxaca City and that it must have been raining hard in the central valleys because the river was very full of muddy, red-brown water.

It had been cold up among the pine trees but now it got hotter as they descended to the River Atoyac. The heat was like home, Tacho thought, and a welcome change after chilly Tutula and that cold mountain pass, but the rivers were quite different. The familiar one at home was just a stream compared to this turgid, greasy-looking mass of liquid mud with the long concrete bridge spanning it. They stopped for a drink at the little town by the bridge and Tacho nibbled some of his tostadas. He shyly offered some to his travelling companions too.

Then they were crossing the bridge and climbing again. They approached a narrow ravine past great casurina trees with their striking, lemon-yellow flowers. The trees stood right in the water of the tributary to the big river which tumbled down the ravine and then spread out on the flat valley bottom into a broad, shallow stretch with signs of flooding. The little houses here, the appearance of the people and the vegetation were all very different from Mulaca, but as they started up the ravine the clear little river looked almost familiar to Tacho. Finally, they topped another majestic mountain and started down again in the welcome shade of

the pine forest. In the valley below they caught sight
of the town of Sola.

'We will stop there for something to eat,' the
priest assured them.

They rounded the next bend and the driver
braked sharply. Ahead, an enormous machine filled
the road. The boys craned their necks to see this
wonder. There was a great blade in the front and it
was scraping off the road surface. They waited till
the machine pulled off to the side and shovelled its
load of dirt and rock over the edge, then they moved
forward onto a much smoother stretch of road. A
bit further down they came upon a bulldozer still
clearing off the remnants of a landslide that earlier
must have blocked the road completely. Tacho
stared open-mouthed as it pushed great piles of rich,
red earth over the edge of the precipice. So that was
how the road had been built! But he still wondered
how they could break up and move such mighty
rocks. Each of those machines must be stronger than
many mules, he thought admiringly.

They were all more than ready to eat when they
reached Sola. The sick man was stoically holding
out for the journey, but they had to bring his plate
out to him in the jeep as he could not manage the
walk into the restaurant. They had been on the road
for more than seven hours now.

As they left Sola a relatively smooth, blackish
ribbon of road stretched out before them. The two
boys gripped their seats as the jeep picked up
speed, and they stared in wonder at the white line
down the middle of the road. Tacho noticed that
they always kept to the right of this, so there was
plenty of room to pass when another vehicle came

towards them, but he still cringed as they whipped round corners. Cattle, goats and donkeys all seemed to wander freely about the mountainside with their young herdsmen close by. Tacho kept expecting one to stray onto the road in the path of the speeding jeep, but they seemed to have learnt some road safety somewhere along the line. They certainly appeared to have less fear of the traffic than he did, he thought ruefully.

Finally the jeep came down into a wide valley where the fields were almost flat. Tacho was fascinated to see men in the fields of young corn plants using oxen to plough out the weeds between the rows. He had heard about men working with oxen like this, but had never seen them or such an expanse of flat, gently rolling land. It was reassuring to have the mountains still in sight on both sides.

Then he noticed a vehicle moving along in a cornfield. It had enormous wheels and a man perched up on a seat on top, and it was dragging some contraption behind it. The priest followed his puzzled gaze. 'That's a tractor, Tacho. In these flat fields it can do the work of many men or several oxen much faster, because it pulls different kinds of machines behind it to plant or weed or harvest. Still, it could never manage the steep mountainside fields your people farm at home.'

Tacho wondered how he could ever adequately describe all this to his family. All these new experiences and impressions were coming thick and fast and this was still only his first day away.

They passed through a town not unlike Tutula, except that there were no hills. The villages seemed to be getting closer together now too. Later the road became continuously lined with houses and shops, and there was much more traffic. Everywhere was brick and concrete and plaster, with big placards and signs. They kept crossing other roads that he was told were streets, while buses and people seemed to be going in every direction. There were a lot of churches too and shops of every kind, as well as houses on top of houses.

They turned into a quieter street and then stopped at a big gate in a wall near a church. A man peeped out with a cheerful greeting for the priest and his friend, then quickly opened the gate so that they could drive into a large courtyard where a couple of other vehicles were standing.

The sick man was transferred to one of the other vehicles and told that someone would take him to the doctor at the hospital right away. Tacho and the other boy were ushered through a big door into the towering three-storey building at the back of the courtyard. Tacho marvelled as he saw that it was divided up inside into lots of rooms off corridors, with stairs winding up to more rooms and corridors above.

They came to a small room with another priest seated behind a desk. Their benefactor explained that he had brought two more boys from the Tutula area for the orphanage.

'This is Anastasio from Mulaca whose mother died recently,' he said as he pushed Tacho forward. 'And this is Pedro from the little community of San Antonio close by. His father was shot last month in a drunken brawl. Both of them like school, but they have not been able to go beyond year four at home, so I brought them to you.'

Tacho did not understand all of the conversation, but he looked at the other boy with new interest. So this Pedro came from San Antonio; perhaps he also spoke Chatino at home then? It would be good to have a friend to share with who understood all the problems posed by this new life in the city that they were starting together.

Soon the two boys were saying goodbye to Padre Juan who had brought them. He assured them that they would see him now and then as he would be staying in the house for the priests on the other side of the courtyard whenever he had cause to be in the city, which was quite often. If they wanted to send any messages home, he would take them with him next time he visited the Tutula area, and they could go and talk to him whenever he was there if they had any problems. Meantime, they should try to settle down to their new life at the orphanage, be obedient to those in charge, and do some study to be ready for school in September.

An older boy was called to show them round and take them to their dormitory to stow away their belongings in the lockers that were assigned to them.

'A bell will ring for supper in half an hour,' he told them as he left. 'You can find your way back to the dining room, can't you?'

They nodded, and he left them on their own.

'Do you really come from San Antonio near Mulaca?' asked Tacho immediately. 'Are you a Chatino person too?'

'Yes, I speak Chatino,' Pedro replied, 'but we won't be allowed to speak our own language much here. Still, perhaps we can help each other when we don't understand the Spanish very well.'

'Yes, it will be good to have someone who under-stands!' said Tacho. 'What with being older than the others in our class, and coming from the country so that we don't know the ways of the city, we have lots to learn – and all in the city language.'

He felt a great wave of relief sweep over him as they chattered on, comparing notes, until they heard the bell ring for supper.

4

In debt

Tacho's father sat on the porch of his house moodily contemplating the downpour. Why had he allowed himself to be persuaded last night?, he wondered. Now he was paying for it with a hangover, and who knew how much he owed that storekeeper now! He had gone to the store to find out what his bill was, but had met a relative there drinking mezcal with his friends. They insisted that he join them and he remembered little else. He knew that all his drinks, plus any that he might have offered to the others, would have been added to his account with the storekeeper. It had already been more than he liked to think about with that big expense from his wife's funeral. Now school was about to start again and he had to get uniforms for his two school-age children. He would have to do that on account too! However many days' work would it all amount to? Well, he had better go and find out the worst, he thought morosely. In any case, he had already lost today for work.

This time he did not go into the shop but round to the private residence at the back. He was received cordially, but was horrified to be told that now his

debt amounted to three months' work, and not
only for himself but for his son Chico as well. The
rich store-owner had a couple of ranches out in
the country with a lot of cattle roaming about
freely, and also a vast coffee plantation on an
excellent mountainside site.

'What would really be a help to me,' said the rich
man, 'would be for you and your family to move
out to my coffee plantation and look after it for me.
There is a house out there that you could use, and
to make it easier for you, I could pay you half-days
and stretch out the repayment of your debt over six
months or so. How does that sound?'

'Well, I have two children at school, so I would
rather live here in Mulaca,' replied Tacho's father
cautiously. 'Also, there are my own cornfields and
crops to see to.'

'Ah yes, Demetrio, but you know that if we take
this debt business to the Town Hall, the authorities
will give you into my charge completely anyway.
They will say that you should have thought of your
private plans before getting into debt. You have
your choice: you can either agree to my plan or we
take the matter up with the town authorities and
your disgrace becomes public knowledge. That way
would cost you more in the end, you know.'

Tacho's father knew that he was outmanoeuvred
and said wearily: 'When did you want us to move
out to the coffee plantation?'

'Well, I think everything is under control until
after the sixteenth of September fiesta, so your
children should be settled in school by then and you
could move out about the eighteenth. See me again
just before the fiesta.'

Tacho's father went home sadly to report all this to his mother. At least their small cornfield would soon be harvested and the weeding of their main crop would be done. They would have a few beans too, and he could worry about the other harvesting later. Another long family conference ensued. At dusk his two brothers arrived home from their work and Granny called them over to hear all about it. Both were very sympathetic, knowing how easily they could have fallen into the same trap themselves.

Chila's father volunteered: 'I think we could manage to look after your two children while they are at school here during the week. But let's call our wives over too,' he said to his younger brother.

So the women joined the conference along with Catalí and her young husband, Tito. It was agreed that Tacho's father, Demetrio, and his mother would move out to the coffee plantation, taking Sana, Chico and the two little ones, and leaving their houses closed up. Chila's parents would look after Demetrio's two school-age children, Nino and his sister Beni, during the week and then Chico would come to meet them on Friday afternoons after school to take them out to the coffee plantation for the weekends. Demetrio's two brothers and Tito would look after his main cornfield as well as their own, which were nearby, and they would keep a watch for the marauding animals that could otherwise do so much damage. Then they would help with the harvesting too, if necessary, when the time came. They would keep part of the proceeds of the cornfield as their pay and to feed the schoolchildren.

Granny said that she would take her chickens and turkeys with her. They would need to take the donkey too to help carry their belongings and the two little ones, as it was a three-hour walk from Mulaca to the coffee plantation. Granny and Sana would also need the beast to get their firewood.

Demetrio was a little comforted by the way his family had rallied round him in his dilemma. From that day on he and Chico worked from dawn till dusk in the fields. They still had a few cartridges for the gun, so they took it with them to hunt wild meat along the way, and they also set snares. Occasionally their dog would scare out a deer, an armadillo or a coati, or they might get a squirrel. All were welcome additions to the family larder. There were wild pigeons sometimes too.

They arrived home early on the day that they got a deer. Granny's eyes lit up at the sight and she called out to her daughters-in-law across the yard: 'Demetrio has shot a deer. Put extra maize corn on to boil tonight. Tomorrow we will make venison tamales.'

Chico and his father were busily engaged in skinning the deer, pegging out the skin to dry, then butchering the meat according to Granny's instructions. Some of it was cut into long, thin strips, salted and hung up to dry, some set aside for the tamales, and some was given to Sana to make a tasty stew for supper. She was also getting the chilli peppers ready to prepare the sauce for the tamale-making tomorrow.

Before it was light the next morning Chico was sent off to the banana patch to cut a supply of the big, broad leaves, while the younger women took

the boiled maize to the village grinder. It was run
by the only motor in the village and owned by the
rich storekeeper. It was certainly a tremendous help
to all the women who had previously had to grind
their corn entirely by hand, so they always tried to
have a few coppers on hand to pay for the grinding
every day. Sometimes this meant selling two or three
eggs first to have the necessary funds, but today they
had the money and went straight to the grinder.
They could hear its motor from a little distance away
and soon they could make out other village women,
each with a plastic bucket or large bowl of maize
corn which had been boiled with lime to soften
it then rinsed and drained. They were all hurrying
towards the house with the grinder and calling out
cheerful greetings to their friends as they joined the
queue that had already formed there.

'Hallo, Sana. Hallo, Chila. Hallo, Catalí. You've
brought a lot of corn for grinding today!'

'Yes, we are going to make tamales.'

'Oh, what kind? Will you have any for sale?'

'Perhaps. Tacho's father shot a deer.'

'Please come to our house first if you have some
to sell. Venison tamales are the kind we like best
and your grandmother's recipe is so tasty!'

'Have you heard any news of Tacho? He's in
Oaxaca, isn't he?' inquired another girl.

'Yes, when the priest came the other day he
brought us a letter. Tacho seems to be settling down
all right. There's a boy from San Antonio there too,
so he doesn't feel quite so lonely. I wish we could
just talk to him though. It took us a long time to
work out from the Spanish what he wanted to tell
us,' sighed Sana.

'That's the trouble with letters,' they sympathised. 'They always have to be written in Spanish. Still, it is good that Tacho can read and write, now that he is so far away. It's good that he does write to you and that some of you can read his letters, even if you don't understand them very well. Perhaps he will speak only Spanish when he comes home after being in that school and with Spanish-speakers all the time.'

'Oh dear, I hope not!' responded Sana. 'Our granny doesn't understand Spanish at all and she would be so disappointed.'

Their cooked maize went through the grinder and the girls hurried home with the big bowls of corn dough balanced on their heads. A small supply of tortillas was quickly prepared. Granny had already cut up the venison into little cubes and set it to boil with salt and herbs. The men had left for work with a supply of bean tostadas for midday as they looked forward eagerly to eating venison tamales with the family that evening.

The banana leaves were prepared, then a thin layer of flavoured maize dough was smeared onto a leaf and a spoonful of the venison stew was added, along with some chilli sauce. The banana leaf was carefully folded to form a little packet with the *tamal* (or pasty) inside. These pasties were stacked up inside an enormous clay pot until it was full. A little water was added – just enough to cover the bottom of the pot – then more banana leaves were tucked in to keep in the steam while the big pot was left over an open fire for several hours.

When Tacho's father returned in the late afternoon he sniffed appreciatively.

'Those venison tamales smell good, mother. Chico, you had better take a plateful round to the storekeeper as a present to show that we haven't forgotten that we owe him money. Then we can all enjoy them. Did my brothers' wives help too? Have they had their share? Good, I'm glad it was a fair-sized deer so it made plenty.'

'Do we have to wait for Chico to come back, papa? We've been waiting all day to eat tamales and I'm hungry!' said Neyo, the four-year-old.

His father laughed as he drew up a chair to the table and Granny put down a large gourd full of steaming hot pasties in the middle. They were still in their banana-leaf cases, so everyone unfolded the leaf on the table and no plates were needed. There was plenty of hot coffee too, and Tacho's father forgot his problems for a few minutes as he looked round at his family all happily enjoying this special treat which he had provided for them.

Suddenly he realised that his schoolboy son, Nino, was animatedly describing the school programme and parade for Independence Day, the sixteenth of September. 'Papa, Beni and I have to have our uniforms for the fiesta parade or we can't be in it. It's less than a week away now. Will you be able to get them soon?'

'Don't worry, son. I'll go and see about it tonight,' replied his father. But his enjoyment of the meal was gone as reality crowded in. He would have to see the storekeeper and arrange more credit to buy the uniforms, and he would also find out exactly when they must move to the plantation. What a good thing that his brothers and their families were being so helpful! And how he would ever manage without his old mother he just did not know.

He washed his hands and hastily changed out of his dirty, old working clothes. Then he made his way to the house of the store-owner.

'Ah, Demetrio. I hope you have everything organised for your move out to my plantation. I really need you there now to make sure that all is clean and clear under the coffee bushes ready for the harvest. You need to pick the few berries that ripen early too – there are some on most bushes. The coffee pickers' shacks need to be looked over as well. Could you go out on the eighteenth?'

'Yes, we will be ready, sir. Just one thing. My two children need their school uniforms for the fiesta parade. Can I have them on credit?'

'Oh yes. Come into the shop with me now. That will only add a few days' work to your bill. Nothing to worry about. Here they are – cream shirts, with maroon trousers for the boys and skirts for the girls. There are two kinds but I don't suppose you want the best quality as it costs more. What sizes are the children?'

'The boy is ten years old and my daughter is seven.'

'These two sets should be about right then. Hmmm, that adds another eight full days of work that you owe me then. Anything else?'

'No, not now. Thank you for letting me have these, sir.'

'Yes, I think we understand each other now. I'll see you next week, the night before you go out, Demetrio, as I will probably have a few things that I want you to take with you and some last-minute instructions.'

'Right. I'll come round then. Good night, sir.'

'And Demetrio, watch out at this fiesta that you don't get into any more trouble.'

Tacho's father left and was very glad that he had not met any old friends who would have insisted that he stay and drink with them. He went home quickly. Nino and Beni were delighted to see their new uniforms and tried them on at once. Then the uniforms were surrendered to Granny for safe keeping till the day of the fiesta.

Chico tried not to think that he would have been in the parade too if he were still at school. He had never been chosen to be in the colour party in the procession, proudly carrying Mexico's flag, but then his father could never have afforded the specially grand uniform required for a member of the colour party, so that was just wishful thinking anyway! Still, he had once taken part in the special programme outside the Town Hall after the procession through the streets. What did it matter, anyway? It was really good to be a man now and to work with his father in the fields all day. He was learning all kinds of things about farming, hunting, plants and animals – useful things for life, not like the things in the school-books that were only for children to answer test questions in Spanish! He was glad that Nino and Beni had their uniforms now. They would represent the family very creditably, he knew. Perhaps they would learn to understand Spanish better than he had.

Then he found himself wondering, as he had many times, how Tacho was getting on in Oaxaca.

What was his school uniform like? How did he like that school and what was he learning there? Was it really worth leaving home and everything that was familiar? How would they be celebrating the Fiesta of the Sixteenth in the city? Would Tacho really come home at Christmas so that he could answer all these questions? And what would he think about the family having had to move out to Señor Tomás' coffee plantation? Would Tacho be willing to come out there too and rough it in the country with the family, or would he feel too grand and citified to live like that after all these months away? Chico just did not know.

5

Christmas

Tacho and Pedro could hardly believe that they had two weeks' holiday from school. Tomorrow Padre Juan would collect them in the jeep so that they could travel back to Tutula for ten days. It seemed ages since the two boys had left home and they had received very little news of their families, so each of them had all kinds of questions in his mind as he thought about the visit.

They had been amazed to see all the Christmas street-decorations in the city. The shops were decorated too and carols were being played over the loudspeakers. In the central square outside the government building there was an almost life-size model of the nativity scene covering about half an acre. There were model sheep and shepherds in one corner and wise men wending their way towards the stable from another corner. All sorts of other animals and people were scattered about. 'And tonight is this radish festival,' thought Tacho. The boys had permission to be out until 11.00 p.m., so they were determined to find out all they could about these famous radishes and to see everything that was going on. They had had so many exciting new experiences; there was so much to tell everyone at home!

They marvelled at the coloured lights strung over the streets and the variety and ingenuity of the displays in the shop windows. Everywhere was lit up tonight. They came back to the central square and went to look at the floodlit nativity scene from all round. Then they heard a band, and a procession of small carts entered the square. Each one came from a suburb of Oaxaca or a village nearby and was decorated entirely with radishes. They were fashioned into wonderful traditional scenes, some biblical and some based on local traditions, with all the people, animals, trees, flowers and buildings made from radishes. The boys were fascinated. They heard someone say that people had all kinds of ingenious methods to make their radishes grow to enormous sizes or grow into the desired shape ready for the competition every year. Pedro noticed a first-prize certificate on one cart which had a splendid Pancho Villa and his army on it, all made of radishes, of course. He gleefully pointed it out to Tacho. Second prize went to a particularly attractive nativity scene, and third to a scene showing a fiesta with traditional Zapotec dancers.

They ambled round the square examining everything, and suddenly both became aware of a crashing sound as of breaking crockery. There it was again! They burrowed their way through the crowd to find out what was going on. They came upon a row of market stalls with charcoal stoves on fire-tables where great cauldrons of oil were kept bubbling. Men were working there. One at a time they were pulling off small handfuls of an elastic kind of dough which they rolled and pulled over a shiny metal ball till each handful stretched out into a circular sheet about a foot or more across. This thin dough-sheet went sizzling into the boiling oil and gave off a delicious smell as it bubbled and crackled. Then it was pulled out, all crisp and brown, and balanced on a traditional Oaxaca plate that looked like a glazed clay bowl. A gooey brown sugar sauce was poured on top. They were called *bunuelos*. A queue of people was waiting to be served and, to the boys' amazement, when someone finished eating his bunuelo he lifted his arm and sent his bowl crashing into the street! The place was littered with pottery shards which crunched underfoot. Tacho's and Pedro's curiosity overcame their timidity and when they spied some other boys watching, they went over to ask them what it all meant.

'Oh, this happens every year at Christmas and the New Year,' the other boys told them airily. 'Everyone is supposed to eat a bunuelo, then make a wish as they smash their plates. If the plate doesn't smash, they don't get their wish. These vendors buy up all the seconds and rejects from the pottery specially for serving bunuelos. They get them very cheaply, and also their defects make sure that the customers are satisfied! Because the plates all break when they get thrown down, the customers are sure they will get their wish for the New Year!'

At that moment Tacho looked up and saw the cathedral clock.

'We'll have to run to get back to the dormitory on time, Pedro! Come on!' he exclaimed and hurried away.

It was hard to hurry without bumping into people in such a big crowd and with so much to look at, but they did not want to cause anyone's displeasure on this last night before their holiday. They arrived at the door panting and were greeted with a welcoming smile from the porter there.

'Good lads. I'm glad you remembered the time,' he said.

Padre Juan arrived with the jeep at the crack of dawn the next morning, but both boys were already waiting with their small bundles. After their short night they were tired by the time they came through the pass into the Tutula valley about mid-afternoon, but both perked up as the familiar fertile abundance of green opened up before them and the jeep plunged down the steep incline towards home. As they neared the outskirts of the county town, the boys respectfully begged to get out of the jeep and continue their journey straight away without accompanying the priest to the centre of the town.

Padre Juan said: 'You know you are both welcome to stay the night at our house and go on to your homes tomorrow. You still have a long walk ahead of you and you both must be very tired.'

'Thank you, but we would rather go on now and surprise our families,' the boys pleaded. 'We can rest at home tomorrow, Padre.'

'All right then, if your minds are made up. I will be visiting both San Antonio and Mulaca during this Christmas season while I am here, so we can make arrangements for the return trip when I see you. Take care on the trail. It's good that you can go most of the way together. God bless you both.'

'Thank you, Padre,' they chorused, and turned towards home as the jeep drove on into the town.

They made their way down a steep trail to the old airfield that was still used sometimes, especially for medical emergencies, then further down to the ford over the familiar little river and up the steep slope on the other side.

'I would love to stop for a bath,' sighed Tacho, 'but we will be hard put to reach home in daylight without that, so we mustn't stop this time.'

As they gained the top of the slope they could see the trail running on round a great fold of the mountainside.

'Look, Tacho,' said Pedro, 'there are some other travellers ahead. Let's see if we can catch them up – we might know them!'

They quickened their pace and soon caught up with a family on their way home to San Antonio. They turned out to be Pedro's neighbours. In fact, this man's brother was one of Pedro's godfathers, so it was a happy reunion. Tacho felt a bit left out as they plied Pedro with questions about the city, the school, the priests and all their 'foreign' experiences, but he knew the same would happen to him if they met someone from Mulaca.

Dusk was descending as they came to the division in the trail. Pedro and his companions took the right-hand fork while Tacho went to the left. This last part of the journey was over very familiar territory and it was no worry to him that it would be dark in a few minutes. He dawdled a bit when he heard the sound of someone approaching from a side trail which took off straight up the mountainside and was obviously the way to someone's cornfield. To his delight, one of his father's brothers appeared with a load of dried cobs of corn on his back and a donkey in tow also laden with corn.

'Hullo, uncle, it's me,' said Tacho.

'Why Tacho! Where did you spring from? I certainly didn't expect to meet you.'

'We have a fortnight's holiday for Christmas and the New Year, uncle. Padre Juan was coming out to Tutula, so he gave me a lift in his jeep.'

Then the questions came thick and fast and in no time they had arrived at the family compound. Tacho stopped short as they went in.

'But where is my grandmother? Where are Sana and the others? Isn't my father here?' he asked in bewilderment as he saw the familiar houses tightly closed up and locked.

Then Nino and Beni erupted from Chila's house: they had heard their brother's voice. The rest of Chila's family was close behind them.

'Tacho, Tacho, how did you get here? We're going home tomorrow and you must come too,' they said, both speaking at once in their excitement.

'But what's happened? Isn't this home? What's happened to our grandmother?' Tacho asked again.

'Oh, we all live out on the coffee plantation now,' his brother responded. 'We had to go there so that papa can work off his debt to the store-owner. He and Chico work for him full-time now so we all live at the coffee plantation. Beni and I are just here with Chila's family during the week to go to school, but we broke up for Christmas this afternoon. Chico wasn't there to meet us so I expect he will come tomorrow. What a surprise he will have to see you as well! It's the Noche Buena tomorrow, you know, so perhaps Señor Tomás will give papa permission to come back here to our own place for the fiesta. Wouldn't that be marvellous?'

Tacho turned a troubled face to his uncle and asked: 'Is all this true? Is my father really so badly in debt to this rich man?'

'I'm afraid so, Tacho, but I think he will let them all come back to the village here for the fiesta.'

'My godfather, Rolando, is appointed as the fiesta host this year,' broke in Nino with an important air, 'so our father, and our grandmother and Sana should all go to his house to help. I hope Señor Tomás allows them to come so that they can fulfil their obligations. It's the tradition.'

'Tacho, come on in and have something to eat and we'll soon see what happens tomorrow,' called Chila's mother.

It was good to have a hot meal in familiar surroundings with welcoming relatives, but this was not the homecoming Tacho had imagined. His uncle explained the situation to him and he was horrified at his father's predicament.

'You had better stay out of sight, Tacho,' said his uncle seriously, 'or that rich man might demand that you join your father and Chico to help work off this debt – then no more school for you.'

'But has anyone checked up on the figures to see if papa really owes so much?' Tacho demanded.

'Rich people don't let anyone look at their accounts, Tacho. They just tell you the amounts. So few people here really understand books and suchlike, or can argue in Spanish, so we have to take their word for it.'

Tacho was confused. He desperately wanted to
help his father, but would it be more help to stay
and work with him or to do well in the city and so
give the family more prestige? Then he would be
able to stand up to these rich Spanish-speakers who
liked to run things their own way. Well, tomorrow
he would see his father and they could talk it all
over, he thought wearily. So he stretched out on a
palm-leaf mat and snuggled into his blanket beside
his younger brother. It was good to be back home,
but he had got rather used to his dormitory bed: he
found the earth floor a bit hard, and all these family
problems were quite a shock.

Next morning he was ready to dash off to the
river with his brother for a bath. There was still no
sign of their brother Chico when they got back, so
after breakfast Chila's mother suggested that they
go for a load of firewood for Rolando, Nino's godfather, since it was their obligation to help him with
his fiesta responsibilities. When they returned they
were delighted to see the family donkey in the yard,
the little children on the porch and Sana hard at
work sweeping out the kitchen under Granny's
direction. Their father came into the yard with a big
bundle of grass for the donkey and was loud in his
praise when he heard that the boys had already
taken a load of firewood to his compadre, Rolando.

'Tacho,' he said, 'we are all very pleased that you
have come back to us for this holiday. We will talk
more later though, because after dinner we must all
go over to Rolando's to see what needs to be done.
But I agree with your uncle,' he added. 'You must
keep pretty much out of sight so as not to come to
the attention of my boss, Tomás. We don't want him

arranging our family affairs any more than he has already, if we can help it.'

On their arrival at Rolando's house they were welcomed heartily.

'Ah, compadre Demetrio,' exclaimed Rolando. 'So you are back with us for the fiesta. How is life out there on the coffee plantation? Do you see anything of the bandits that people say are hiding out in the countryside? And your son, Tacho, is back with us again. That's good. Come in, come in. There is plenty to be done and we can chat later. I have to go over to the church now because Padre Juan is due to arrive any time. Very early this morning I sent my son to escort him here, and I sent a mule for him to ride, so they should arrive very soon now and I must be on hand to welcome the Padre.'

The women went round to the kitchen to help Rolando's wife with the festive supper. They would need lots of food as the entire village was invited. A bullock was being barbecued in a big pit and mountains of tortillas were being prepared, along with large pots of black beans each bubbling on its own fire. There were bowls of spicy, hot chilli sauce being made and great cauldrons of hot chocolate and ready-sweetened coffee. Large bamboo baskets full of sweet bread rolls stood along one wall, and a constant stream of men was coming in with boxes and buckets filled with earthenware bowls borrowed from neighbours and relatives in which to serve the food to everyone.

In the main house tables and benches started arriving from nearby houses. Demetrio, Tacho and Chico doused the earth floor with water to settle the dust and gave it a thorough sweeping with wide palm leaf brooms. Then they did the same for the porch outside and under the big shelter of palm fronds that had been erected in the patio. Other men arrived with bamboo poles and greenery from the countryside and started constructing a special arbour leading onto the porch. An altar table was placed there and beautifully decorated with a nativity scene complete with shepherds and wise men, but the manger was empty. The tables were arranged in rows under the palm shelter along with the benches and any available chairs.

Friends and relatives arrived with helpful dona- tions of maize corn, salt, beans, chilli peppers, crates of beer and soft drinks, bottles of potent mezcal and a home-made brew called *tepache*, together with cigarettes and firewood. Many people helped to lighten the burden for the fiesta's host. Rolando's family carefully noted all the gifts so that they, in their turn, could help the givers when they found themselves responsible for a fiesta later on. This co- operative system bound all the families in the village together with mutual obligations, and it gave Tacho a warm feeling to be part of it all again.

The church bell began to clang to say that the priest had arrived. All those who wanted to go to the preliminary service at the village church made their way to the kitchen for a quick snack, then set off for the centre of the village. Tacho, Nino and their father stayed behind to help with the final details of the preparations.

'Now remember, Tacho, just stay inside here in the corner where you won't be noticed, and if the storekeeper does come, you can skip round the back of the kitchen. The women need someone to fetch

more water and bring in more firewood anyway,'
said Demetrio.

'All right, papa. I'll be careful, because I really
want to go back to school, even though I am angry
with that Tomás for the way he is treating you. You
are almost his slave – and Chico too!'

'Steady on, son,' cautioned Demetrio. 'I do owe
him a lot of money after all. Listen, that's the village
band. Here they come!'

Lighted torches of pitch pine flickered in the
darkness as the Christmas procession made its way
towards them. Rolando arrived just ahead of the
crowd and was there in the arbour to greet them all.
Paraffin lamps with glass chimneys had been lit and
set on the tables, but the torches gave much more
light as the sacristan boys from the church carried
forward the images of St Joseph and St Mary.

A church official then formally asked Rolando:
'Is there room for Joseph and Mary to stay here?
She is going to have a baby.'

'Yes, come in, come in. They can stay in this
stable,' replied Rolando, leading the way into the
main room of the house which was clean and empty
except for a table ready to receive the statues of the
holy couple. The village band set themselves up on
the porch, but as many other people as could do so
squeezed into the main room and knelt on the earth
floor as Padre Juan conducted a short service.

Then Rolando led the priest to the head of the
tables in the patio and all the men followed. A small
pile of sweet rolls and a bowl of hot chocolate had
been laid out at each place. There were palm mats
and extra benches round the edges to accommodate
the overflow: there would be a second sitting at the

tables, and probably a third, until everyone was
served. The women and children sat down on the
mats to wait and watch, while Rolando's brothers
and Demetrio started circulating the bottles of
mezcal and the cigarettes to the men on the extra
benches. Each man took a swig and then passed
on the bottle. He took a cigarette and lit up to
wait in comfort. The women from the kitchen were
hovering, and cleared the chocolate bowls as soon
as they were empty, as they needed to wash them
up ready for the next sitting. Each man at the table
picked up any rolls at his place that he had not
finished and stashed them away in his striped bag
as was the custom. Rolando's wife brought a basket
covered with a beautifully embroidered cloth for the
priest to put away his share.

Meanwhile, a procession of women was bringing
steaming bowls of barbecued beef for each person
at the table. Down the centre of the tables they
placed piles of fresh tortillas wrapped in special
cloths to keep them warm, along with bowls of chilli
sauce, containers of salt and big bowls of black
beans. Everyone was served a bottle of beer or a
glass of pop spiked with mezcal. As they were
finishing, Rolando's wife brought the priest another
bowl of beans, more tortillas in a special, clean cloth
and a little blue enamel pot containing more of the
barbecued beef. She packed all this in the basket
with his extra rolls and a little jug of chocolate for
him to take with him. Then all the men stood up,
said, 'Thank you for the food,' and received the
traditional reply: 'No, thank God.' Then they moved
away from the tables. The women swiftly put the
tables to rights and Rolando moved round the

benches inviting another group of men and boys to take their places. The band had been playing during the first sitting but now the musicians were invited to the table to eat too.

Tacho sidled into the kitchen and caught his grandmother's eye. She sat him down on a little stool in a corner and served him there. Chico had taken his place at the table with their father, and his younger brother and sister were running wild in the brilliant moonlight outside along with their excited school-friends. Tacho thought of his friend Pedro and wondered if he was at a similar celebration in San Antonio. Suddenly Tacho became aware of Rolando saying goodbye to Padre Juan. It seemed that the priest and a couple of the church officials were going over to San Antonio now to be part of the Christmas fiesta there as well. They would return tomorrow.

The band was playing again and some of the women and children were having their supper as Tacho wandered outside to see if any of his old friends were about. Men were sitting or standing round the edges of the patio and continued to pass round the bottles of mezcal and tepache. Some of them were getting quite loud and boisterous with so much to drink. Tacho saw his young brother Chico being handed a bottle to take a little swig. No doubt it gave the boy a real sense of satisfaction to be accepted among the men, but did these fiestas always have to end with strong men helplessly drunk just because of tradition?, Tacho wondered. Was that really all there was to having a good time? Was that really what custom demanded?

A bit later the sound of cane pipes and small drums was heard approaching and another little torchlit procession arrived. It was all small boys dressed in very old-fashioned clothes, each carrying a small load and a walking stick. They were organised by a church official and came right up to the arbour where the church cantor stepped forward to greet them.

'Look, the Baby is born,' he said, and sure enough there was now a baby doll in the manger. It was midnight.

'We have brought gifts for the Baby,' the boys chorused.

They unloaded their packs in a pile in front of the altar table, then all knelt there on the ground. Everyone had gathered round by this time.

'It's a miracle – the Baby is born!' they were saying to each other.

Then the cantor led them in reciting the rosary together as they knelt before the altar in the arbour. Many of the men were too merry to join in and continued to drink and smoke under the palm shelter in the background, but no one seemed to consider their behaviour a disturbance.

After this the women brought out coffee and sweet rolls for anyone who wanted more food. Rolando's wife also brought out a great bowl of pieces of sugar cane, peanuts, bananas and oranges for the children. She just set it down on a mat for them to help themselves, which they did with gusto.

All of a sudden loud, angry voices were heard from a group of men that had been drinking heavily. Rolando and some of the others rushed over to try to calm them down, but one very belligerent drunk upended a bottle of beer over Demetrio's head and slapped his face. Tacho's father had been drinking as well and this indignity made him furious. He ran to the side of the patio, grabbed a machete hanging there and charged at his tormentor. The big drunk was looking round for a weapon of his own and with an empty beer bottle in each hand stood his ground. Everyone was shouting and trying to hold back the two assailants, while the women scurried about worriedly shooing the little children out of range. The big man managed to crash a beer bottle down and it broke on the handle of Demetrio's machete. In a fury of superhuman strength Demetrio threw off the men holding his arm and chopped at his opponent. He sliced off the man's ear and the blade continued on and sank into his shoulder. As the blood spurted out, all the fight left Tacho's father and he staggered to a bench and put his head in his hands.

The wounded man collapsed in a faint and was carried to Rolando's bedroom. Tacho's grand-mother slipped out and found some herbs to use for a poultice which they applied to the bleeding shoulder. It helped to stop the bleeding and they left the man to sleep it off. The party broke up as village officials took Demetrio in hand and he went with them, unresisting. He soon found himself locked up in the village jail. Tacho and Chico were shocked and horrified at the turn of events. They had seen their father helplessly drunk plenty of times, but never fighting mad like this. Whatever would happen next? He would certainly be fined. Would they send him to jail in Tutula to come before the county judge? Who was going to pay for all this?

Granny called to them sharply to come on home.
She already had Nino and Beni in tow. Sana was
trying to cope with the little ones, but both were
fast asleep so she needed help to carry them. The
sad little group wearily trudged home to bed. It was
Christmas Day.

6

Out of jail – but not free

Tacho awoke in the morning to find his grandmother and Sana hard at work in the kitchen as usual, in spite of the short night's sleep.

'Chico will have to take your father's breakfast to him,' said Granny, busily bustling round. 'We can't have Sana going over there to the jail with those policemen on guard, and you must keep out of the way even more now, Tacho.'

Chico came in just then. He was not feeling too good after the drinks he had been given the night before, and he wanted a cup of coffee.

'No, your father needs it more than you do!' said Granny impatiently. 'Take this over to the jail and see what you can find out.'

She thrust into his hands a rope bag containing his father's breakfast, along with a little enamel pot of hot coffee.

'I expect our local officials are waiting to consult Padre Juan about it all, because he knows what happens in these affairs in the outside world. I do hope they don't need to send your father to Tutula, because we are supposed to return to the coffee plantation tomorrow and start on the main coffee-

picking. The berries are really ripe and ready now
and Señor Tomás made arrangements for a lot of
people to arrive tomorrow to start picking, so your
father must be there to supervise. The señor will be
very angry if things don't work out as he planned.
He is a Spanish-speaker and he will never understand our customs or our way of looking at things.'

Chico found his father in a very sorry state. There
were two other men in the jail as well: they had been
arrested for being drunk and disorderly at the fiesta
the night before. One had been sick in the night, so
their cell was a mess. It had an earth floor and the
door was a heavy wooden lattice open to the
elements. With no blankets, they had not been very
comfortable and all three were suffering from
hangovers. Demetrio put his hand through the bars
to grab the hot coffee first.

'I don't think anything will happen till the priest
gets back, so go home and have your own breakfast,
Chico,' said his father. 'You could go past Señor
Tomás' shop though and see if you can find out
whether he already knows that I am in here. He will
probably have something to say about it too!'

Chico went reluctantly and, sure enough, the
storekeeper knew all about the matter.

'Hello Chico,' he said. 'So your father is in jail
now. I hear that big lout Lino has lost a lot of blood,
but he'll live. Since he started the fight and there are
plenty of witnesses, I think I can persuade the
officials not to take the case to the county court. I
have a plane coming for my first load of coffee-beans
tomorrow, so we can fly Lino out to Oaxaca to the
doctor. I will see about your father's fine too, so tell
him not to worry: I want him back out there

overseeing the work on my coffee plantation. I'll let him know what the bill is later because both he and you will certainly owe me a lot more days' work with all this expense. Those other two in jail also work for me, so you can tell all three that I will have them out of there by this afternoon.'

Chico rushed home to get some breakfast and report to his grandmother first.

'Yes, such foolishness always has to be paid for, and the poorer you are, the more there is to pay,' she commented bitterly. Then she called Sana. 'Let's go to the river and wash the clothes so that we are ready to go back to the coffee plantation tomorrow. Tacho, you take the donkey with Nino and get some firewood, then you both can have a bath too, but don't go through the centre of the village. Come on Beni, you can give me a hand with the little ones. They need a bath too.'

Chico returned to the jail with clean clothes for his father. Their grandmother would never allow her son to appear before the village council in soiled clothes, even though he was not allowed out for a bath. Chico noticed activity at the priest's house as he passed and a mule tethered outside, so he knew that Padre Juan had returned. Some of the town officials were sitting on his porch waiting to speak to him. Chico guessed that they wanted to talk about the prisoners. The rest of the town council were gathered in their big office next to the jail. Chico told his father all that he had learned and then stayed at the door waiting for further developments. He noticed a familiar figure casually making his way towards the village office to speak to the officials. Everyone he met greeted him respectfully and he

stopped to speak kindly to several people on the
way.

'Here comes Señor Tomás to speak to the officials
now, papa,' Chico alerted his father. 'He doesn't
seem in any hurry though.'

'No, he wouldn't be,' his father replied. 'He
knows that it will all work out as he has planned for
his own benefit. Part of me is glad that he has
enough influence to arrange things and get me out
of here, and part of me despairs of ever becoming
an independent man again!'

'But papa, we only have to work for him long
enough to clear your debt and then we can work in
our own fields again.'

'We are not clever enough to get out of the
clutches of a rich man, son,' responded his father
sadly. 'We will never finish paying back that debt
now. I'm glad your brother is away at school so that
he can learn all about money and learn enough
Spanish to be the equal of these scheming plantation
owners. They think they own everything, including
the land – that's why they fence it in – but no one
can really own the land. It is there for us all to use,
except that Spanish-speakers don't seem to understand that either.'

The officials returned from the priest's house,
conferred with Señor Tomás, then sent the police
guards to get Demetrio and bring him in to their
office.

'This kind of conduct must stop, Demetrio,' said
the mayor seriously. 'Señor Tomás has kindly taken
responsibility for you as you are his overseer, so get
back to his plantation and get to work. He is also
seeing about Lino's wound, so you can sort out

everything with him and we wash our hands of you. Since the fine is paid, you are free to go.'

Demetrio stumbled out and followed Tomás to his house.

'Yes well, Demetrio, you really do get yourself into some tight situations. Still, I don't mind helping a bit. I hear your son Tacho is at home again, is that right? Well, he can help with the coffee-picking too while he is here. It's too bad that the priest is taking him back to Oaxaca shortly or his work could help to shorten your indemnity. Still, the few days he is here will help a little. Of course, he will earn less than you as he is still an inexperienced lad. So you will all leave here first thing in the morning because the other workers that I have under contract will arrive out there tomorrow afternoon. I'll send a mule train out with you to collect the remaining sacks of coffee that you picked earlier. It did all get hulled and dried before you came back for the fiesta, didn't it?'

'Yes, Señor. The sacks are all ready for the mule train.'

'Good, because my plane will be flying the early coffee out to market during the next few days, so it needs to be here at the airstrip ready and in good condition. That's all then. I'll see you just before dawn when you come for the mules.'

Demetrio was afraid to ask how many months of work he was in arrears – or was it years now? He merely turned away and trudged home. At least the priest had made it plain that Tacho was to return to Oaxaca, so Tomás could not keep him back. It was the only bright spot in a very dreary prospect for his family's future, he thought. He cheered himself

with the thought that perhaps it would be possible
for his son to become a priest like Padre Juan,
and then he would be a match for such rich people
as Tomás. Then their family could regain their
dignity.

Tacho was glad to go with them next morning.
He was especially glad to have the chance to work
with his father in the country again and to feel that
he was helping the family get rid of this crushing
load of debt. His father had taught him many things
out in the fields and, even though his life was so
different now, he did not want to forget all that. He
wanted his father to know that he was glad to be
Demetrio's son, a Chatino from Mulaca. He told his
father and Chico about his friend Pedro from San
Antonio, and how good it was to have someone
from the same background to talk things over with
in their own language. As Demetrio had never spent
time away from Mulaca, he found it very hard to
understand this need.

'But you should always speak Spanish together,
Tacho,' he said. 'You want to learn all the Spanish
that you can so that they can't accuse you of being a
dim-witted Indian from the country who knows
nothing!'

'Don't worry, papa, we are learning fast, but
sometimes we are so tired from all the schoolwork
and trying to think only in Spanish and in the
Spanish-speakers' way that our heads really hurt.
Then we just go off together for a bit and chat in
our own language. That seems to relax us so that
we can continue with it all again. It's pretty hard to
stick it out there sometimes with all the misunderstandings!'

'Just keep it up, son,' encouraged his father. 'I so much want you to do better than I have here. I want you to become someone of importance, an independent man in charge of his own destiny. Perhaps you can become a priest and be really influential. Then I could die happy, even if I am still in debt to this rich man!'

'I'll try, papa. Perhaps I can get a job in the city during the next holidays and send you the money, although I wouldn't be able to come out to visit you then. That might be more help to you really.'

'Yes. It would give you a little money of your own also, because I can't give you anything to take back with you, Tacho. You realise that everything that we need here we have to get from Tomás' shop and he adds it to our bill. We never see any actual money any more because he just subtracts work done from that bill. Your work too will just go into his book: he won't pay you anything and it will always be the same when you come back here. He will expect you to work for him whenever you come home, never in our own fields, but he won't pay you any actual money.'

The days passed rapidly and the afternoon of 6 January found Tacho, Nino and Beni following a mule train loaded with coffee back to Mulaca. It was another fiesta day for many in Mexico, a day for giving presents to the children to commemorate the visit of the wise men to the infant Jesus, but for Demetrio's children it meant only the end of the holidays. School started again in Mulaca the next day for Nino and Beni, while Tacho was to meet Padre Juan and Pedro in Tutula to travel back to Oaxaca. He had decided to leave Mulaca at about

3.00 a.m. so that he would arrive in Tutula by dawn, then there would be no need to stay the night at the priest's house as he had done before.

Tacho and Pedro had lots of news to exchange when they met again by the priest's jeep, but they felt a little inhibited with Padre Juan for company. They contented themselves with a little stilted conversation in Spanish that included the priest.

It was a long and weary day of travelling and everyone was glad when they drove into the city just before dark. Padre Juan deposited the boys at the orphanage gate, saying that he would see them again soon, and they made their way inside to find supper and bed.

7

The city

Tacho discovered that he was welcome to stay at the orphanage during the holidays and the priest in charge encouraged him in his plan to find a holiday job. When the Easter break came Pedro returned to Tutula with Padre Juan, but Tacho ran errands for a butcher in the main market during the day. For this he only received a little pocket money and a somewhat sketchy midday meal, but these were his first earnings and it felt good to have money in his pocket that he had earned for himself.

Pedro returned to find a much more assured, streetwise Tacho. But he was still eager to hear all that Pedro had to tell him about the Tutula valley.

'You will be coming home in the summer, won't you, Tacho?' asked Pedro.

'Yes, but just for a few days at the end of the summer, I think. The butcher said I could work for him again and he would give me a regular job cutting meat, so I think I will work for several weeks first and then go back home for the last few days before we start school again. I can always go to Tutula on the bus if Padre Juan isn't going again just then, now that I am earning a little. It will be hard facing yet another year at the primary school, but I really want the certificate for finishing satisfactorily. I feel so conspicuous being older than the others in our class, don't you? Missing those four years after finishing only the fourth year in Mulaca was quite a disadvantage, but I'm determined to make it up and go on to secondary.'

'Yes, me too,' responded Pedro, 'although I don't like the taunts from those little city kids either.'

'Well, anyway,' Tacho went on, 'it's not so hard to understand what the teachers say now, and I think our spoken Spanish has improved no end. It is good to have these last years of primary here in the city, in spite of everything.'

There were lots of festive occasions during this term at school, what with Children's Day, Mothers' Day, Teachers' Day and May Day. These were followed rapidly by the fiesta of 5 May with its parade to commemorate the Battle of Puebla, when the French were finally defeated in Mexico in the middle of the nineteenth century. These fiestas all culminated in a special programme on the last day of the school year when those leaving received their certificates. Everyone in the class had family and perhaps other visitors attending, except Tacho and Pedro.

The following year sped past in much the same fashion. Tacho and Pedro were getting good marks now as their Spanish really improved and they fully understood what they were being taught. They had become much more assured and articulate in class and asked many intelligent questions which their teachers welcomed. Tacho continued to work for the butcher in his spare time and had become quite a favourite with the butcher's family.

'I think we will both be awarded our certificates without question,' Tacho said to Pedro with satisfaction one day after Easter. 'I'm going to ask my employer, the butcher, to be my godfather for the closing ceremony at school because he is being very kind to me now. Who will you ask, Pedro?'

'Oh, I think I'll just ask Padre Juan,' Pedro replied rather off-handedly. 'I don't know anyone else to stand up for me, unless I ask one of our teachers.'

'It certainly will be good to get into secondary school and start learning some useful skills as well as all this academic stuff!' said Tacho.

The final day of the school year dawned at last and it was a warm, satisfying feeling for Tacho and Pedro to have their own visitors for the first time. They were proud to have their new godfathers on hand to support them in all the excitement of this important occasion and they took every opportunity to present them to their teachers. At last each of their names was called and they walked forward to the platform to receive their certificates. Then they were congratulated publicly by their godfathers and received gaily wrapped presents from them to mark the occasion.

Later they bought special plastic covers to store away their precious certificates and then Pedro was gone with Padre Juan again and Tacho was working in the market at the butcher's stall full-time. The summer weeks sped by. One day Tacho met Padre Juan in the market.

'I'll be going out to Tutula for about a week later this month if you want to go as well, Tacho. You haven't seen much of your family this past year. How about coming with me? That's when I will be bringing Pedro back for the next school year too.'

'Yes, Padre, I would like to go then. Thank you.'

'I'll see you by the gate next Friday at dawn then,' and the Padre was gone.

Tacho decided to buy exercise books and pencils for his little brother and sister who were at school and a big bag of marbles for everyone. He knew Chico loved to play marbles with his friends, and even their father would join in a game with them sometimes. The younger boys delighted to copy their elders, although their 'marbles' were usually the red seeds of wild plants. One or two little plastic dishes would make the little girls' eyes light up, he was sure. He was careful to keep most of his earnings hidden away for use at the secondary school next year. The orphanage priests would pay for his uniform and school-books, but he knew there would be things that he would need which he would not like to ask the priest in charge for. He also knew that his father could give him nothing, but he would be able to reassure his father that he had his own funds now.

Tacho enjoyed his visit home. He went directly out to the coffee plantation from Tutula and hoped that Señor Tomás would not find out that he had come. The family was very pleased to see him and Granny immediately set about making his favourite food for him.

Young Neyo looked a bit puzzled after a day or too and finally said: 'Tacho, why do you keep using foreign words that we don't understand? Don't you speak like us in Oaxaca?'

'No, little brother. Nobody speaks our language in Oaxaca, so I only know the Spanish names of all the new things that I have seen there. I'm sorry, but I can only tell you about them with Spanish words.'

'Will you forget our language then, if you are learning all these new things?' Neyo was becoming distressed. 'Please don't forget, because I won't be able to talk to you if you speak only Spanish!'

'Neyo, listen, and you too Rita. Even if I don't speak our language all the time I am studying in Oaxaca, and even if I can't come home to visit you very often, I will never forget my family here.'

'Oh good, I'll remember that you told me that,' responded the little boy. 'I will learn some Spanish too because I am starting school next week.'

With a quick smile Neyo rushed off to join in a game of marbles with his brothers, and Granny called Rita into the kitchen.

Tacho and Pedro quickly got into the secondary school routine. The discipline was stricter here and it was an all-male private school where all their teachers were priests. There was considerably more homework and more emphasis on sport. The two boys enjoyed the athletics, the drilling and particularly the football field. They each had other friends now and no longer spent all their spare time together. Tacho was glad that he had that little bit of money of his own when his new friends introduced him to smoking, gambling at cards and spiking the bottled soft drinks with whisky, rum or tequila. The butcher was glad of his help during the Christmas holidays and on any other free days, so that topped up his funds again.

During the following summer he found he was using up his money almost as soon as he earned it, so he decided to write a loving letter to his family and send it out with Padre Juan in August. He explained that he could not manage to come himself this year with his job and everything. He felt slightly embarrassed that he had no surplus money to send to his father to help pay off his old debt though. He understood peer pressure a bit better now and could sympathise more with his father's predicament and how easy it was to fall into such a situation. Now he considered it almost inevitable in view of the village customs. At least he himself was independent and had not added to his father's burden, he thought with satisfaction. He had lots of friends too and they didn't even notice any more that he was a countrified clodhopper; but drinking, smoking and gambling cost money and he would have to keep on a part-time job during school term next year to come out even. He had enjoyed sports at school this past year, but now he would need to work during the games practices because he wanted extra money to be even more independent. The butcher was glad to hear that Tacho wanted to work extra hours and was happy to employ him: the butcher's wife was more tied at home with the growing family and rarely accompanied him in the market nowadays.

8

Riot in Mulaca

One day as Tacho was working after school he
saw a newsboy selling the evening paper. 'Riot
in Mulaca!' he was shouting. 'Uprising in Tutula
county! Read all about it. Plantation owner hounded
out of his home. Riot in Mulaca!'

Could his home village be in the news? What did
the fellow mean by 'riot'? He must buy a newspaper,
Tacho thought, and rushed after the vendor. He
was shocked to see a picture of Mulaca on the front
page and there were the remains of Tomás' big
house and shop. It had been burnt down and not by
accident, the report said. It went on to say that a
great crowd of villagers had surrounded the house
at night. Then the family and retainers had been
roused out of their beds at gunpoint, ordered to
dress and leave the house. The shop was looted and
a barrel of paraffin was emptied over everything
that was left so that it burned to a cinder, in spite of
the downpour on the previous afternoon. The
gunmen stood guard so that no one would take pity
and help the rich family. The members of the family
were told they could spend the rest of the night in
the village office and they would be given enough

of their horses to carry them to Tutula in the morning. They must never try to return.

'All our debts are cancelled now, so don't try to collect anything when you get to Oaxaca City,' Tomás had been told. 'All your lands and animals have been confiscated because you didn't keep the laws and customs of this place. You wanted to make us all your slaves and give nothing back to the town. You fenced in our town land and registered it as your own in the county archives, but this is communal land and cannot be used to discharge debts. So we are claiming it back.'

The next morning Tomás and his family had left with just what they stood up in. As soon as they reached Tutula, Tomás had reported to the county offices there and registered his accusation against the autonomous village of Mulaca, and a detachment of soldiers had been sent from Tutula to sort things out.

Tacho was horrified and rushed to show the report to his friendly employer.

'I don't know if this has affected my family!' Tacho gasped. 'I don't know if they will be counted as enemies of the village because my father worked for Tomás, or whether my father became so angry at Señor Tomás' treatment that he joined those rebels. What shall I do? Would you mind if I took a little time off to go round to the priests' house and see if they have heard anything more?'

The butcher gladly gave permission and Tacho dashed off, bumping into people on the crowded city pavements in his anxiety and impatience to learn more of this terrible event. Suddenly a voice of authority called out: 'Slow down boy. You'll cause an accident!'

Tacho realised that he had become conspicuous, so he slowed down a bit and tried to curb his impatience, even though frantic thoughts of all the awful possibilities still churned round in his mind. He knew that everyone would have been very afraid when the soldiers arrived in Mulaca. He knew too that the village loyalties would be divided. Some would be standing out against the injustices that so many had suffered and would back the rioters, whether they themselves had taken an active part in the riot or not. They would feel that Tomás' family had deserved this summary treatment and that any interference from outside lacked local understanding and was not to be tolerated. Others would reason that Tomás was part of the establishment and therefore knew the outside authorities and something about the law: they would be afraid that he would cause the whole village to suffer. It would be better to be known as his friends, even if the land did rightfully belong to Mulaca for the use of all its inhabitants.

Tacho arrived out of breath at the priests' house and gasped out to the gatekeeper that he needed to see Padre Juan urgently.

'You can't today, young man, because he is out in Tutula and no one knows when he will get back with all this trouble out there.'

'But that's what I want to see him about! The trouble is in my home village.'

'Well, come in anyway and speak to Padre Pablo, his superior. He might have some news. Through that door across the courtyard and his office is the second door on the right.'

Tacho had never met Padre Pablo before, but the urgency of his distress overcame his timidity and he went straight up to the office door and knocked as he had learnt to do in the city, although resentment surged up inside him. At home we would just call out and get an answer, he thought sullenly. Why are all the customs different here in the city? Why are all the doors closed anyway?

A kindly voice called: 'Come in.'

Tacho entered a small, plain office to find the priest at his desk. He greeted the boy with a smile: 'Hallo, young man. What can I do for you? Have we met before? You look a bit worried.'

'Good evening, Padre. Yes I am very worried. Do you know any more about this riot in Mulaca that is reported in the paper? I am Anastasio Ruíz, one of the boys that Padre Juan brought from there for further education and I am concerned about my family. You see my father works for this Señor Tomás and I don't know which side he finds himself on now in all this trouble, but I do know the way feuds work out there.'

'Yes, I understand your concern, Anastasio. We wonder about the safety of Padre Juan too.'

Tacho's head jerked up in shock. He burst out: 'But everyone knows and likes Padre Juan – he has helped so many people! No one there would hurt him. This trouble is just an internal village affair and doesn't affect anyone else-where. For many years people have resented Señor Tomás and his manipulations! It's just that so many were in debt to him that they always had to agree to whatever conditions he laid down for them.'

Padre Pablo looked puzzled at this outburst.

'Surely this Señor Tomás was a kindly man, Anastasio. He paid the fines for many of your fellow villagers so that they would not be sent to the county jail. It is only fair that they should work for him to pay back the money. They were fined because they were at fault in the first place.'

'Yes, Padre. They were at fault and it does seem like kindness that he helped them. But he sold the drink to them at extra high prices in the first place and encouraged them to get it on credit. Most of my people speak very little Spanish and cannot read or write, so Señor Tomás just keeps records of all the goods they get from his store on credit, all the fines and any money that they may need to borrow. Then he deducts a little from the bill for any work done. They never see any actual wages, nor know what they might have earned and they don't know the actual balance of debits and credits or have any other evidence for them. They are caught in a trap forever with no hope of escape, no hope of ever repaying those debts!'

'I can see that life is very difficult for them, but violence and destruction solves nothing,' said Padre Pablo thoughtfully. 'I'm sure Padre Juan will use his influence to help sort things out and clear up any misunderstandings. We shall get news from him as soon as possible, so try to be patient and carry on at school. He will know of your concern, so don't try to go out to Mulaca now in the middle of all this. You know, what you are learning here in the city is preparation for you yourself to be a bridge of help and understanding between your village and everyone outside it. So just stick to it and learn all that you can. You may come and inquire for news from Padre Juan as often as you like.'

Tacho left in despair, wondering if non-Chatino speakers would ever understand his people's thinking. He was still full of questions and fears but felt a bit calmer. He decided that his employer would not miss him for the rest of the evening so he went to find Pedro to talk over the situation. They had not seen much of each other recently, with Tacho working in the evenings and spending any spare time with his newer, city friends. Pedro was concentrating on his homework, as he was determined to prove that country people could manage schoolwork just as well as those who had grown up in the city. It made him rather sad and a bit lonely that his old friend Tacho seemed to have so little time for him lately, so he greeted him with enthusiasm.

Pedro's expression soon changed when he saw the newspaper that Tacho thrust in front of him. School and city were forgotten as the two lads resorted to their own language to discuss all the implications for the village of Mulaca and the surrounding area now that this detachment of government troops had moved in. They knew that many families would have fled from the village when they heard the soldiers were on their way. The soldiers would take no notice of people who could speak so little Spanish, so the villagers expected neither understanding nor consideration. They judged it easier, in the midst of their fears, to take refuge in the familiar wildness of the mountains, even if that caused them to be branded as outlaws by the authorities. The boys agreed that it would be better to follow Padre Pablo's advice and wait for news from Padre Juan, but it was hard to concentrate on their usual routine in the next day or two.

A few days later the sight of the dusty jeep in the courtyard of the priests' house greeted Pedro as he came in from school. He dumped his bag of books at the orphanage and rushed down to the butcher's stall in the market to find Tacho.

'Padre Juan must be back, Tacho,' Pedro told him urgently. 'I've just seen the jeep in the courtyard.'

Again Tacho begged time off from his tolerant employer who understood Tacho's anxiety.

'Yes, go on and talk to the priest, Tacho,' the butcher urged. 'See if you can find out the truth. You never know how much to believe of what these newspaper reporters write. Things are not so busy tonight anyway, so I'll see you tomorrow.'

Tacho and Pedro hurried off and found Padre Juan just about to drive out in the jeep again. He stopped when he saw the boys and told them all that he knew. Yes, Señor Tomás and his family were now in Oaxaca City staying with relatives. Yes, the soldiers had stayed in Mulaca about a week and had questioned many people. They had returned to Tutula with some prisoners for the county jail, including the village secretary. All the rest of the village authorities had fled rather than be held responsible for the riot. Rumour had it that the secretary would be sent to the state security prison in the city as an example. In the absence of the real culprits he would be held responsible for the rebels and the damage done. This seemed very harsh as it would mean years in prison and Padre Juan was about to go to visit Señor Tomás to find out more.

'What about my family?' asked Tacho. 'Do you know if they were involved?'

'I believe your father was in the village and among those who tried to save things from Señor Tomás' house, so he and all your family have fled to Jaguar Mountain in the Señor's territory. They are counted as outlaws now since most of the village was against Señor Tomás.'

'He must have been desperate to do that!' Tacho replied. 'He is a very mild man usually and wouldn't dream of turning against his own people. Perhaps Señor Tomás promised to cancel the debt if my father stood by him.'

Padre Juan drove off on his errand and Tacho turned to Pedro.

'Well, it's plain that I can't go back to Mulaca again now. I don't even know how to get to Jaguar Mountain except that it is the really huge coffee plantation that Tomás owned towards the Pacific Ocean. How could I ever look for anybody there? I must just forget my family now and get on here in the city as well as I can. I think they must have forgotten all about me too!'

'Tacho, how can you say that?' Pedro remonstrated. 'Of course they haven't forgotten you, but it is too bad that people couldn't wait with their complaints till we are properly educated and could help them legally. When will there ever be real understanding between the city Mexicans and their country cousins who they call Indians? We are all Mexicans, but our ways of life, our customs, our very thought patterns and points of view are so very different.'

'Yes, well, I'm just a Mexican here in the city from now on!' said Tacho bitterly.

9

Work

Their secondary school was a trade school and Tacho decided to specialise in plumbing. He had noticed all the building work going on around the city, and he reasoned that there would always be work for a good plumber. Since he was adamant about not continuing with further schooling, the priests encouraged him in this course and the three years at secondary school were soon over. His employer and friend, the butcher, was happy to be his godfather again as he received his certicate at the graduation ceremony and Tacho was very proud that he now possessed this proof of his academic abilities. The kindly butcher had a photograph taken of them both, with Tacho holding up the certificate for all to see. Secretly Tacho admitted to himself that he would love to show it to his family and to tell them all about his achievements, but he stored it away carefully among his most precious belongings, which were few. He hoped that Padre Juan would mention his graduation in Mulaca and that the news would somehow reach his father and grandmother. Were they alive even? he wondered miserably. He shrugged off the sad feeling and sombre thoughts and deliberately thought of the future.

The priest in charge of the orphanage knew someone in a building firm and the next day he took Tacho along to where they were working. It was a large new development and the firm employed a vast work force. After a short interview Tacho found himself with a job as a plumber's assistant.

'Start on Monday here at 7.00 sharp,' were his new boss' parting words. Tacho was elated.

He soon discovered that it was no easy task to get up, out and across the city to the building site by 7.00 a.m. The buses were crammed with other people on their way to work or school. He found that a number of his workmates lived together close to the site and he decided to move out of the orphanage and join them. The priest in charge was quite pleased that he had found a place to stay nearer to his employment: the orphanage was there to help boys of school age, and really expected them to make their own way if they found a job after finishing school.

'But keep in touch with us, Anastasio, and if you later find that you would rather continue your education, come back and see me about it. You must be really sure that you do not have a vocation to become a priest – we need people in the Church with your kind of background, you know,' the priest said with a smile, then gave him his blessing. Tacho knew that his new living quarters were rather rough and ready in a room shared with several others, so he asked to leave his few books, his certificates from school and a few other special things in a box at the orphanage for safe keeping, and then he was away.

The end of the week and pay-day soon came. Tacho went out and spent most of his earnings on expensive new clothes such as he had never owned before. Then he decided to visit his godfather, the kindly butcher in the market. Tacho was welcomed by the whole family who had got to know him well while he worked with them during his schooldays. His godfather knew some of Tacho's weaknesses too, and sensed that the young man had lost some of his drive and direction. He was also rather concerned to find that Tacho had no definite idea of what to do with his earnings other than to buy new clothes.

'Do you ever hear from home?' he enquired. 'How are your father and brothers getting on now? What did they think of our photo when you received your school-leaving certificate?'

Tacho looked a bit startled and suddenly realised that he hardly ever thought of his family or of Mulaca now.

'Oh, they don't write letters,' he replied. 'I expect they would like the photo though. I must go and visit Padre Juan and see if he has any news. It is Sunday and I should let him know how this job is going anyway.'

Tacho had never told his godfather that his family was probably outlawed now, and that the chances of contacting any of them were very slight. It was all too complicated to explain, even to these kind friends, since they were city people and knew nothing of the ways of people from the Tutula area. Before Tacho left, the butcher reminded him of all the pickpockets to be encountered in the city, especially in the market, and urged him to look after his money carefully.

'You need to eat every day you know, so you must keep some in reserve. I know you are buying these things this week, but if you want to save up for something worthwhile, like a bicycle or radio or something, perhaps you should start a bank account. Come and see me next weekend and we can talk about it again.'

Tacho went away thoughtfully. Perhaps it would be best to go straight away to the priests' house where Padre Juan lived. He knew they kept a room there where people from the Tutula area could stay overnight. Perhaps it would be better to stay there tonight, then he would not need to join his room-mates in any carousing they might have planned. He might even meet someone he knew from his home area. Also he could slip into the church first thing in the morning before returning to work, and he knew that his presence there would please Padre Juan. What with the butcher's family and the priests, it was good to feel that he had somewhere definite to go and friendly people to visit in this impersonal city. He wondered vaguely if Pedro had found a job too. Perhaps he should visit the orphanage as well and find out what had happened to his old friend and his contemporaries. He had been too busy all week to give them a thought.

He quickened his pace as he headed along the familiar streets towards the orphanage. The door-man greeted him as if he had never left, so Tacho enquired if Pedro had gone out or not.

'I haven't seen him go out so you will probably find him about here somewhere,' he was told.

It was all so familiar and yet in another way it seemed ages since he had moved out to his job. He found Pedro in the common room and learnt that he had a job for the summer, but had opted to continue his education at the college preparatory school. At the end of that three-year course he would decide whether or not to become a novice and prepare for the priesthood. Tacho realised that he had not really talked to Pedro for quite a long time: he had no idea that he was thinking seriously about becoming a priest. In fact, the two boys had a lot of catching up to do to know what had been happening in each other's lives. It turned out that Padre Juan had made a quick trip out to Tutula that week. Pedro had gone with him and spent a day or two in San Antonio. They had just returned that very afternoon.

'They say that the people of your village are rather unhappy at present, Tacho,' Pedro told him. 'They are grumbling about all those who fled to Jaguar Mountain and took over the big coffee plantation that Tomás used to have there. They have claimed that whole mountain and guard it with guns now.'

'But it has always been the same. Tomás didn't let anyone else onto that land either,' responded Tacho. 'Is there some reason that they are especially unhappy now? Did Padre Juan visit Mulaca while he was out there? Perhaps he can tell me a bit more about it. He may have heard something about my family. I was going over to the priests' house for the night anyway, so perhaps I should get on now. It was good to see you again, Pedro. We must keep in touch.'

Tacho made his way out and crossed the street to the other house. He saw a couple of men that he knew in the courtyard. They were from the Tutula area and had come to the city to look for a few weeks' work to get some ready cash for clothes for the family, and particularly for the new uniforms their children would need for the coming school year.

'Padre Juan arrived an hour or two ago and he brought someone with him from your village, Tacho. Go on in and find them,' one of them said.

So Tacho went over to the door to enquire for Padre Juan and was taken inside to a large room with tables, benches, beds and a large roll of straw mats in the corner. Suddenly he noticed Beto, a neighbour from Mulaca, sitting on a bed, but there was no time for more than a smile of recognition as Padre Juan appeared at that moment.

'Hello, Tacho. I haven't seen anything of you for a long time, but I mentioned you while I was in Mulaca recently.'

'Well, I have a job with a builder now as a plumber's mate,' Tacho replied. 'I don't know when I shall get any time off to visit my family again because we are working on a big development.'

'I see. Anyway, your family seems to be well except that your grandmother appears rather frail these days. Apparently your father has taken another wife now, so your grandmother and Susana decided to return to their old house in the village again, as they personally have no real quarrel with anyone there. Demetrio and his family are out on Jaguar Mountain, but I think your grandmother knows how to contact them if you have a message for them. I'm very glad that you have come, Tacho, because I want you to meet Padre Hilario. I will be leaving in a week or two and he will be taking my place here.'

'You are going away, Padre? You mean that you won't be going out to Tutula any more?' exclaimed Tacho. 'But then, how will I get news? This new padre doesn't know my village, or the ways of my people or my family. He can't understand the situation out there! Do you have to leave?' he pleaded.

'Yes, it is time that I moved on now and I'm sure Padre Hilario will soon get to know everyone. You can have full confidence in him. Here he comes now.'

A stocky, pleasant-faced priest was walking towards them. Tacho stood stonily for the introduction, said he hoped that Padre Hilario would soon get to know the people in the Tutula area, and left as soon as he could. No point in staying the night at the priests' house now, he thought dispiritedly. I'm really on my own, so I may as well return to my workmates.

He hopped onto a bus and made his way back to the earth-floored room near the building site. It was crammed with camp beds but empty of people. It was getting late now but the men were still out enjoying themselves and Tacho vowed that he would be among them next weekend. He slowly crawled into bed feeling very lonely and sorry for himself. He wondered if his grandmother ever thought of him. He was glad that at least she and Sana were back in their old home in Mulaca.

He was drifting off to sleep at last when a crash against the wall, accompanied by loud voices, cursing and swearing, brought him wide awake again. His workmates staggered in, complaining vociferously as they dragged along one completely

incapacitated companion. All were the worse for
drink and in an ugly mood, so Tacho kept quiet in
his corner bed. He gathered from their angry talk
that they had been involved in a fight at a funfair.
The police had come and caught one of them. He
resisted so they had hauled him away roughly. He
was in jail tonight and who knew how much he
would be fined tomorrow? And he a skilled brick-
layer! It was all the fault of these funfair people and
they got off scot-free!

Finally they settled down. Dawn came all too
quickly and there was much grumbling as they
dragged themselves out of bed and stumbled over
to the building site to report for work. Tacho listened
and wondered if all city workers were like this? Yes,
he remembered the hangovers his father and uncles
had after a fiesta, but at home it did not happen often
and they were usually rueful and sad if it caused
them to lose time at work out in the fields, not
resentful nor trying to blame society and other
people for their misfortune. His workmates seemed
to think that God had the workers in the building
trade specially marked out for punishment, and had
ranged all the rest of society against them. 'Perhaps
they don't enjoy themselves so much on their nights
out after all,' Tacho thought.

The foreman had put Tacho to work as assistant
to a master plumber, so he spent a lot of his time
bringing long, heavy pipes of various sizes to this
plumber. He learned to measure and cut them to
the required length, metal ones one way, plastic ones
another, and how to fit each kind together. By the
end of each day Tacho was exhausted but pleased
that he was really starting to do the job that his

training at school had prepared him for. Because of that plumbing course he understood why he was doing some things in the particular way that the master plumber insisted, and that gave him confidence in his work and a good feeling inside.

The master plumber took to this young man from the country who worked so hard and willingly. He himself had grown up in a rural area and it was only after many long years of hard grind that he had gained his present, more skilled position. He had his own house in one of the new *colonias* surrounding the city and he invited Tacho to come and visit him at the weekend to meet his wife and family. Tacho accepted gratefully, thinking that not all the workers on this building site were like his room-mates after all. So for some weeks Tacho just kept on good terms with his companions, paid his share of the rent promptly, but always had places to go and people to visit at the weekends, rather than carousing with them.

One day he realised with a shock that the new school year was beginning. The plumber's family was preoccupied with new school uniforms for their two older children now in primary school and Tacho knew that many new, overawed, country boys would be arriving at the orphanage to continue their education in the city. Pedro would be starting his three years of college prepa. school. Perhaps he had been out to the Tutula area again? It would be good to have news from there. He would go and find out what was happening next weekend.

He found Pedro full of all the challenges of life at his senior school and all the possibilities for the future. He tried to take an interest in Tacho's job and workmates, but they had really grown apart now and their experiences were very different. Pedro had soon finished telling him about the couple of days spent back in San Antonio with his family. He was finding it increasingly difficult to fit in there now with all his city experience and education, as he no longer had the same way of thinking as his relatives, nor did he use the same frame of reference, but he did not share this unease with Tacho.

'Oh yes,' Pedro suddenly remembered, 'a new little boy from Mulaca came back with us this time so perhaps you know his family. I expect you will find him in the common room.'

At this news Tacho left Pedro to his books and went in search of the new boy. When he looked into the common room he spied a rather tubby little boy of eleven or twelve sitting solemnly in a corner by himself. The youngster looked vaguely familiar, so Tacho went over to him and asked him in Spanish: 'Where do you come from? What is the name of your home town?'

'I'm Ernestino González from Mulaca in the county of Tutula,' the boy replied politely.

'Not Tino, Rolando's son?' said Tacho excitedly in his own language. 'I'm Tacho, Demetrio's son. Remember me?'

Yes, it was indeed Tino and he was delighted to meet someone from home who spoke the language of his heart. Tacho plied him with questions and the boy was only too eager to answer at length. Yes, Rolando and his family still lived in the village. Yes, Tacho's grandmother was still alive but very frail now. Sana was married and together she and her husband looked after Granny. No, there was very little news of the outlaws on Jaguar Mountain. If they happened to meet Mulaca men on the trail there was often a gun-fight, so all the village people were afraid of them now. Who knew what their children did about school, or where they went to buy clothes and other supplies? They certainly did not come to Mulaca, and probably did not go to Tutula either, for fear of being recognised and reported to the police or the soldiers there. They were a separate community now.

Tacho remained cheerful for the sake of young Tino, remembering how lonely he himself had felt during those first few weeks at the orphanage. He reassured Tino that he would quickly catch on at school and learn more Spanish, that he would soon feel at home there in the orphanage, and that he would easily adjust to life in the city. The boy seemed comforted to hear all this and to see how Tacho had prospered. To think that Tacho now had a proper job and was accepted by city Spanish-speakers! Finally, Tacho left with vague promises to return another weekend and chat with Tino about familiar Mulaca things. He returned to his lodgings, however, with bitter feelings about how life had treated his family. He no longer knew what was happening to them and felt utterly bereft. He might as well become a real Oaxaca City worker, forget Mulaca and everything about it and just join in with everything that his workmates did, he decided.

10

Weekends

'Coming with us today, Tacho?' said one of his workmates the following pay-day.

Tacho went. He knew that he was still welcome at the home of the plumber that he worked with, and he could still go to his godfather, the butcher in the market, but this time he chose to be independent and join the other young men that he lived with. They all dressed up in new clothes because they were going to a dance. Tacho did the same and was pleased to see that he looked no different from the rest. They went by bus to a part of the city that was new to Tacho and got off in the local square. The basketball court had been screened off for the dance floor where a band had set up its battery of loudspeakers and was trying out its equipment.

'Let's get a table so that we have somewhere to sit and to bring the girls back to,' said Chucho, who seemed to make most of the decisions for their group of five young men. 'It doesn't cost that much and it will be more comfortable.'

They ordered beer straight away and sat watching the crowd gather. The dance was to celebrate the annual patronal fiesta for this section of the city and all the local girls were out in force, looking happy in anticipation of a good time. The dancing began and Tacho's four companions soon found dancing partners, but Tacho stayed at the table sipping his beer and watching. Even had his companions stayed with him, conversation would have been impossible while the band was playing; the loudspeakers saw to that! The giggling girls accompanied their partners back to the table for more refreshment between numbers.

Soon one of his companions said to Tacho: 'You take young Emma here for the next dance. I want to finish my beer.'

Tacho had been swaying to the beat and felt that he could easily keep up with this kind of dancing, so he took Emma's hand and led her out with a shy smile when the music began again. It was reassuring that she accepted him just like the rest. 'Mulaca Indian makes good,' he thought wryly and whirled her round at the edge of the dance floor. He had been watching carefully and now found it easy to copy the steps and motions of everyone else as he seemed to have a natural sense of rhythm. By 3.00 a.m. when things closed down they were all rather merry, including the girls, but no one was helplessly drunk. All four girls were related and lived close by, so the men left them at the door and took a taxi back to their lodgings.

Next morning Tacho was a little alarmed to realise what a dent one night out had made in his week's pay. 'I won't go out again tonight,' he thought. 'I'll just join in a game of cards here. I might even win some money.'

As the weeks went by Tacho's confidence mounted. He joined in more and more, visiting a local *cantina* and frequently getting drunk, such that his friends often had to drag him back to their room protesting wildly. A few weeks later they went to another Saturday night dance and mixed their drinks. This time he got very drunk and obstreperous when a more sober companion tried to lead him away. Others got involved and a fight ensued, knocking over one of the tables so that the girls started screaming. Help soon came in the form of the police, at which Tacho's friends melted into the crowd. He and two other helplessly drunk belligerents were taken into custody and woke up to reality the next morning when they were hauled before the local authorities. Tacho's new clothes were ruined and he had a raging headache along with various bruises, which made him feel very sorry for himself. He was fined, and to his relief, found that he had just enough money left in his pocket to pay. He was released and found his shambling way back to the building site. No taxi this time; all his money had gone.

The following weekend he again went home with his friend the plumber. After hearing his rueful tale on Monday morning, the plumber determined to help him to see that such expensive, aimless roistering was not the only way to use his hard-earned pay and free time. Tacho was quite touched by the family's concern and friendliness, but it made him homesick for his own family. Again he returned to his lodgings full of bitter thoughts about the rough trick that fate had played on him. He worked hard during the week but at the weekends he seemed to challenge himself to wilder and wilder excesses. He became well known in the various local jails, but tried to limit such escapades to Saturday nights so that he was always on the job on time on Monday mornings.

A year passed and his friend the plumber recommended him for promotion as a master plumber. The company had many houses to finish in this vast new development, so they were taking on a number of new youngsters. Both Tacho and the plumber got new assistants and Tacho had more money to spend with his increase in pay. He remembered his godfather, the butcher, and decided to visit him again and tell him the news. He was rather embarrassed that he had left it so long, so he bought presents for the entire family. He was welcomed joyfully and able to boast of his recent promotion.

'We thought that you had forgotten all about us in your busy new life,' the butcher said jovially. At heart he was saddened by Tacho's evasiveness regarding his friends, his free time and any contact with his family and home area. He referred again to the advice he had given Tacho earlier about setting up a bank account now that he was earning more, but the younger man shrugged it off.

'I never seem to have any money left by the next pay-day. How would I live in between if I put all my earnings into this bank account?' he asked. 'At least I have managed to keep out of debt so far,' he added proudly.

More years passed. With the good recommendation from his first job, Tacho was quite easily able to get more plumbing jobs with reliable, big building firms. One Saturday night he was at a dance in an outlying town when a friend approached his table.

'Tacho, you are wanted outside. It's an old friend, I think,' he said with a grin.

Puzzled, Tacho went out into the street and found a girl standing there who looked vaguely familiar. Had he ended up spending the weekend with her the last time that he came to this place, or was that someone else?

'Hallo, Tacho, if that's your real name,' she said. 'I need to know your full name now though.'

'Why? What do you mean? We haven't met for months even though we had fun that one weekend.'

'Yes, we did, and as a result I'm going to have a baby soon, so I need your name as the father to register the birth at the Town Hall.'

'What? How can you be sure that the baby is mine? I know that you have slept with lots of men! I don't want to be a father anyway!'

'It's not a matter of likes and dislikes. I'm sure you are the father, so you must help me, my mother says.'

Tacho was stunned, but he thought quickly. It sounded as if money was what she wanted and he wasn't prepared to check into her story.

'Here is all the money that I have on me,' he said, emptying his pocket into her ready hand. 'I'll come back for the next dance in a month's time and we can talk more about it then. How about that?'

He dodged back inside the dance area and returned to his table, but left soon afterwards, not waiting for his friends this time. He caught the first bus that he saw and got off in the centre of the city. Then he walked along, thinking hard about this new

development. Did he want the responsibilities of a
wife and family? There would be the added com-
plications of his wife's relatives, but he was not
ready to get married or set up a home! No, he
certainly had no inclination to be saddled with
this girl and her child even if what she said was
true. He would just keep clear of that place in
future and hope that she did not remember who
his friends were and approach them for information about him. This was the first time that any
question of responsibility in an event had been
raised. In fights or drunken rages when things got
broken, he just paid the fines to Authority and
endured till the next pay-day when his funds were
replenished. No, he was not ready for anything
different now either.

Next day he hunted up a workmate who owed
him some money and used it as his stake in a card
game. He won, stood his mates drinks all round and
felt in charge of his own destiny again. During the
week he decided that it was time to find his own
room and to start doing a few little private,
plumbing jobs on his own. This current contract
with the building firm would end soon and he
wanted his reputation to be solid enough to be able
to start up his own business if he could. At least he
could put out feelers this way. He found a cheap
room on somebody's flat roof with access from a
small courtyard via a rickety iron staircase. His
next few weekends were exemplary as he searched
around for second-hand bargains. First he acquired
a small table, a gas ring and small butane gas tank,
a saucepan, a bowl, a cup and a straw mat to sleep
on. With these new belongings he was ready to

move in and set up housekeeping. He soon added cloths to act as curtains for the window and door because it was late March and well into the dry season, so he could not sleep with the window or door closed. The concrete roof and brick walls got very hot during the day and had barely cooled down by morning. Little by little he added shelves, a chair, a few more things for his 'kitchen', another little table and finally a bed. He did not plan to sleep on the bed till the rains began at the beginning of June and cooled everything down a bit. For the moment it was cooler on his mat on the floor.

Below him was a two-storey house where the owners lived. It fronted onto a large, pleasant courtyard with plants and a shady porch, and often he could hear the children playing. There was another room on the roof next to Tacho's where their servants lived, a man and his wife. At the side of the tiny back courtyard was another house full of rooms to let with communal showers and toilets just inside the main door, while the flat roof of that building was given over to laundry lines. A shelter for the owner's vehicle further reduced the courtyard and overshadowed the ground floor windows, but Tacho noticed a small space at the back of this makeshift garage that seemed to be unused. It looked as if it had been some sort of workshop once and he wondered if they might let him use it for his plumbing equipment, if he ever managed to acquire some of his own. He got quite adept at avoiding his old friends at the work-site on pay-day and slipping away on his own errands.

He was rather proud of his new living situation and decided to go and see his old friend, the plumber, and his godfather, the butcher, to report on his changed circumstances. And could it be three and a half years since young Tino had come to the city? Perhaps he should offer to be Tino's godfather when he received his secondary school leaving certificate this summer? He remembered how hard it had been for Pedro and himself not to have their own visitors at school functions. Then too, he remembered guiltily that he had promised to visit Tino at the orphanage. 'Was that really three and a half years ago? I will go there this Saturday,' he vowed to himself. 'And I should take a little present for Tino.'

Saturday afternoon came and Tacho set off for the orphanage. He had found a nice set of coloured ballpoint for Tino. The doorman laughed when he enquired for the boy.

'Oh, you won't catch that one back yet. He's off to work for somebody in the market. He'll do his schoolwork in the middle of the night if he has to, just so long as he can keep that job!'

Tacho was a little taken aback, but decided that he could visit the butcher and look for Tino at the same time if they were both in the central market. So he set off along the familiar streets noting all the little changes of the past three years. Suddenly he quickened his pace. What if the butcher was no longer in the market? Perhaps something had happened to him or to his family? He had not thought of them for so long and was filled with compunction that he had forgotten their kindness to him so quickly. Threading his way through the market he looked up and caught sight of the familiar smiling face of the butcher. He heaved a sigh of relief and relaxed into a smile himself as he approached the stall.

'Tacho? Is that really you?' his surprised god-father greeted him. 'We have talked about you so often at home, but we thought that you must have moved on to some other place as we never heard anything. We did hear a bit about your village though because I have another Mulaca boy from the orphanage working here with me now.'

Now it was Tacho's turn to be surprised. 'Not young Tino?'

'Why yes. Do you know him?'

'His father is my brother's godfather,' Tacho responded. 'Tino is just like another little brother to me. I feel bad about not keeping up with him since he has been here in the city, because I know how lonely village boys can get here,' he added shame-facedly.

'Well, he will be back from a delivery for me in a minute and then you can talk. I'm so glad you have come now, and he will be too. Better late than never, young man!'

Tacho was heartened by his godfather's reception and began to tell him animatedly of his dream to branch out on his own. The butcher encouraged him and made several helpful suggestions. Then here came a taller, much more assured Tino towards them with a hesitant smile.

'It is you, Tacho, isn't it?' he said. 'I'm really glad to see you because I have lots to tell you.'

'I'm sorry it has taken me so long to come back to see you, Tino, but I have a few things to tell you too.'

The kindly butcher interrupted: 'Look, Tino, there are no more deliveries for this evening, so I can

manage alone here. You take an early evening. Off
you both go and have a good chinwag together.'

They went, but Tacho found it a little difficult to
lapse back into the language after his years of no
contact with home and having thought little about
it. The conversation was therefore mostly in Spanish.
He was glad that Tino did not seem to be put off by
this. The situation between Mulaca and Jaguar
Mountain was still just as bad, Tino reported sadly
– really acrimonious, with bitterness on both sides.
Mulaca men went out to work in their cornfields in
twos nowadays, and one kept guard with a gun all
the time while the other worked. Even so, several
had been shot and some killed. Of course, they had
retaliated, so some on the other side had died too.

'What of my family?' Tacho asked. 'Even my baby
sister is not so little any more. It's over six years
now since I saw any of them,' he added reflectively.

'I think your grandmother said that you have
another little sister and a new baby brother,' volunteered Tino.

'When did you see my grandmother? How is she?
What about Sana and her husband? Did they ask
about me? And to think that I don't even know who
my stepmother is!'

Tino answered this barrage of questions as
well as he could since he had visited Mulaca at
Christmas. Padre Hilario still went there regularly
and Tino seemed quite fond of him. The trip was
easier now because the road to Tutula had been
upgraded. A logging company had opened a road
right into the village of Mulaca, having made a
contract with the village to cut a certain number of
their great pine trees for timber.

'The village owns its own lorry now and the authorities employ a driver to carry people or whatever is needed to and from Tutula. Lots of people have their own chain-saws too, so getting firewood and house-building material is a lot easier as well. Actually, with the road a lot of cement and other building materials are coming in, so that many more families are building brick and concrete houses which are reinforced against earthquakes and tremors. They have flat roofs which make it easier to dry out the coffee beans. Coffee fetches a good price these days, so what with individuals getting coffee money and the village getting timber money from the logging company for co-operative projects, there are lots of changes for the better in Mulaca now. You should see that lovely primary school building they have and the new village office-block for the authorities!'

'Wow, that sounds like a lot of progress!' Tacho exclaimed. 'Do you think I would still recognise the place?' Then he added wistfully to himself: 'Or would anyone there still recognise me?'

He suddenly remembered the other matter. 'I'm very sorry that I wasn't on hand when you finished primary school, Tino, but if you still want me, I am willing to be your godfather for your graduation ceremony from secondary school.'

'Would you really, Tacho?' said Tino excitedly. 'You know, getting my certificate from primary school was a special event, but I felt rather bad that none of my own people were there to witness it. Padre Hilario was my godfather, but it would be terrific to have you this time.'

11

Romance

True to his resolution, Tacho went to visit the plumber and his family the next day. He knew that they enjoyed fruit, so he took a large papaya along with him. The eyes of the plumber's wife lit up when she saw it.

'How lovely to see you again, Tacho. I'll make us all cool drinks with this straight away,' she said, taking the fruit.

The children all greeted him happily and the plumber himself was very welcoming. 'Why didn't I come back sooner?' thought Tacho. 'These people seem to genuinely like me and are pleased to see me again now.' He was soon seated with the plumber on the shady porch and lost no time in telling him of his ideas and his new independence.

'My contract ends at Easter,' he said. 'After that I'll see how I get on freelance.'

'Look, Tacho, you see that I have built a shed by the gate now? I am quite well known among my neighbours here as I have done many little jobs for them at the weekends, so I was thinking of setting up my own business soon. How about if we go into partnership? It wouldn't be too far for you to travel out here each day, would it? We could advertise in the little shop on the corner of this street.'

Tacho was quite overcome by this generous offer, and to be so thoroughly accepted by this kind and skilled man.

'Thank you very much, sir. I would really like to work with you like that,' he replied unsteadily.

The plumber beamed and invited Tacho to stay for a meal with the family while they discussed details of their business arrangements.

Later that day Tacho was sauntering through the centre of the city on his way home when he noticed a girl ahead of him. She was neatly but attractively dressed and tripped along as if she were anticipating something good. Tacho was just thinking about passing her to see what her face looked like when she greeted a boisterous group of young people coming round the corner and walked on in the middle of them. Tacho crossed the street and kept pace with the group to see where they were going. Suddenly they all turned into an open door along with various people approaching from the other direction. 'They must be going to a fiesta in there,' Tacho reasoned. 'Someone's birthday perhaps, although they aren't carrying gifts.' Then he looked up and saw the words 'Baptist Church' on the wall above the door. 'But this house doesn't look like a church,' he thought. 'And what is a "Baptist Church" anyway? I've heard of St John the Baptist. Is St John their patron saint perhaps? But why put a sign like that outside?'

He lounged against the lamp-post and watched several other people go in. Then a middle-aged man came along with some books under his arm. He

noticed Tacho on the other side of the street and
came over. Smiling, he greeted him courteously and
said: 'Would you like to join us, young man? The
service is about to begin.'

'Service? Oh well, it does say "Church" and it is
Sunday after all,' thought a slightly confused Tacho.
He decided to be frank with this friendly stranger.

'Well, sir, I don't know what a "Baptist Church"
is and I was just wondering what was happening in
this house.'

'Come in and see then. You can sit by me,' the
man responded.

Tacho went with him, thinking to himself: 'Well,
I do want to know what that girl looks like and I am
curious to see why she came here. Those young
people with her looked very happy and carefree – I
doubt that they have to work for a living! Just rich
kids, I suppose. Still, this man is not wearing new
or expensive clothes, although they are very neat
and tidy.'

The group of young people, including the girl
that he had followed, sat up in the front facing the
rest of the people. They turned out to be the choir
and sang a couple of songs on their own as the
service went on. The whole congregation sang lots
of songs from a book, and Tacho was able to join in
a bit because the man beside him suggested that he
look over his copy of the song-book. Tacho discovered that the man sitting up on the platform in
front was their 'pastor', but he was not wearing
any special robes and there were no candles or
images anywhere. It was all very strange. The
pastor stood up to read from the Bible, and everyone
found the place in their own books and stood up

too. Again the man beside him shared his copy with Tacho.

'So these were the books that he was carrying under his arm,' thought Tacho. 'Everyone here seems to have their own copy of these books – do they read them at home as well then?'

During the sermon Tacho looked his fill at the petite young lady that he had been following. 'She is just as attractive from the front,' he thought, as he watched her vivacious face reflect some of her reactions while she listened to the pastor. 'I must get to know her,' he vowed to himself.

When the service finished the kindly man who had invited him in turned to him with a smile and said: 'I am Amadeo Gómez. What did you think of what goes on in this house then? A "Baptist church" is not such a strange place after all, is it?'

'No sir. Thank you for inviting me here. I am Anastasio Ruíz.'

'Would you like to come again next Sunday? I could meet you outside at the same time as today so that we could sit together and you could share my books again.'

'Yes, thank you. I think that I would like to come again,' Tacho replied.

Amadeo continued in his friendly fashion: 'Let me introduce you to some of the young people here. My niece is among them. They have their own young people's meeting here on Saturday afternoons too and they all seem to enjoy that.'

He started to move across the church and Tacho followed.

'Hey, Paco and Emilio, this is Anastasio Ruíz who just came here today and doesn't know anyone yet.

Anastasio, this is Francisco (usually called Paco) and Emilio, Fermín, my niece Marta and her friends Ana, Raquel and Yasmín. I told him about your young people's meeting on Saturdays. I hope to see you next Sunday then, Anastasio. Goodbye all.'

Tacho was elated by the introduction, as Marta was the very girl that he had been watching. The group of youngsters chatted to Tacho in a friendly way and urged him to join them on Saturday afternoon. It gave him a warm feeling to be made so welcome and he agreed to come. It would also give him the opportunity to get to know Amadeo's niece better without forcing a meeting.

Tacho soon discovered that Sunday morning services at the Baptist church were much better attended, but he preferred the smaller, more casual gatherings in the late afternoon when he could watch Marta as much as he pleased. He enjoyed the youth group too and found to his surprise that they were not all from rich families. Paco was a full-time student at the university studying law, but one of the others was a carpenter's assistant. Another was a shop assistant in a men's clothing establishment down near the central market, and another had a part-time job in the market so that he could afford to go to an afternoon prepa. school. The carpenter's assistant and the prepa. school student were also country boys, the former lived in the city with an uncle and his family, while the latter was in lodgings like Tacho.

The girls were a mixture too. He found that Marta had always lived with her family here in the city and now worked in a restaurant kitchen while still living at home. Ana was also a city girl and lived at home. Her family all belonged to the Baptist church and she had attended there all her life. Ana and Marta had been in the same class all through secondary school and were great friends, so Ana had introduced Marta to her church and the young people's group as well. Neither Marta's mother nor her sisters were very keen on Marta going to her friend's church, but they were persuaded as her uncle Amadeo went there. They were glad that she had some nice friends and did not just roam the streets with other girls from the restaurant when she had time off. Marta's mother was a widow and worried about her three unmarried daughters. The eldest daughter was successfully married to a young architect who seemed to have the right contacts and a will to succeed. The mother was very proud of her son-in-law and his wife but she knew that she could not expect much help from them with regard to the younger girls until the architect was well established. Her brother-in-law, Amadeo, could not help much either as he was a widower and childless himself. He had never made much of a mark on the world anyway, she felt.

The weeks went by and Tacho was now working with his friend, the plumber. They made a good team and their little business was flourishing. The plumber was intrigued by Tacho's change of life-style and weekend activities. Tacho told him about this lovely girl that he had met, but he did not say much about the church. The plumber was pleased that Tacho seemed to have made a break from his former wild and carousing friends in the building trade. Perhaps this girl would be a steadying influence.

By now Tacho had furnished his little room to
his satisfaction and he began to wonder what to do
with his money. It was time to visit his godfather in
the market again and find out more about bank
accounts. The following Sunday morning he was
back at the butcher's stall in the market recounting
his recent good fortune. His godfather was delighted
to hear all the news and agreed to meet him on the
Wednesday morning to go to the bank and put in
his first deposit.

'The money earns interest for you, you know,'
the butcher said.

'Yes, I've heard that,' Tacho replied, 'but I don't
understand how it all works. How can I be sure that
I am not being cheated?'

The butcher explained patiently. Then he looked
hard at Tacho and surprised him by saying: 'How
come you have just started thinking about saving
your money, son? You weren't interested the
other times that I suggested it. Have you met a nice
girl? Are you saving up to get married?' He smiled
knowingly.

'Oh no, marriage never entered my head!'
countered Tacho quickly. 'But yes, I have met some
nice girls lately. They are friendly and helpful, but
I'm sure they don't think seriously about a country
boy-cum-plumber!'

'But you like one of them specially, don't you,
Tacho?' his godfather persisted.

'Well perhaps, but I don't know her very well
yet and she's a city girl too.'

'Just take it quietly and honourably then, son. If
you get a chance to take her out, bring her to visit
our family so that she can let on to her mother that

you have a godfather at least, even if you have no other family members nearby.'

'Thanks, I'll remember that,' Tacho said gratefully. He knew he would need all the credibility he could get if he was to impress Marta's mother. Then he became aware of young Tino hovering nearby and suddenly realised that his own turn to be a godfather was rapidly approaching. He asked Tino about school and his exams, and then about the date of the important closing ceremony. He remembered that the butcher had given him a shirt of the latest cut for his graduation present and that he had been inordinately proud of it. Perhaps he would go out and buy one for Tino right now and get it giftwrapped for the great day. Tino's eyes were shining and he seemed very pleased that Tacho had remembered about the event, but he did not detain him when Tacho said it was time that he went.

Tacho soon found the shirt he was looking for, got it wrapped and was just leaving the shop when he almost collided with a familiar figure. It was Chucho, his old friend from the building site.

'Tacho! It can't be really you! How is life treating you these days?' he greeted him exuberantly.

'Why Chucho, are you still working for the same building firm?' Tacho responded.

'Yes, lad, and it's another big development. A government contract this time, I think. But come and meet the others for old times' sake. It's Tito's birthday today, so we are all eating lunch together at a place just down here. You must come and join us!'

Tacho found himself propelled along and into a small café with a big bar along one side. He was hailed from a long table at the back and found a bottle of beer in his hands before he had finished greeting everyone. He gave the parcel to Tito as if he had planned it for his birthday gift and fervently hoped that the shirt would be big enough. They all ate a hearty meal which Tito paid for as the birthday host, and then left the café merrily with a table full of empty beer bottles to mark their passage. They moved on to a cantina nearby and soon it was night.

Tacho woke up to find himself sharing Chucho's bed in a dormitory room at the edge of a building site. The scene was very familiar, but the place was not. He must have got dead drunk last night and they must have brought him back with them to their lodgings. Oh, his aching head and his mouth like cotton wool! Where could he find water? Nobody else stirred as he staggered out. It must have rained in the night as it was muddy outside, but it was bright moonlight now and there was a hose in a big metal drum. He carefully made his way to it and sloshed water over his face and head. His clothes were a mess, but he decided to start walking and find out where he was. He got his bearings from the lights of the radio mast at the eastern edge of the city and began to trudge towards the more brightly lit streets and so to his own room. Dawn was breaking as he finally fell gratefully into his own bed.

'Why, oh why did I go with Chucho?' he remonstrated with himself. 'What will I tell my partner now? How can I get over there to work this morning in this state? I'm just a failure all round. How can I ever face Marta again? What excuse do I have for missing church yesterday? Well, I'm not a member of their church and I don't have to be at every service. I can't let Marta run my life anyway! Why should I tell her anything about it and just look like a weak fool?' With this thought he drifted off to sleep and awoke at midday feeling ravenously hungry.

After a meal and a shower he felt a lot better and decided that he must go over to the plumber's house for a few hours at least. He would just tell him that he went to a birthday party and made a night of it. Everyone understood about fiestas! But they were partners and he must carry his full share of the load because this work relationship was going so well. The plumber accepted his explanation without comment, but guessed the whole truth. He knew how impossible it was to avoid convivial drinking with friends who insisted. He had hoped that Tacho's new friends were different.

On Saturday Tacho was back at the youth group meeting.

'I just couldn't make it last Sunday,' he told them, and they accepted his word without question.

They were full of the plans they had for the Sunday in two weeks' time when it would be Ana's eighteenth birthday. After the late-afternoon service the entire congregation was invited back to her home for supper and some kind of programme was to be put on by the young people. There was much discussion about what to include. When they had decided and made a list, they began to practise the items. Tacho was roped in for the singing and found himself cast as a passer-by in the sketch. It was a good feeling to be included in the fun, especially as Marta looked at him so approvingly. Afterwards he managed to join the group leaving with Marta and they all continued chatting about the forthcoming party as they walked along the street.

When the others turned off Tacho said quickly: 'I go along this street too, Marta. May I walk the rest of the way with you?'

'Thank you, Tacho. I'll be glad of your company,' she replied and so he found out her address quite naturally.

The following afternoon he contrived to wander along that same street on his way to the church and sure enough Marta left her house just ahead of him. After that it was natural for them to walk to and from church activities together. On the way home after their final practice for the birthday-party programme he asked her advice about an appropriate present for Ana.

'Oh, flowers would be nice. She loves carnations,' Marta said with an encouraging smile.

Next morning Tacho called in to see his godfather and Tino on his way to buy the flowers. 'I must get another shirt for Tino too,' he reminded himself.

'The closing ceremony is fixed for Thursday 18 July,' Tino told him. 'It will start at seven in the evening.'

'Right, I'll be there,' replied Tacho. 'It will be strange to visit the old school again after all these years. I wonder if any of the teachers will recognise me?'

'I expect so,' Tino responded. 'It wasn't that long ago and some of them have been there for ages, but even those that are quite ancient seem to have good memories for their old students.'

Tacho went off to make his purchases, whistling as he walked jauntily along. Later he walked to the church with Marta. He was quite surprised at the end of the service when the pastor said a special prayer for Ana, then they all trooped out and made their way to Ana's family house a couple of streets away. Tables were set up in the large patio and everyone took a seat. Then to Tacho's amazement the pastor prayed again. He thanked God for the food and the opportunity to enjoy it together.

'Surely it's enough to talk to God in church,' Tacho thought.

He was further amazed that only bottled soft drinks were served all through the party and they were not spiked either! Everyone seemed to be enjoying themselves though, and they particularly appreciated the youth group's programme. No drunks, no smoking, no quarrels! Amazing! It was a revelation, another new and unexpected experience for Tacho. Nobody would have any regrets or bad effects as an aftermath of the party. This was quite a novel idea that needed to be considered again later. However, it was plain that he could never share any details of his other life and friends with these people!

The weeks passed rapidly and he was thinking more and more about Marta. He told her about Tino's graduation and that he would be his godfather on that occasion. Then, greatly daring, he asked if she would be free to accompany him on that evening. It turned out that Marta had cousins at the same school and one of them was in the graduating class too. Her uncle and aunt had already invited her to go to the ceremony, so she would meet him there.

Tacho got to the school in good time and found a platform and loudspeakers set up on the basketball court. Schoolboys were bringing out chairs for the guests and Tacho soon spotted Tino hard at work. He waved, and then a voice behind him said: 'Why, Anastasio Ruíz! What are you doing these days?'

It was his old science teacher. So somebody did still recognise him! An animated little conversation ensued and then the teacher passed on. Tacho spied Marta arriving with a group, so he moved in her direction. She called to him and introduced him to her uncle, aunt and cousins, explaining that he also was part of the same youth group at Uncle Amadeo's church as she was, and that he was godfather to one of these boys graduating here today. It created a very convivial atmosphere and they all moved towards the chairs together. When the time came to present the certificates, the students' names were read out and their godparents' along with them. The students received their certificates on the platform, shaking hands with the school director and other officials seated there, then met their godparents at the edge of the platform to receive a hug and their graduation presents. Official photographers were on hand to capture this important event for each student. Afterwards there was an exhibition of the students' work inside the school and refreshments were served.

Tacho kept close to Marta and her relatives and was glad to see that Tino seemed to be on good terms with her cousin in his class. Apparently they had chosen to study the same subjects and were now discussing the merits of continuing their education at a prepa. school. Marta's uncle encouraged both boys to do this as he was especially eager for his own son to become a priest.

'I was older than you are now when I left here,' Tacho said to Marta with a rueful grin, 'because I didn't have the opportunity to finish primary till I was sixteen. I had been out of school for four years when that priest brought me to Oaxaca for more schooling.'

'How do you know my age?' Marta asked quickly.

'Well, you were in the same class as your friend Ana, so I guess you must have your eighteenth birthday this year too.'

'That's quite true,' and Marta laughed, 'but I am a couple of months younger than she is.'

'So what date is your birthday then?' Tacho asked eagerly.

'August the twentieth, but it won't be a big party like Ana's because our family can't afford all that. Anyway, I don't want the kind of party that my mother and godparents would arrange with a big band for a disco and lots of drinking!'

Greatly daring, Tacho suggested, 'Could you just get the day off from the restaurant kitchen and let me take you out somewhere? I have some friends that I would like you to meet and we could walk a bit in that big park up on the mountainside.'

'That would be marvellous, Tacho! I have never been up to that park and they say that you get wonderful views of the city and the whole valley from up there.'

'Would you be happy to be with just me, or would you want a friend to come too?' Tacho asked anxiously.

'I trust you, Tacho, and I would enjoy being just with you,' she said with shining eyes.

Marta's aunt and uncle were ready to leave, so Tacho and Tino said goodbye and made their way back to the orphanage.

'I'm going home to Mulaca on Saturday to stay for a few days before I start work in earnest for the summer,' said Tino. 'Can I take a letter to your grandmother or anything?'

'I'll have it ready,' Tacho replied. 'Perhaps you can get an extra print of your graduation photo with me on it to take to her as well. Here's the money to pay for the photos by the way, because that's a godfather's expense.'

Tino grinned, but he was very glad to accept the money and thought that he must be sure to mention to everyone at home in Mulaca how kind and helpful Tacho had been to him. Tacho wrote a long letter to his grandmother with a short covering note to Sana, as he knew that she would be the one to read it to the little old lady. He said that if there were any chance of passing it on to his father, he would like him to read all the news as well. He also enclosed the photo of himself with his godfather, the butcher, at his own graduation ceremony. Then he rushed over to the orphanage with it just before 'lights out' on Friday evening.

'Have a good trip, Tino. I'll see you when you get back.'

12

Proposal

Tino's report from Mulaca was quite heartening.
Tacho's grandmother was still alive and very
alert, although unable to do a lot now. Sana had
two little children. Everyone was delighted to
get news direct from Tacho himself. His grandmother was especially proud of the photos, and
yes, they would certainly send the letter on to
Demetrio. He and his young family seemed to
have settled down well on Jaguar Mountain, but
Tacho's teenage brothers had a very bad reputation
as hard-drinking, trigger-happy young bucks with
little patience and no sense of humour. It was
rumoured that they had actually killed some
Mulaca men; in fact, it was said that Nino never
missed. It was said that they always rode beautiful horses with lovely tooled leather saddles and
that they dressed very stylishly, so a number of
girls found them rather attractive, despite their
violence.

Tacho thought to himself: 'Well, at least, it seems
they are no longer short of money. My brothers seem
to be dabbling in the same sort of diversions as I do,
maybe more, even without the city's influence. I

suppose they will just have to find their own way,
like I must here!'

He continued to go to the Baptist church where
Marta's uncle Amadeo was consistently friendly and
encouraging. Tacho was really looking forward to
his special date with Marta. Her birthday fell on a
Tuesday, so the preceding week he arranged with
his business partner to take the whole day off on 20
August. The plumber looked at him enquiringly,
but Tacho did not enlighten his friend further.
On Sunday morning he went to see his godfather
again. After chatting generally and catching up on
family news Tacho plunged in.

'Once, you said that if ever I got to know a nice
girl I should bring her to see you. Would you be
very busy this Tuesday afternoon? Could I bring
someone then?'

'Why of course, Tacho,' the butcher replied
heartily. 'You must both come for lunch, about 4.00
p.m. My wife and the children will be delighted to
see you again. Who is this charming girl then? We
really want to meet her.'

'I met her at the church – and her uncle too.'

'That's a pretty good recommendation. Does she
live here in the city?'

'Yes, she is a city girl. She lives with her widowed
mother and works in a restaurant.'

'Have you met her mother then?'

'No, not yet, but her cousin was in the same class
as Tino at school, so I met another uncle and aunt at
the boys' graduation the other night and they were
quite friendly,' Tacho responded a little defensively.

'Right. We'll see you both on Tuesday afternoon
then,' the butcher said as he left.

Tacho finalised plans with Marta on their walk home after church.

'I'll meet you on the corner at nine o' clock and take you to breakfast at a nice café that I know,' he said. 'Then we can pick up a couple of *tortas* for a snack, and some bottles of Coca Cola or something, and go up and explore the park.'

Tacho was up early on Tuesday morning. He dashed down to the central market and made his unaccustomed way to the flower section. He chose two different but equally beautiful flower arrangements and appeared before his godfather with them.

'Could you possibly look after these for me and take them home with you?' he asked the surprised butcher hurriedly.

'Anything you say today, Tacho. But why two?' he asked.

'One is for Marta and the other is for your wife.'

'How very thoughtful of you, son. She will be delighted. I don't know when anyone last gave her flowers! What a good idea.'

Tacho rushed off again and the butcher thought to himself: 'Looks like an important day for that young man. I'm glad he chose to spend part of it with us.'

Tacho waited on the street corner with studied nonchalance. He was in good time but still anxious: 'Will she be held up? What will she tell her mother? What if there is some last-minute hitch – how can she get word to me? Perhaps she was just being kind to this country boy all along and doesn't really want to come out with me at all?'

His wondering was interrupted by a neat Marta tripping towards him.

'I do hope that I haven't kept you waiting, Tacho. I have been looking forward to this day out so much!' she greeted him happily.

Breakfast was delicious and then they ambled up the hill to the park entrance, buying their *torta* snacks at a roadside stand on the way. Once inside, they branched off the main path and made their way round the side of the hill. The track got rough and Tacho reached out a hand to help Marta, then it seemed natural to keep hold of her hand and she did not resist. They enjoyed the view over the city, picking out the well-known landmarks. They talked a bit about their families and shared some of their hopes and dreams. Soon after midday they flopped down in the shade of some trees to share their snack.

Suddenly Tacho said: 'Marta, you are eighteen now. Have you thought about getting married?'

'Well yes, Tacho. Every girl has, I'm sure, but no one has said anything to me about it before.'

'I'm saying something now, Marta. I really love you and I want to marry you. Do you think that your mother would listen to me? Are you willing? I have a good job now and a furnished room and my godfather helped me to start a bank account. Soon we would be able to buy one of those plots of land on the edge of the city to build our own home. Do you care enough to trust yourself to me? You know that I have no family here nearby to help us out.'

'Yes Tacho, I care very deeply for you, but I never believed that you would want me to marry you. I really want to be your wife, but we must talk to my family about it.'

'Marta, you make me so happy to think that you love me too. May I kiss you?'

They continued to share dreams and then Tacho told her of his godfather's invitation, so they reluctantly left the quiet mountainside and came down to the busy city again. Tacho led the way and stopped in front of a shop with necklaces on display. Some weeks before he had noticed one with blue stones the very same colour as the dress that Marta had worn that he admired most.

'Look at all these. Which colour and design do you like best?' he asked her.

'They are all so beautiful!' she exclaimed. 'I love to admire such things in shop windows. I do own one necklace that my godfather gave me at my first communion long ago, but I am almost afraid to wear it in case it breaks or something, and then I would be left with none at all.'

'I know you must like blue because of that pretty blue dress you wear,' he said. 'Do you like that blue necklace there?'

'Tacho, I've never seen anything prettier!'

'Then I will buy it for your birthday because you have said that you will marry me. It's the sign of our promise.'

'But won't it be very expensive? You mustn't spend all your money on me, Tacho.'

'My dearest, I want to spend my money on you, so let me worry about that. Come on, let's go in and get it.'

He took her hand again and pulled her into the shop. He bought the necklace and put it round her throat straight away.

'Now I know that you belong to me,' he said, beaming.

On they went to his godfather's house where the kindly butcher and his wife were on the look-out for them. It was a proud but very self-conscious Tacho who introduced Marta to them. The butcher produced the flowers and Tacho presented one basket to his hostess, who was quite overcome.

'Tacho, are these really for me? However did you know to choose my favourite flowers!' she exclaimed.

'And these are for you on your birthday, Marta,' he said.

'But you shouldn't! You have already given me this beautiful necklace today,' she said, embarrassed but pleased and proud at the same time.

'Yes, I should. The necklace is a pledge because today Marta promised to become my wife, if I can persuade her mother that I need her more than she does and that I will really take care of her,' Tacho told his friends with pride.

'Oh dear! I didn't realise what an important occasion this is!' wailed the butcher's wife. 'Here we are, celebrating two important events, and I didn't get a cake!'

'But your meals are always so delicious. They are always celebration meals,' Tacho said sincerely. 'Just being with you two and the children makes it a special occasion.'

'Yes, this couldn't be a happier day for me,' put in Marta. 'And it is extra special to share it with you knowing how kind you have been to Tacho. I shall always remember this as a golden day.'

The children came in just then so there were more introductions followed by the festive meal. The hours sped past till Tacho noticed the time.

'I must take Marta home – it is almost dark. Would you come with us to formally speak to her mother?' he shyly asked his godfather.

'Now? Of course, let's go.'

Tacho thanked the butcher's wife again profusely, but she just laughed as she gave them a goodbye hug and said she hoped to see them again soon. It was fully dark as they came to Marta's house.

'Mama, I have visitors with me,' she called as she let herself in.

Her mother came forward to greet them with surprise. Marta's sister Honoria was there too, watching television with her mother, but now she came across the room with a puzzled look as Marta introduced the men. They all sat down and Marta told her mother and sister of the lovely afternoon that she and Tacho had spent with his godparents and showed them her lovely flowers. They looked even more surprised since she had been so vehement about wanting no party for her birthday.

'I think you can see, Señora, that these two young people have become very fond of each other,' said the butcher. 'That being the case, I came to tell you what I know of young Anastasio here, because he would like your permission to marry your daughter, Marta. It is true that his home was in an obscure country village in the county of Tutula, so he has no family here in the city. But I am his godfather and I can vouch for him that he is a hard-working young man who has been saving his money in a bank account. All of our family is very fond of him. I am sure that he would really look after your Marta and be a good son-in-law to you. He and his partner have their own plumbing business and they must be quite good at their work because they never seem to lack clients.'

Marta's mother broke in at this point, having recovered a little from her initial surprise. 'This is all very sudden, Marta. Where and when did you meet this young man? Why have you never mentioned him before?'

'Uncle Amadeo introduced him to me at church one day, mama, and he joined the young people's group there, so we all know him. Then he found out that today is my birthday and wanted to take me to meet his godparents. That's when he gave me these gorgeous flowers.'

The widow now turned her austere gaze on Tacho.

'So, Anastasio, what do you have to say for yourself? Do you really think that you could support my daughter? I am a widow you know, so there will be no help from me. Where would you live? There certainly isn't room in this house. And have you thought about the wedding? The expenses would be your responsibility, you know.'

'Yes, Señora, I have considered all these things. I have a furnished room, a good job and some money saved, as my godfather said. I think we should manage very well, but we do want your blessing.'

'All right, you may continue to come here and see Marta and we will think about the wedding. But it is all very difficult, not having your family here!'

'My mother died when I was a child, Señora. That is why the priest brought me to the orphanage here in the city to finish my education.'

'I see. Well, we couldn't expect much from your family then, so it's a good thing that your godparents here take such an interest in you.'

'Yes, Señora, you can rely on us to stand by these young people,' chimed in the jovial voice of the butcher with conviction. 'No, Anastasio is not entirely without friends and resources.'

'It is good that we have had this little discussion,' continued Marta's mother. 'Now we need a little time to get used to the idea. So when you have further thoughts about the arrangements you may return to discuss them.'

She stood up to put an end to the interview, so Tacho and the butcher took their leave. But Tacho knew that he would see Marta again on Saturday. As they walked away along the street Tacho invited his godfather back to his room for a chat.

'I'd like to see where you live, Tacho. You know, you should take Marta's mother some flowers next time you go there, and perhaps some fruit another time, or some sweet rolls straight from the bakery, or some other special thing – just to show her some consideration. Perhaps you could take something for Marta's sisters occasionally too. Women like that kind of attention.'

He was glad to see how attractively Tacho had arranged his room with the little improvements and conveniences that he had contrived.

'Oh yes, you two could live here quite comfortably to start with,' was his verdict.

Tacho quickly made a cup of coffee, then settled down to talk seriously about the wedding and all the necessary arrangements. They talked for a long time.

'We'll have to go and talk to this pastor at your church pretty soon, Tacho, and see what he has to say about it all.'

'I'll see him on Sunday and arrange an appointment with him,' Tacho said eagerly. 'I had no idea there was so much involved in just getting married. There are lots of customs to follow in my home village, but I thought it was different in the city.'

'Marriage is supposed to last a lifetime, son, so there are a few things to see to and several people that have to be consulted. My wife and I are very glad to be in on this, you know, so come round any time and keep us informed as things develop. I'll be off now to tell her the latest news.'

The next day Tacho could not help but tell his partner, the plumber, of all the recent developments in his life. When the plumber's wife heard, she immediately issued an invitation to Tacho to bring Marta to dinner with them on Sunday.

On Saturday Tacho took flowers for his future mother-in-law and boldly knocked on the gate when he went to escort Marta to the youth group meeting. The lady was suitably impressed and they left her in a good mood. At the meeting the other young people quickly wormed the news out of the happy couple and started talking to each other excitedly to plan their own contribution to the affair.

On Sunday the dinner with the plumber and his family was a great success. 'You picked a winner there, Tacho,' the plumber said as they left. 'Look after her, young man.'

They were a little late arriving at the church that afternoon but Amadeo was still lingering at the door. He greeted them with a smile and said, 'Have you got news for me, Marta?'

'Dear uncle, Tacho has asked me to marry him and my mother is not opposed. I am so happy!'

'I must congratulate you both,' Amadeo said, embracing Marta and kissing her affectionately. 'Could I have the honour of giving away the bride on the great day, since my brother is no longer with us to fulfil that responsibility? I will speak to your lady mother, my sister-in-law, about it. She is sure to agree.'

'Uncle, that would be marvellous, because we want to be married here at this church.'

After the service, Tacho booked an interview with the pastor and, having seen Marta home, rushed over to tell his godfather the details.

'We can meet him at the church on Wednesday evening at 7.30. Is that convenient for you? I could always change the date or the time if that doesn't suit, I think,' Tacho informed the butcher.

'Don't worry, son,' replied the butcher. 'I'll be there.'

Wednesday came and a very pleasant interview with the pastor ensued. He seemed genuinely pleased by the turn of events. He arranged a time in the following week when his wife would be available also, they could talk to Tacho and Marta together. On the next Saturday Tacho remembered his godfather's advice and took a big papaya with him when he went to call for Marta.

'My mother is beginning to speak quite well of you, Tacho,' Marta told him with a smile as they walked along together. 'Also, she is very pleased that my uncle Amadeo has volunteered to act in my father's place and it reassures her that he really seems to like you. As a result she is almost reconciled to our wedding being quite soon. After all, she will still have my sisters Honoria and Estela at home.'

At a street corner near the church Ana greeted them excitedly. 'I want to talk to you two. Look, I'm your oldest friend, Marta. Can I be your attendant at your wedding? And I've been talking it over with my parents. We know that Tacho's family isn't here and that you lost your father a few years ago which leaves your mother on her own now. So, can we please give you the wedding fiesta as our family's wedding present? There is plenty of room in our patio.'

She finished breathlessly, then laughed at their stunned expressions. 'Oh come on. It's not such a big thing and we would love to do it.'

'But, but we hadn't even considered a big party . . .' Marta stammered as she and Tacho stared at each other in disbelief.

A wedding feast? At Ana's home in those rich surroundings? Why should Ana's family do such a thing? Why should they give them a present at all? The unspoken questions swirled round their minds in their amazement.

'Now that's all settled, isn't it? We really do want to do this, you know,' Ana said with satisfaction. 'And did you remember, Marta, that Raquel is a seamstress? She wants to make my dress as your attendant and she would like to make your wedding dress too, if you trust her.'

'Now wait a minute!' put in Tacho. 'I don't know the city customs for a wedding, but at home the bridegroom always went out to a big town armed with his fiancée's measurements and bought all the bride-clothes. She didn't see them till the day of the wedding.'

'No!' the girls cried out together. 'The bridegroom pays the bill, but *he* doesn't see the dress until his wedding day. The bride has to have several fittings to make sure it is absolutely right. We will let you come with us to choose the material so that you can pay for it, and that's all!'

Tacho was a bit disconcerted, but decided to do things their way since he wanted to fit in with city customs and he was hopelessly outnumbered anyway. He had better ask advice about his own attire too. He didn't want to let anyone down, and everything was moving so fast now. But how generous of these new friends at the church to help him so much! He and Marta had better decide on a definite date fairly soon. They moved on to the church and Raquel came running to meet them at the door.

'Did you say anything to them, Ana?' she enquired shyly.

'Yes, and they want you to make the dresses, don't you?' Ana replied promptly.

'Yes please, and thank you very much for thinking of it,' said Marta, hugging Raquel.

'Now you understand that making them is my wedding present, because I couldn't buy you a nice gift, but I can do this work,' Raquel said breathlessly.

Marta could only hug her again saying, 'It's a most wonderful present! Thank you, oh thank you, dear Raquel.'

'I want to thank you too, Raquel. I'm just over-whelmed by everyone's thoughtfulness,' Tacho said, hugging her in his turn.

After the youth meeting Tacho and Marta walked home with Ana so that they could thank her parents for their amazing generosity.

'Jesus Christ helped at a wedding when His young friend got married, so as His followers, we want to do the same,' said Ana's father. 'We want this to be a really happy occasion to the honour of God. Just let us know how many extra guests are invited, and we'll take it from there. We expect to invite the whole church here for a start.'

Tacho privately thought: 'This is like a fiesta at home when they invite the entire village – and I expected just a quick, quiet family affair!'

As they arrived for the afternoon service the next day they were met at the church door by a beaming Amadeo.

'I heard what Ana's family are doing for your wedding. Well, my present will be your wedding cake. I will go and order it as soon as we know the date.'

'I can hardly believe this!' Tacho exclaimed. 'Everything is falling into place without us arrang-ing anything!'

Marta was hugging her uncle, incoherent with gratitude.

They met the pastor and his wife later in the week as arranged, and decided on the last Saturday in October for the wedding date.

'There is the civil ceremony to consider as well, Anastasio,' the pastor reminded him. 'We are will-ing to be your witnesses, if you like. I could drive us all down to the Town Hall – the Friday just before would be the best time to arrange it. Marta, your mother would need to go with us and perhaps your uncle Amadeo as well. Would your godparents be available then, Tacho?'

'If the appointment is in the afternoon, I'm sure they could come,' Tacho said.

Later the butcher assured Tacho that they could fit in with whatever arrangements were made. When the plumber and his wife heard of all that was happening, they wanted to contribute something too.

'Listen, Tacho. It would be good to have a quiet celebration after the civil ceremony, you know. Why don't you all come here from the Town Hall and eat supper with us? I mean you two, Marta's mother and uncle, Tacho's godparents and this pastor and his wife. Will there be anyone else in the wedding party?'

'That would be terrific, but can you cope with so many extra people – that's at least eight of us?'

'Oh yes,' the plumber assured him with a smile. 'We can send the children over to their grandmother for the night. Her house is just round the corner there. So that's all settled. It will be just a country celebration here, a bit like they do it in your home village, I shouldn't be surprised. You know, it might be good to invite Marta's two sisters as well because ten people is no more trouble for my wife than eight. So do that, Tacho.'

The weeks flew past and in between all the necessary errands Tacho worked hard with his friend at their thriving plumbing business. They seemed to have won the confidence of the entire *colonia* and were never short of work.

One day the plumber asked Tacho: 'Have you got your guest list finally decided? I know that Marta has all her friends and relations, and there are all the friends at your church, plus our family and your godparents. Do you have anyone of your own to invite?'

'There is Tino at the orphanage from my home village, and perhaps my old school-friend Pedro from San Antonio is still there, although I seem to have lost touch with him. There's no one else though.'

'How about your old workmates from the building site? I know they are a bit wild, but perhaps this very special occasion merits inviting them for old times' sake,' the plumber said gently.

This was a new idea for Tacho, but he agreed that the plumber should invite Chucho and the others, since he knew the site where they were working.

'I have never known them to go into a church though. Do they even know what a Baptist church is? I didn't,' Tacho said tentatively.

'That doesn't matter,' the plumber reassured him. 'I'll just tell them the date, time and address. They will be a bit surprised to find there's no strong drink at the reception, and no smoking, but I think they will enjoy the novel experience. They need to see whole families enjoying themselves together.'

13

Marriage to Marta

The invitations were delivered, flowers ordered,
dresses made and Tacho had his own clothes ready.
In the end his godfather had insisted on buying the
new white shirt, black trousers, socks and shoes, and
a tie for this special event. 'The appointment with
the judge is for 3.30 this afternoon, and tomorrow
the wedding at the church, then Marta will be my
wife!' Tacho thought with a great sense of well-being
and wonder. He arrived at Marta's house in good
time that afternoon, feeling distinctly nervous, and
clutching a little box with a gift for her mother. In it
was an obsidian necklace and brooch that quite
charmed the lady.

'You are really very good to me, Anastasio,' she
said. 'I would never have expected such thoughtfulness from a country boy. I think that I would have
liked to meet your mother. Tomorrow you will meet
my dear daughter Isabel along with her husband,
Hector, the architect, you know. They are such a
comfort to a widow like me. Hector is a great success
in his profession for such a young man. He is very
popular and really getting ahead. I think he may go
into local politics later. And dear Isabel is a great

success socially too which is such a help to him. A wife that is an ornament to his career is just what an important man needs, I feel.'

'Yes, Señora, I look forward to meeting them,' Tacho replied dutifully.

Privately he wondered just what his in-laws would think of him, not to mention what they would think of his friends – a butcher for a godfather, a plumber as partner, and labourers from a building site. Not quite in the same league as the architect's friends at the golf club!

Marta appeared as a welcome interruption to his thoughts. She was wearing the blue dress that he admired so much and her birthday necklace. 'She must be very different from her sister, Isabel, since she is content to marry me and live in one rented room,' he thought humbly. Then Amadeo arrived along with the pastor in his pick-up which was shiny and clean for the occasion. Honoria and Estela came running to join them, and they all climbed into the vehicle, laughing. Marta's mother rode in front with the pastor and his wife, while the others piled into the cab at the back with its plank seats on either side. Estela's tight skirt caused a moment of concern but, giggling, she hitched it above her knees and climbed in, adding to the general hilarity. The butcher and his wife met them outside the judge's office, and the party was complete.

The ceremony only took a few minutes. The marriage certificate was signed, witnessed and sealed and the judge congratulated Señor and Señora Anastasio Ruíz. Tacho and Marta stared at each other, trying to take in the fact of their married state while everybody was giving them hugs of congratulation. They all piled into the pick-up again, making room for the butcher and his wife too, and Tacho shouted directions to the pastor through the little back-window of the driver's cab.

They arrived at the plumber's without mishap and were greeted warmly, then seated on the roomy porch for a few minutes with cool glasses of hibiscus drink called 'jamaica' so that they could recount the latest events for the plumber. Soon they were called inside to a bowl of thick soup with a small mountain of tortillas to accompany it. These were kept warm in beautifully embroidered cloths set at intervals down the long table. The pastor suggested that they give thanks to God for this joyous occasion and for the company and the good food provided. 'Jesus Christ is glad to see us here, you know, and He is here with us,' he said.

Delicious rice followed, along with turkey in the traditional black molé sauce. It was a real feast and everyone tucked in with enthusiasm, while chatting happily. There was homemade crème caramel to finish, for which the womenfolk were loud in their praise. They asked the plumber's wife for her private recipe as they vowed that their own efforts never turned out as beautifully as this. She was delighted that everything had gone so well and that all the guests had enjoyed the meal. The bridal party left soon afterwards, knowing that tomorrow would be a big day.

It was. Tacho had been invited to breakfast with his godparents as he needed to collect the flowers from the market. Also, they wanted to check with him that no detail had been forgotten that was his responsibility. There would be the bouquets for

Marta and Ana, buttonholes for the bridal party and family with a special corsage for Marta's mother, and flowers for the church. The young people had offered to decorate the church and would meet him there at midday to receive the flowers. Before breakfast Tacho rushed round to Ana's house to offer to do any last-minute jobs or errands.

'Now you run along, Tacho. We have everything under control here and we will see you this afternoon at the church,' Ana's genial father told him.

The butcher and his wife were equally kind and encouraging, so that it seemed no time at all before Tacho was meeting his friends at the church with the flowers. Young Yasmín seemed to be in charge there today and had several people cutting up white tissue and crêpe paper to make streamers and other decorations. She was very pleased with his choice of flowers and assured him that they had plenty of vases for them. She would also see that the buttonholes were kept fresh, although she advised him to deliver enough for Marta's family to her home right away along with the bouquets.

He was a little disconcerted to find a stranger answering Marta's door, but she quickly introduced herself as Marta's elder sister, Isabel, and pulled forward her husband, the successful architect, to be introduced too.

'I don't suppose you thought of anything to decorate the car did you?' she asked.

Tacho was deeply chagrined that it had never entered his head, being so unused to travelling in a car. She just laughed at his crestfallen expression and added: 'That's all right. We expected to transport the bride in our car, so we came prepared. I'll see that these flowers get put in water, but it is really strange to see the bridegroom delivering them personally. Why didn't you get a delivery boy? Much more dignified, you know.'

Tacho decided to leave before he disclosed any more of his shortcomings, so he just said, 'I'll see you at the church later then,' and made his exit.

He found a very dapper Tino waiting for him when he got back to his room.

'I've brought you this, Tacho, but I didn't want to give it to you at the actual wedding,' he said as he handed over a flat package. 'Please open it now because it is really just for you to help in your trade.'

Tacho looked questioningly at Tino as he took the box. He opened it to find a gleaming new Stilson wrench. It was the first tool that he had ever owned and he knew that it must have made a hole in Tino's savings. Tacho remembered the day his gas tank had run out and how he had had to borrow a spanner to change it; and when he had wanted to put up his shelves he had paid a friend for the use of his hammer for a day to do the job. He was very touched that young Tino should have thought of this useful gift and that he had wanted to bring it here privately.

'I shall always remember who gave this to me,' he said, and Tino looked happily uncomfortable. 'I must change now but I am really grateful to have someone to walk down to the church with me,' Tacho continued. 'I feel so self-conscious when I am all dressed up like this.'

They arrived in good time and Tacho insisted that Tino sit in the front row with himself and his godfather. Tacho was thinking contentedly: 'This

Christianity is a good thing. All the people in this church are so friendly, generous and helpful. Our young friends have done all this beautiful decorating especially for Marta and me, even though they didn't know that I existed a few months ago! I'm still not sure what this "following Jesus Christ" is all about, but it's certainly different from what I knew about Christ before and it's different from what I know about church. It seems to affect their whole lives and not just be a set of customs to keep.'

The pastor smiled at him reassuringly from the platform. The piano was being played softly and the church was already quite full. He gave a quick glance behind him as the music changed and he heard a rustle. Everyone was standing up.

'Come on, son,' said the butcher.

They moved to the front and turned to see a radiant bride at the door on her uncle's arm. Ana came forward first as the attendant and moved on to the other side. Then the lovely vision in white that was Marta followed slowly. Amadeo took Tacho's hand and put Marta's into it, then turned them to face the pastor and the service began. This included several symbolic acts such as being tied together with a *lazo* of artificial flowers. Later each lit a candle with which they together lit a third candle and blew out the original two. The joint candle was left burning for the rest of the service. Tacho listened to the pastor's homily more carefully than he had ever done before and found that he was being reminded of his responsibilities as a husband.

'Yes, I do want to take care of this wonderful wife of mine,' he vowed to God, or was it to himself? He was not sure, but he was serious about it.

They sang the last hymn and then he was proudly leading the way from the church with his new wife on his arm. Friends took photos, then they all formed up in a procession for the short walk to Ana's house. The patio there was tastefully decorated and filled with small tables with two big tables at the front. There was a space beside the main table and the bridal couple was positioned there to receive their guests. Most of them came with presents in their hands and these were passed to Ana to arrange on the other big table. Marta found herself well occupied introducing her many relatives to Tacho, as well as her friends from the restaurant where she worked. It helped that he knew the church people already. Then he noticed five well-dressed young men approaching and recognised Chucho and his other former workmates. Now it was his turn to perform the introductions as the men handed over several bottles wrapped in white paper with big ribbon bows on the necks and a separate square box. Tacho knew that these must be tequila, whisky or brandy along with a big box of cigarettes. He realised suddenly that no one else had brought this kind of gift and he remembered that they had all been served soft drinks at Ana's birthday party. With a little embarrassment he handed them to Ana now to put on the gift table and tried to thank all the givers heartily.

When everyone was seated and the young people from the church were busily serving tables, Ana's father clapped his hands for quiet. He welcomed everyone to his house for this happy celebration, then thanked God for all that He had provided and

asked His continued blessing on Tacho and Marta
as they set up home together. The delicious meal
was consumed with plenty of extra servings for
those who were hungry, and then Tacho and Marta
were guided to uncle Amadeo's cake on a little table
of its own to the side. It was a magnificent wedding
cake and they were reluctant to cut into it but a big
knife decorated with a white ribbon bow was thrust
into their hands to cut out their 'first mouthfuls'.
Then they had to feed each other simultaneously!
The cry started: 'A kiss, a kiss!' Soon it became a
chant as all the guests joined in until a bashful Tacho
grabbed his wife's shoulders and kissed her lips
spreading sticky, soft icing from the 'mouthful' all
over her laughing cheeks.

As people finished their cake the guitar group
formed up. There were one or two solos, duets and
quartets interspersed with well-known songs from
the church when everyone was encouraged to join
in. Then Tacho and Marta were called to the gate to
receive many more hugs and good wishes as some
of the guests took their leave.

After most people had gone, they went to gaze
again at the table full of presents.

'How good God is to give us all these friends!'
exclaimed Marta.

'And how kind our friends are to us,' added
Tacho, 'but I don't know how we will fit it all into
our one room!'

Ana came up just then: 'Your case is in my bedroom ready for you to change, Marta. Would you
like us to put your presents into this spare room
here that opens onto the patio? You could come back
and open them at your leisure and there is room

enough for you to sort them out and pack things together more to take them home.'

'That's wonderful, Ana. How thoughtful you are, and how helpful you have been to us. Thank you again,' said Marta.

'Well, I am very fond of you both and so pleased to see you married now and setting up another Christian home.'

Tacho was somewhat startled to hear her say 'Christian home' as if it was special and different, but he was reminded of some of what the pastor and his wife had been saying to them the other day. He had rather dismissed it at the time as the standard that applied to church leaders, perhaps, which he and other ordinary people could admire, but Ana seemed to think this was the norm for everyone. Still, she had grown up in a 'church' family, which made all the difference, he was sure. Also, she had never had to work for her living and things were always different for rich people, he told himself. So he smiled and thanked her again, then helped her to move the presents, while Marta went off to change.

Ana's parents urged them to leave, having assured them that everything was under control and no, they could not help with anything more. They sauntered slowly along hand in hand and stopped at every street corner for Tacho to kiss his bride again. 'No need for anything clandestine now because she is my wife and we are going home together!' he thought jubilantly.

They soon settled into a routine with Tacho off early to his work at the plumber's house and Marta continuing at the restaurant. Saturday morning came and it dawned on them that they could no longer be counted among the young people of the youth group at the church.

'We should go and open the rest of our presents this evening and bring them home,' said Marta. 'In future this time will be free for us to visit people.'

'I've been thinking,' Tacho said. 'Everybody helped us so much with the wedding that I still have money in the bank. With you working as well, it will soon mount up and we can start looking for our own plot of land somewhere. We won't be able to put all those presents to use in this one room, so we must build our own place as soon as possible.'

'That's really something to look forward to, Tacho. It will be exciting to visit some of the areas on the edge of the city where they are selling land! It looks as if our Saturday evenings will be well occupied.'

Tacho talked to his partner about the idea and the plumber was very encouraging with lots of good advice. He warned Tacho of all the pitfalls too. He described the racketeers who were selling land that they had no right to, then absconding with the proceeds, but he did know of land legally available in a small town just across the river and a little beyond the edge of the city.

'This city is growing fast, Tacho. I'm sure that small town will soon be swallowed up by the city itself and then you would be in a very good position,' he said.

Tacho and Marta visited a number of the new *colonias* and saw lots of plots where they would have been happy to settle. Tacho's experience from working on a building site in an area that was being developed helped him to describe to Marta how things might look later on. He wanted her to see not just a bare hillside with a few shacks here and there and a muddy, or dusty, track meandering through the middle but to visualise neat little houses with gardens arranged along concrete streets with shade trees and street lamps. It was fun dreaming together, but they never seemed to track down an actual vendor or agent, and so the year ended.

It was well into the new year when one day the plumber said to Tacho, 'You remember that I told you about a place they are developing? Have you been out there to look at it yet?'

'Not yet. We've been looking more to the north of the city.'

'Well, my cousin bought land out there, but now he has a family emergency so he can't possibly put a building on it in the stipulated time. In fact, he wants to sell his plot so that he has the money in reserve as ready cash rather than having to borrow more. Would you be interested? We could go and see the land this Saturday morning and then go on and see him in the afternoon if you wanted to. I'll come with you so that there is no mistake or mix-up.'

'I'll tell Marta tonight, but I'm sure she will like the idea,' Tacho responded excitedly and then added doubtfully: 'I wonder if we will have enough money though?'

'You can sort that out when we find out more details. Let's go and fit this pipe for Señor Roberto in the meantime.'

When Tacho told Marta the news that evening she was excited too, so with great anticipation they met the plumber at the central bus station on Saturday morning and rode out to the edge of the small town that the plumber had mentioned.

'You know, I have lived in Oaxaca all of my life but I have never crossed the river before,' Marta said.

'Have you never been up to Monte Albán then?' asked the plumber with some surprise. 'Everybody has heard of those famous ruins and I thought that all the Oaxaca City people knew them well! So many visitors come long distances to see them, from other countries even!'

'No,' she confessed shamefacedly, 'I've never been up to Monte Albán. I think that's true for a lot of the Oaxaca residents. We think it is good that the visitors come, but we are so immersed in our own lives and work that we never find time to go there ourselves. I think they often take the schoolchildren now, but they didn't take us on trips much when I was at school.'

They walked down a track through the fields almost as far as the canal. Then they saw plots and potential streets marked out where several houses were in various stages of being built. There were shed-style buildings on most of the other plots and people were obviously living in some of them. A neat two-roomed concrete-block house stood on the corner and was already doing trade as the local shop.

'Just down here,' said the plumber.

They walked past five or six plots beyond the shop to come to a double one that had a fence round it, but nothing else except a small tree in one corner.

'Of course, the town centre with the Town Hall and offices is over there on the main road in the old town,' the plumber explained. 'But they are planning a town bypass on this side because of the traffic bottleneck in the town square, so then the main road and bus services will be much closer. They also plan to build a new school near here on what is to be the main street of the *colonia*, and soon there will be plenty of shops nearby as well.'

Finally, Tacho looked at Marta and she nodded with shining eyes. So he said to the plumber: 'We brought *tortas* with us and one for you too, so let's sit down under that tree and eat them. I'll just run down to the shop for some soft drinks. Then after that we can go and talk to your cousin about this land.'

The cousin was overjoyed at the prospect of selling quickly to such a reliable buyer vouched for by the plumber, but Tacho found that he only had enough money for one of the plots.

'You will need both of the adjacent plots, Tacho,' the plumber said seriously. 'Why don't I pay for the other and then you can buy it from me gradually in instalments?'

They agreed a time and date to go to the Town Hall together to arrange the transfer of land deeds and also the transfer of the money.

'You don't know what a relief this is to me,' the former owner said. 'I was at my wits' end to know how to lay my hands on some ready cash quickly, and to borrow money means exorbitant interest. To sell through an agent takes time and there's lots of red tape, to say nothing of the search for a reliable agency that doesn't demand an enormous cut.

Thanks so much, cousin, for coming to my aid by means of this young man.'

Tacho was thinking: 'I'm very fortunate to have this man as my partner. He always seems to be coming to someone's aid, including mine!'

Marta was in a daze on the way home. They were actually going to have their own home out there on the edge of the city in sight of Monte Albán. If they were to live on that side of the city, perhaps she and Tacho would go and visit those ruins. His friend the plumber seemed to consider it a real lack in their education that they had not been there and knew so little of their own history that was represented by the ruins. 'Perhaps someone will dig up the ruins of our house one day hundreds of years in the future and wonder about the people who built it,' she thought to herself with a smile. 'How strange that would be. But I'm more concerned with getting it built here and now so that we can move onto our own land!'

Tacho was busy with his own thoughts too, planning and calculating: he was very conscious that he needed to get a building on the site quickly to establish ownership. 'If I go to see the timber merchant tomorrow morning I can order poles and beams and boards,' he thought. 'Then we need corrugated tar-paper for the roof, although metal roofing material would be better if we can afford it. We will need nails and a spade too. Those wedding present tools will come in useful now and some of the plastic utensils too. I won't need to pay for the wood till it is delivered and we will have more money by next weekend. Or perhaps it is cheaper or more convenient to hire one of those pick-ups and take the wood out there myself? I shall have to find out. We must have at least a shed up on that land before the end of next month, that's certain.'

'Let's visit my godfather on the way home, Marta, and tell him the news,' Tacho said.

'Oh yes, if I don't tell someone our good news soon, I'll burst!' she replied.

The butcher was delighted to hear their news and volunteered a suggestion: 'I can manage without young Tino for the next two weekends, Tacho, then he can help you with this building. I'll send him round to see you tomorrow evening. You can borrow my wheelbarrow and any other tools that I have, so don't buy anything new till you check with me first.'

Tacho was touched that the butcher should think of such helpful, practical details. 'Thank you, and I'll be back often for advice,' he told him.

The next morning they went round to visit Marta's mother to tell her their news and then on to the timber yard. They were rather late for the afternoon service, but afterwards they lost no time in telling Amadeo their news along with the rest of their friends there. Ana was determined to get the rest of the youth group involved, so the young people decided to scrap the following Saturday afternoon meeting and go out to help Tacho and Marta on their site instead.

One of the young men, Emilio, said: 'My father has a pick-up which I drive to make deliveries for him. I'm sure he would let me collect your lumber in it and take it out to your site if it is ready by Saturday morning. He would only want the cost of the petrol. Remember that Fermín is an excellent carpenter, so he will be especially useful to you. Perhaps my father would let me have the pick-up all day then I could transport other things for you as well. I could even come back here in the afternoon and pick up all these friends of ours to bring them out to help and that would save time messing about with buses.'

They decided on times and meeting places and Amadeo added, 'I think that I could help you a bit then too.'

'Thank you, uncle,' replied Marta happily. 'Everyone is so kind to us.'

Things were definitely making progress and she was really looking forward to the next weekend.

14

Building

Evenings were occupied with enquiring about prices, ordering, making small purchases such as nails, making lists and planning the actual building. One evening Ana appeared, lugging a large shopping bag.

'We saved all the tops from the soft drinks bottles at my party and your wedding fiesta in case they might be useful. People always use them when they nail on corrugated roofing and such-like my papa says. So perhaps you will need some, Tacho? Anyway, he sent me round to ask you.'

'Thanks a lot, Ana. We can certainly use them,' Tacho replied enthusiastically. 'Actually, I had forgotten all about them. We need them so that the nails won't tear the roofing material too much. How very thoughtful of your father – please thank him for us.'

When Ana had gone, Tacho said to Marta: 'I never would have thought that a rich man like Ana's father would even know how to put a simple corrugated roof on using bottle tops! Most people just throw these tops away, yet he collected them all up and kept them just in case they might be useful to some

poor person. It's certain that he had no plans to use
them himself! I don't suppose he has ever been
under such a roof, let alone owned one! But he
really is concerned about people less fortunate than
himself.'

'We must remember to thank God more often,
Tacho. He must be looking after us, especially with
so many good things happening to us,' Marta said
thoughtfully. 'Ana's father is always thanking God.'

'I suppose so,' responded Tacho. 'It does seem a
bit more than coincidence that we have so many of
the right friends at the right time.'

'Perhaps if we read the Bible together we would
understand God a bit better,' Marta added.

'Well, we hardly have time to eat and sleep at
present, but once we have moved out to our own
place we must try to do that, like the pastor suggested,' Tacho agreed.

Saturday came and Tino arrived with the wheelbarrow. Then Emilio called for them in the pick-up.
Off to the timber yard, then out to their plot with
the first load. Emilio and Tacho went back for the
rest of their building materials and Tino set to work
making wooden pegs from the first plank, while
Marta got out a measuring tape and a ball of string.
Then Tino cleared off the site with a spade to make
it as level as he could before they set out the pegs
definitively. Soon Tacho and Emilio were back with
the next load. Tacho approved their measuring and
marking, so the boys started digging holes for the
corner posts.

They had to beg buckets of water from the
friendly owner of the little shop on the corner to
soften the ground, which set Tacho thinking: 'Yes,

the very next thing is to dig a well. We can't go on begging or buying water by the bucketful if we are to live out here. We'll need a latrine too.'

An hour or so later Marta announced to the men: 'I've brought *tortas* for everyone. Let's sit over there under our tree and have them now. I've made lemonade too.'

Then it was time for Emilio to go and collect Amadeo and the young people from the church. Even with such unskilled labour they got quite a bit done, but Tacho was preoccupied by the water problem. Amadeo noticed this and said: 'I helped to dig wells when I was younger and helped to make the cement rings to line them. I have a week's holiday owing to me because I worked all through Christmas and the New Year to let the family men be at home then. Why don't I take my holiday time as soon as possible and help you with the well? You need to get hold of a few bricks though, as well as sand and cement to make the rings, because it is best to put them in as you dig. I could bring my crowbar and you already have a spade and your godfather's wheelbarrow.'

By nightfall the framework of the building was completed. Everybody enthusiastically agreed to continue the operation the following Saturday. Several of the youngsters volunteered to come earlier next time so that they could finish the shell of the building in just the one day. The next afternoon Ana met Tacho and Marta on their way to church.

'You know what?' she greeted them excitedly. 'We have a spare door in our storeroom. It's the one that my papa replaced with a more attractive one when we had our kitchen redone last year. I asked him if he is ever going to use it or could I give it to you for your new place, and he said that he was just keeping it for someone who needed it, so to go ahead and take it if it is useful. How about that? Why don't you come and look at it after the service? I'm sure it would work.'

'We owe your father a great deal, Ana. He seems to have taken us on as a special project, and we are very grateful.'

'Oh, he loves to help people!' she responded.

'I wonder if Fermín would be free to come with us and give a carpenter's opinion. I would value uncle Amadeo's advice too,' said Tacho, thinking aloud.

Later on they all trooped round to Ana's home and inspected the door. She produced a tape measure and Fermín assured them that the door would fit beautifully. It even still had its door frame and hinges. Ana's father came along in time to hear this verdict and was very pleased.

'Ana's mother told me to invite you all to stay on for hot chocolate and sweet rolls as it is getting late now,' he said.

'But she shouldn't go to all that trouble for us!' exclaimed Marta.

'No trouble, my dear. She has the table all ready, so come along now while the chocolate is still hot.'

The following Saturday they collected the door first. While they were there, Ana's mother called Emilio into the kitchen.

'Take this crate of soft drinks along with you, Emilio. You will all be needing some refreshment this afternoon,' she said.

They went on to pick up the roofing material and then were on their way. Tino, Amadeo and Fermín were all with them on that first journey, so they got to work right away while Tacho and Emilio went back to the timber yard. They were going to bring out a pile of cut-offs from the squared logs because these worked out much cheaper but still made good walls. Sure enough, by nightfall their smart little one-roomed house was complete. Fermín had even managed a shutter-type window and Tacho proudly fixed a padlock on the door.

Emilio agreed to make one more trip early the following morning with Tacho and Amadeo to bring the various things that they would need to dig the well. So next day Amadeo met them with his crow-bar, a large sheet of plastic, a woven palm-leaf sleeping mat and a blanket, as he planned to camp out in the new house for the entire week. When they arrived at the site Tacho was eager to get started, but Emilio and Amadeo went back for the morning service at the church. To Tacho it seemed like no time at all before he saw Amadeo and Marta arriving.

Marta had brought a picnic again and after they had eaten it Amadeo told them: 'Now you two run along so that you are in good time for the service this afternoon and I will settle in here. I'll see you on whatever days you can manage a few hours here, Tacho, and don't worry about me: I'm used to living alone and fending for myself.'

Tacho had already told his partner about the well project, so they had not taken on quite so much work that week, allowing Tacho to get out and work with Amadeo for a few hours each day. He could go home when night fell, he thought. He really wanted to learn all that he could from Amadeo, especially about making the rings for lining the well. Amadeo spent the first day preparing the rings so that the cement could dry out. When Tacho arrived in mid-afternoon, he watched the process carefully.

In the digging they averaged about half a metre each day. A well ring took up about a third of a metre, and the two of them were needed to place each one into the hole for the well. They were very glad to see that it was just plain earth that they had to dig through, and not rock, although they knew that they might come to that later. Fermín turned up on Saturday morning early, armed with a tin of paint and his saw.

'This paint is for the door and I thought that I could make a few rough shelves inside with some of those leftover boards,' he announced. 'You really should paint the whole thing with wood preservative, but that can come later,' he said as he set to work.

That evening Amadeo remarked: 'I'll stay on here, Tacho. I don't mind camping and it is not far to my work from here. Then you won't have to worry about leaving the tools and the wheelbarrow here. They will be all right inside with the padlock on during the day, but it will be good for the neighbours to see that someone is already living here. In the evenings this next week I can dig the hole for the latrine over in that corner of the plot. There are still enough boards and roofing material left to make a little house for it.'

Tacho did not know how to thank these two friends. He was thoroughly delighted to see all this happening on his land. Suddenly he thought of his father and wondered how Demetrio was faring out on Jaguar Mountain. 'I wish he knew about my wonderful wife, and could see our land here and talk over the plans for our home in this place,' Tacho thought wistfully.

Amadeo broke into his reverie: 'In a couple of weeks it will be Holy Week and then I will have a few more days off,' he said. 'We can do some more work on the well then. Next Saturday we'll put up the little house for the latrine and then make some more rings for the well so as to have them ready in advance. But we need another bag of cement and a few more bricks for that.'

Tacho and Fermín made their way out to the main road to catch the bus back to the centre of the city and left Amadeo on his own again. It was good to be able to report all this progress and their plans to Marta that evening.

They struck water at a depth of three metres and managed to dig out another metre and a half for reserve. The new supply of bricks and cement held out so that they could finish off the top of the well properly with a little wall. This pleased Amadeo who liked to have things look tidy. On 'glorious Saturday' of Holy Week the plumber brought his family out to view the proceedings. He had told Tacho earlier that he would like to visit the site and see how they were getting on.

'Take Marta out with you on Saturday,' his wife had said, 'and I will bring a picnic for us all.'

The plumber was full of admiration for all that had been accomplished so far. 'It's very good that you have your own water supply now, Tacho,' he said, 'but you will need a pulley for that well. I think I've got one at home that I don't need any more, and the rope too. And haven't we got some of that iron pipe left over from that last job we did? That would make a good bar for the pulley wheel.'

Tacho and Marta decided to make a little cornfield on the empty part of the land, with beans and squash in between the maize plants. Tacho had noticed a type of squash, rather like a pumpkin, that seemed to grow extra well in the Oaxaca valley. With their own water supply they could irrigate the land, so there was no problem if it did not always rain at the right time for their crops. They could also plant some other things along the edges.

'I can get some plants from my mother's house and from Ana,' Marta said happily. 'Then we can have flowers along by the fence.'

So they worked away companionably at the weekends, getting the soil of their garden ready. The rains began at the end of May, so they rushed out to the plot to plant their seeds. Then Marta shyly voiced her idea: 'Tacho, it will be your birthday a week on Saturday. You made mine such a special day last year. Why don't we celebrate by moving out here? Then we could look after our cornfield properly and be in our own home. We know that the roof of our little house is watertight . We have your furniture with the stove and gas tanks, so we could manage very well. We could store our electrical things like the blender and any other special items with Ana, till we get electricity out here.'

'But what if it floods here in a heavy rainfall? The canal is very close,' Tacho responded.

'Can't we dig a trench round the house?' countered Marta. 'We could add a little porch too for extra space. These shelves Fermín put up make very good storage,' she added in a satisfied tone.

'Well, I planned to have a cement floor put in for you first,' Tacho said doubtfully.

'No, let's come here on your birthday, then we can save the rent money as well. We want to pay your friend the plumber for the other half of this land as soon as possible.'

'That's true, dear. If you really think that you can rough it out here we will ask Emilio if he can help us once more with his father's pick-up and move out here then,' Tacho said, smiling at her fondly.

Emilio was very willing and Tacho's birthday morning found them filling cardboard boxes and tying up bundles of bedding for the journey. It took three trips to get everything out to their new home including the food supplies that Marta had just bought. It was a tight squeeze inside their little house, but they found a place for everything in the end. Tacho had just got the stove connected up to the gas tank and levelled on its little table when they heard a cheerful shout of greeting from outside. It was the butcher and his family. The sky had really clouded over but the daily shower had not yet fallen, so the pathway that they had worn to the fence was not too muddy.

After birthday hugs all round the butcher said: 'Looks as if you are settling in nicely. We won't stay long, but we brought you a birthday dinner, Tacho. We left young Tino to look after our stall in the market for us because we wanted to see how you were managing. Moving in the rainy season can be hard sometimes. Your corn plants seem to be thriving though. We shall look forward to some young corn cobs later on.'

His wife put the food down on their little table and the children looked round in amazement. They exclaimed over the carpenter's cleverness in putting up so many sturdy shelves and asked their father why the rooms in their own house did not have this innovation.

'Mama always wants things tidied up off the floor,' they said, 'and look, Tacho's little house has the perfect answer!'

'No, Marta, thank you. No time for coffee if we are to beat the rain,' they said as they turned to leave. 'We can see that you are quite snug here and that the stove works. Happy birthday, Tacho, and we will see you soon.'

Marta and Tacho gratefully attacked the delicious food so lovingly prepared for them by the butcher's wife and then they decided to go to bed as the rain was drumming on the roof and they had only candles for illumination. It had already been a long day and they were dog-tired.

'This is our very own place, Marta my dearest. It's not very grand though. Do you really think that you can cope? This is much more isolated and primitive than anything that you have been used to,' Tacho said, both proud and worried at the same time.

Then Marta dropped her bombshell.

'Oh yes. It will be lovely for the three of us!'

'Marta? What do you mean? Surely you are not . . . ? When did you know? Why didn't you tell me? Am I to be a father then? Really?' stammered Tacho taking her into his arms.

'Yes, my dear husband. This news is my birthday present and I am especially glad that I can tell you in our own home.'

They worked harder than ever after that and saved all that they could for construction materials as they dreamed of a house of bricks. They got to know some of their neighbours and Tacho picked up a few extra little plumbing jobs locally. It was exciting when the first load of foundation rock was delivered a few weeks later. With Amadeo's help Tacho had already built a shelter over the well. It had a cement sink and water tank next to it for Marta to do the laundry more comfortably. The shelter had a concrete floor so that they did not have to stand in the mud to pull up the buckets of water or to use the sink. Having a bath was made easier when they put up opaque plastic sheeting on the other side of the water tank. This formed a little shower room where a bucket of water and a gourd dipper were all that was necessary.

Towards the end of July the rains let up a little for the few weeks of the *canícula*, so Tacho and Amadeo set to work to dig trenches for the foundations of the first permanent building. They planned to do one room first with a flat roof, then add on other rooms as money became available. The final stage would be a second storey. The plumber had lots of friends in the building trade and soon put Tacho in contact with a mason who contracted to build the foundation for a very reasonable fee if he could work only at the weekends and stay with them on Saturday nights. Tacho himself could be his assistant. This meant missing the services at church, but Tacho was obsessed with getting the house foundation in before the heavy September rains began.

They finished it on the last Sunday afternoon of August and the mason said: 'Let's go out and get a celebratory drink, Tacho. We've earned it and your wife won't be home to congratulate us for a while yet.'

'How about if we just get *refrescos* at the little shop on the corner?' Tacho replied.

'No, that's not a celebration! You've given me those all the time we were working. Come on man, I want a real drink!'

'I've just remembered,' said Tacho, 'I still have a bottle that was given to us for a wedding present. We have never opened it, so I don't know what we will find,' he said leading the way into the house. 'Yes, here it is at the back of this shelf. Will tequila do?'

'That's more like it,' said the mason, beaming as Tacho handed him the bottle and a glass. 'But you must join me, Tacho! It's no fun drinking alone, even when the drink is the best wedding present tequila.'

'Just a small one then, to celebrate our achievement,' agreed Tacho.

They toasted each other and the bottle stayed open between them on the table, so they could not stop with just one glass. The light was beginning to fade as the mason lurched to his feet.

'Must go, old man. Let me know when you have the bricks and want to build the walls of your house,' he said as he set off for the bus, leaving Tacho slumped over the table.

Tacho was fast asleep when Marta arrived a few minutes later. She was appalled to see the empty bottle and glasses and was not quite sure what to do next. She cleaned off the table and set about making coffee to go with the fresh sweet rolls that she had brought back with her.

'I will just try to act as normally as I can,' she thought.

When all was ready she gently shook her husband's shoulder. He started awake and she offered him the steaming cup of coffee.

'I feel terrible,' he said, taking a gulp.'But it is good news. We finished the foundation this afternoon. Oh, I remember, we had a little drink from one of the boys' wedding presents to celebrate. This hot coffee helps – and fresh rolls too. Good!' he said heartily, but a bit shamefacedly too.

Afterwards he went quietly to bed while a confused Marta put things away and locked up for the night. This was the first time that he had shown no interest in the church or their friends there. There were no eager questions and she had never known him to drink like this before. She had forgotten all about those bottles of liquor brought by his old workmates as wedding presents. Well, tomorrow would be another workday, so she must sleep too.

They followed their usual routine in the morning and Marta admired the completed foundation, but neither made any reference to the previous evening. September passed and in October the first load of bricks was delivered.

A few weeks later Tacho said: 'I'm going to contact that mason, Juan, again to find out how much cement and sand we need. I think we have enough bricks now to do the walls, but we have to make the concrete supports first and they need reinforcing bars, and gravel too. Then we must have planks to make the moulds. Perhaps I should talk to your uncle Amadeo again first, because he really knows about these things and I need some advice.'

'Come to church with me on Sunday, then you can talk to my uncle. You haven't been very often lately and everyone always enquires after you and about how things are coming along here. They are really interested too,' Marta coaxed.

'That's a good idea, Marta. I'll come.'

Amadeo was pleased to see Tacho back at church and to hear their news. He was especially glad that Tacho wanted his advice again.

'If I can get off work an hour early tomorrow I can come straight out to your place and we can do all the measuring while the light lasts. Then we can make our calculations,' he told Tacho. 'If Emilio's father is willing to loan his pick-up again we could get those young people organised to collect sand and gravel from the river bed on Saturday, which would be one less expense.'

'What a good idea,' Tacho responded with relief. 'And my partner the plumber knows the best yard to go to for the construction materials.'

They talked to Emilio, who was delighted to be of use again. He rushed off to round up the members of the youth group and tell them about this latest project.

'I'll go with them on Saturday to get them started,' Amadeo said. 'I have a sieve for the sand and I know where I can borrow one the right size for the gravel. I'll see that they have enough shovels too because these city youngsters often don't know

much about the practical details,' he added with a
grin.

Amadeo turned up at the house the next day soon
after Marta got home. He looked at her sharply and
said: 'You look rather tired, my dear. Are you sure
that you should still be working at the restaurant?
It makes a long, hard day for you with the bus travel
as well. When do you expect the baby and what do
they say at the clinic?'

'I'm going to leave the restaurant at Christmas,
uncle, when they take on extra people for the
Christmas rush. The baby should come in the new
year, about the middle of January, I think.'

'Well, don't overwork and don't cut it too fine. It
isn't worth it,' he advised rather anxiously.

Marta insisted that he stay to eat supper with
them after he and Tacho had done the measuring
and calculating to their satisfaction.

'It's going to take those youngsters more than one
Saturday's work to get this pile of sand and gravel
together,' he told Tacho. 'But it is good that they are
so interested and want to be involved, even though
it means hard work.'

'I must make enquiries about prices and see to
ordering the rest of the things that we need,' Tacho
said, and added as he glanced at Marta: 'It would
be so good if we had that first room built before the
baby is born.'

Juan was available full-time from the last week
of November, so Amadeo arranged with his boss to
be free to work with him for a week then. Amadeo
told his boss that he would work over Christmas
and the New Year as he had done before. That
would give his workmates time with their families,

so his boss accepted gratefully. Juan and Amadeo got the main supports done during that week together so then Juan could start laying bricks. Tacho helped when he could, and the walls went up quickly. Amadeo made himself available the following Saturday, so that was when they made the rest of the concrete beams. By Christmas they were ready to pour the concrete roof.

'I'm going to ask the men of the church to help with the roof on the first Saturday of the New Year,' said Amadeo. 'Thanks to the young people you have plenty of sand and gravel, but you will need more bags of cement. Can your partner arrange to borrow scaffolding for roof supports from one of his builder friends, do you think? And will Juan be available again to supervise it all?'

'I'll see about the scaffolding and contact Juan again. I really wouldn't have got very far without all your help and know-how, Amadeo,' said Tacho in admiration. 'Thanks again for everything. Do you really think all those men from the church would help us pour the roof? They don't all have experience at this job though. Perhaps my old workmates from the building firm would come too. Did you meet Chucho and the others at our wedding? I must see about contacting them.'

The plumber was sure that he could arrange for the scaffolding and assured Tacho that he would be on hand to help as well. He also volunteered to talk to Chucho and the others. His wife, Petra, looked hard at Tacho when she heard of the plans: 'Does Marta realise that all these men must be fed at the roof-pouring?' she asked. 'She's in no condition to cope with all that work though, so don't mention it.

I will go and talk to your godparents about this. Have you spoken to them yet, Tacho?'

'Not yet, and I hadn't thought about the food at all!' said Tacho in consternation.

'Well, don't worry about it. You go and see your godfather tonight. His wife is Irma, isn't she? Tell her that I will come on Wednesday afternoon to discuss things. Then we can tell Marta about it later on, when we have it all organised. On no account must Marta fret in her condition, so just leave her in ignorance for the present. I expect those girls from your church would help too – they certainly pitched in before, and enjoyed it.'

Tacho followed Petra's advice and went to see the butcher and Irma that evening. He gave her Petra's message and she began making plans immediately.

'We shall certainly be there with you to help at the roof-pouring,' the butcher assured him. 'If we just close the stall for that day, Tino can come too. He will still be on holiday from his school.'

'Yes, and we can use that day's meat for the dinner,' said Irma enthusiastically, 'so there won't be any left to sell or any wastage either! Now don't get excited about costs, Tacho. We should be able to manage this for our godson.'

A week or so before the roof-pouring, Petra and Irma came to see Marta and found Amadeo visiting the young couple as well. As they explained things to Marta, she burst into tears as she was suddenly faced with the idea of all this entertaining and her own inadequacies. The ladies hastily reassured her and outlined their plans.

Then Amadeo chipped in: 'Yes, when I asked the men to help, all their wives volunteered to come too and asked how they could help with the food. Also the girls from the youth group expect to be here and to do their share, so there will be no lack of contributions and hands to help.'

'Well now, just so that we can keep tabs on things, could you ask each of those wives to come with a pot of beans and a pile of tortillas, please,' said Petra. 'We have the meat part arranged, but the beans and tortillas are a problem with only Marta's little stove to cook on here. Perhaps the girls could do something about the chilli sauce and the drinks too?'

'Yes, I will tell them and I am sure that you can leave all that to the church ladies, Petra. You and Irma seem to have really thought this through,' Amadeo said appreciatively.

Marta was smiling again and Tacho looked relieved.

'Thank you all so much. It looks as if you dear people are rescuing us once more, because we have taken on yet again something much bigger than we realised,' said Tacho gratefully.

Two days before the roof-pouring a truck arrived at their gateway. Ana's father got out of the cab to greet an incredulous Marta affectionately. With him he had a large canvas awning, folding tables and chairs, and five cases of soft drinks.

'We thought this might help with your Saturday guests,' he said, gesturing to the load and smiling.

Then he directed his men to erect the awning over in the corner of the spare lot and to set up the tables and chairs under it.

'I heard that there is going to be a big dinner here that day and if my daughter is to serve food she needs tables to put it on. So here they are. I really am delighted to see the progress on your house, Marta. Ana needs to find a young man as enterprising as your Tacho. We'll come back and collect this furniture and the empty bottles on Monday, so you needn't worry about that. Goodbye now, and greetings to your husband.'

Marta found the rest of the afternoon dragging as she waited for Tacho to return and see this latest development. He was suitably overcome when he arrived.

'You know, Marta, Ana's father is a really good man!' said Tacho in amazement. 'He has no reason to be so kind to us. When I was growing up there was only one really rich man in our village and he just manipulated everybody. He managed to get a lot of people in his debt, including my father, and then arranged things so that it was impossible for them ever to pay off their debts to him. I thought all rich people must be like that.'

'But being a real Christian does make a difference, Tacho,' his wife replied. 'Whether they are rich or poor, Christians want to please Jesus Christ by all that they do and say, so the pastor teaches, and that seems to be how Ana's father lives.'

'I think that is your uncle Amadeo's goal too,' said Tacho thoughtfully. 'Anyway, they have both helped us tremendously.'

Juan arrived with the scaffolding on Friday afternoon, so at first light on Saturday he and Tacho started erecting it. Others soon arrived to help and by mid-morning they were tying the reinforcing bars together on the roof. Petra arrived with a huge container of chicken tamales and, when the other women had arrived with their pots of beans and piles of tortillas, breakfast was served.

After that they started mixing concrete. Soon there was a steady stream of men heaving five-gallon tins of concrete mix up onto the roof to the experts. About mid-afternoon Irma arrived in a taxi with the cooked meat and molé sauce, as well as a pile of bowls to serve it in. She also brought a big bag of apples and a whole stalk of bananas, so with more beans and tortillas it was a substantial meal. They decided to carry on so they could finish pouring the roof in one go. This made the dinner rather late, but it was a very joyful and relaxed meal as they had finished the job and everyone felt a great sense of satisfaction.

Juan cautioned Tacho that he must wet down the roof with a few buckets of water several times each day so that it would not dry out too quickly or unevenly and crack.

The plumber suggested to Tacho, 'Let's both come over here on Wednesday afternoon to take down the scaffolding. Then I can return it to my friend the builder ready for use on Thursday morning. You wouldn't need Juan to come back just for that.'

It was night before everyone had gone. After a quiet cup of coffee Tacho and Marta went out together and walked round their new house in the moonlight.

'Now I must order the doors and windows from the metal worker. And I want to get the inside walls plastered and the floor put in as soon as possible,' said Tacho.

'But our house is built now and the finishing touches can be added when it is convenient,' said

Marta with a happy smile. 'Thank you, dear, for working so hard to get it all ready before our baby puts in an appearance. I really thank our Lord God for all His kindness to us and for the help of so many friends. It's a bit overwhelming really, to be the object of so much loving kindness, but I am very glad our baby will grow up knowing all this.'

15

The family

The next morning, as Marta was reheating the leftover tamales for breakfast, a taxi drew up and her mother and sisters got out. This was a great surprise as they had never shown any interest in the young couple's acquisition of land or in the building project up till now. Marta was very glad that she had the tamales on hand to offer them. Tacho apologised for the untidiness everywhere, but explained about the roof-pouring the previous day.

'You mean that all those people came right out here just to help you with this house?' Marta's mother exclaimed incredulously. 'You certainly have some good-hearted friends, I must say. Most people have plenty of better things to do on a Saturday!'

Honoria and Estela were looking round in amazement.

'So you have been living in this little shack all these months without even a floor, Marta! You must really miss your old home!' Honoria said.

'Oh, I expect it is fun to camp out with Tacho,' countered Estela.

'We'll be moving into our new house very soon now,' responded Marta, goaded by their comments. 'We have been quite busy, you know!'

'You should have stayed in the city proper and rented a decent house near to us,' said her mother reprovingly. 'I'm not at all sure that I approve of my grandchild growing up in this uncivilised district with no streets or other facilities. And what arrangements have you made for the baby's birth, Anastasio? The time must be getting very near now.'

'Well, Marta has been attending a clinic for the last few months and the doctor said to go over there when the pains start,' said Tacho self-consciously.

'Do you mean a clinic in this little country back-water? And how do you know that this doctor is reliable? Do you even have proof that he is a qualified doctor? Like any mother, I expect to help at this time, but I certainly cannot come and stay in this shack, and your other building has yet to be finished, so what are you going to do?'

'Mother!' Marta broke in. 'I am very happy in this "shack" as you call it. This is my home and I am not ashamed to live here with my husband and baby. It is good for a child to grow up on his own family's land in a place of their own, however humble that may be. I am very glad that you want to help and are interested in your grandchild, but we are quite content with our situation here and we are the baby's parents, so we decide what is best for our child!'

'I'm sorry that I am not a successful professional like Hector, Señora,' Tacho said woodenly, 'but you did know my position when I married your daughter.'

'Yes, well, she and the baby must come to us of course. The clinic will only keep her for one night, I expect, and then she can come to us by taxi because she will need proper care. I'm afraid there isn't room for you as well, Anastasio, but you can visit us on your way home from work each day.'

Tacho and Marta were bowled over by this idea, but finally agreed to it as Tacho did not want to antagonise his mother-in-law further. After eating their tamales rather fastidiously, the ladies were ready to leave. Tacho ran out to the main road and flagged down a taxi, while Marta showed them the things that she had made ready for the baby.

The next day the men collected the awning and the tables and chairs. On the Wednesday Tacho and the plumber removed the scaffolding so that they were able to tidy things up. They moved their bed into the new house and put a curtain over the doorway. Their original little house would serve only as the kitchen from now on.

A week later Tacho arrived home from work to find Marta doubled up with pain. He took one look at her and said hastily as he turned to the doorway again: 'I'll get a taxi right away. It looks as if your time has come. Do you have everything ready that you need at the clinic?' he called over his shoulder.

A few minutes later they were on their way. At the clinic the nurse recognised Marta and ushered them inside with a welcoming, reassuring smile.

'We have a bed all ready for you, Señora,' she said.

Tacho found that his help was unnecessary, so he decided that it was time to inform his mother-in-law. He was very nervous about the whole business, so he decided to hurry along to the central market first to tell his godfather the news and rally some moral support. The nurse had said that there were hours to wait yet. It was a great relief to talk to the butcher, who calmly assured him that Irma would be along to the clinic a bit later to sit with them. Then he suggested that Tacho use his telephone to speak to his mother-in-law and so save the time needed to walk over to her house.

'Thank you,' responded Tacho. 'What a good idea. I never thought of that. I am not used to being near to a telephone.'

Marta's mother herself replied and said to be sure to let her know when the baby was born and all the details; and yes, all was ready to receive mother and child when they left the clinic.

'Does your partner the plumber have a phone?' the butcher asked afterwards. 'Perhaps you should let him know how things are, so that he won't expect you at work tomorrow.'

The plumber was most understanding and assured Tacho that he could handle things for the next few days and not to worry. So Tacho hurried back to the clinic to find Marta in bed and fairly comfortable between pains.

'In an hour or two they will be more frequent,' the nurse told her. 'You can get up and walk about a bit then if that helps and I will check back every little while. But you must call me if things get really bad suddenly,' she said, turning to Tacho.

It was not until early the next morning that Tacho called the nurse, who checked Marta's progress and moved her smartly to the delivery room before calling the doctor. A little daughter arrived with the dawn, and soon mother and baby were comfortably tucked up in bed. Irma had arrived in the late evening and stayed the night with them, a motherly, encouraging presence. She left with the happy news and Tacho went off to find a telephone and some breakfast. He told his mother-in-law that they would come to her house the following day at breakfast time unless some complication arose. Petra came to visit with little presents for both mother and baby and was delighted to hear that all was well. Irma returned in the afternoon with messages and greetings from all the family. Then in the evening Ana came with Marta's youngest sister Estela, who was thrilled to hold her little niece. Knowing that Ana was Marta's best friend, Estela had kindly passed on the exciting news and the two girls had decided to visit the clinic together. Now they cooed over the baby and fussed over Marta while the proud father looked on in delight. He was very pleased that his young sister-in-law had taken the trouble to visit them there in the clinic. It lessened a little his awe of his mother-in-law and the dread of leaving his wife and new baby daughter at her house and in their care.

While the girls were visiting Tacho decided to go back and check his house. He had promised to do a little plumbing job for the man at the shop on the corner, so he could just call in and explain the delay. He knew that the job was not urgent, but he really wanted to build up a good reputation locally as a reliable plumber. There would be extra bills now with the baby and he wanted to finish the new house as soon as possible.

Marta was duly discharged from the clinic the next morning and they made their way by taxi to her mother's house. Once there, her mother insisted that she stay for a month, so Tacho worked hard at his extra jobs in the evenings and at the weekends to offset his loneliness. Amadeo came to help him and they plastered the inside walls of the house. The doors and windows arrived and it took several evenings to set them in. Amadeo had also alerted the young people at the church to the need for more sand and gravel. So once more Emilio had them organised down at the riverbed and delivered loads in his father's pick-up.

'We'll do the floor next Saturday, Tacho,' Amadeo said. 'The young people will help mix the concrete if you just get the cement. Then it will be all ready for Marta and my new niece, María, when they come back.'

'That's what I was hoping,' Tacho said smiling. 'It will be marvellous to have my family here in our own home.'

On Saturday the plumber and the butcher came to help pour the concrete floor, and their wives brought food for everyone. The job was done by dusk and everyone left in high spirits. Tacho was bone tired and had just decided to clean up and go straight to bed when he heard a shouted greeting outside. To his surprise his old friends Chucho and Tito were standing there.

'We came to see if your house was finished yet,' said Chucho. 'After seeing this place when we helped with the roof I decided to find out about settling out here too. An old acquaintance got into debt to me at cards, so he let me have his bit of land pretty cheaply and it is on the next street. It just has a lean-to on it at the moment. Tito and I thought that if we could get a more substantial hut built there, with all the building that is going on round here we could probably find plenty of work locally bricklaying and plastering. Can we come in and talk about it?'

They soon produced bottles of beer and a deck of cards and settled down for the evening. Tacho went for some bottles of soft drinks from the corner shop, but when he returned he found that his friends had been looking round and discovered an old wedding present bottle of whisky, so they doctored his Coca Cola and fruit drinks to their satisfaction. Tacho wondered what else they had found if they had been searching his shelves, but he was soon persuaded to drink with them and forget about everything else as they played cards together.

The stakes were not high but Chucho won that evening, so when they finally left Tacho's pockets were empty. Cursing himself for a fool, he drained the whisky bottle and fell onto the bed. Next day it was very late when he finally woke up. He ruefully surveyed his domain. He did have coffee, but he would just have to go hungry till he got to his mother-in-law's to visit in the afternoon. He ought to go to the church too, since everyone had helped him so much and Amadeo would be expecting him. Perhaps Marta and the baby would be allowed to accompany him. He must have a bath and see if the cold water would get rid of this headache and the aches in his bones. Nausea threatened to overcome him, but his spirits rose a little when he checked his new concrete floor and wet it down. Somehow he would have to avoid Chucho and Tito, but if they were going to live on the next street . . . He shook his head: it was all too much when he had so many really good friends and had managed to get along so well up till now! Still, the new friends need not know about this other part of his life, he comforted himself, and he began to get ready to leave for the rest of the day.

Soon the month was up and, after a long lecture from his mother-in-law on the duties of a father and son-in-law, Tacho was allowed to take Marta home along with his lovely little daughter, María. Marta's delighted praise when she saw her new house was music to his ears.

'Dear Tacho, you have worked so hard!' she exclaimed. 'And it's so light and airy with the walls all white and these new windows. A concrete floor is so easy to keep clean too. It is just perfect for our little girl to grow up in!'

'Your uncle Amadeo helped a lot and the young people from the church too,' said Tacho. 'I certainly couldn't have managed without them! My godfather and the plumber and their wives all pitched in too.'

On Saturday Amadeo came to see his great-niece and to talk over with Tacho the next project that he had in mind. However, Tacho was determined to buy the rest of the land from his partner before doing any more improvements and Amadeo encouraged him in that resolve.

On Sundays they dutifully went to visit Marta's mother, as she had told them in no uncertain terms of their need to plan time for the grandmother to be with her granddaughter. They went on to the church service later and so their weekends settled into a routine, with Tacho doing local plumbing jobs on Saturdays. Often they would visit the butcher's or the plumber's on Sunday morning and then call in on Marta's family for a little while before church. They were invited to Ana's house a few times too. The months flew by, and each week Tacho put a little in the bank and left a substantial amount with the plumber.

One day Tacho brought a hammock home and slung it on the little porch outside their kitchen. He put the baby into it and rocked her. She gurgled with glee and Marta was delighted.

'At home in Mulaca every family had a hammock on the porch,' Tacho told her. 'It's the best kind of cradle and it's quite useful for visitors too. I haven't seen them much here in the city, but during these hot months it will be much better for our little Mariquita.'

The young parents watched, marvelling, as their baby developed. Soon she was crawling and pulling herself up by whatever she could grab onto. The usual summer rains began, so it was often muddy outside and Marta had a hard job keeping María indoors and out of the mud. Then Tacho made low gates for the doorways out of the cane that grew alongside the canal nearby, and these proved a good deterrent, even after she started to toddle.

Christmas came and soon it would be María's first birthday. The plumber and Petra had wonderful news for Tacho: he would be the rightful owner of the entire double-plot of land by the day of the baby's birthday, as he had finished paying off all that they had put in to buy it. Petra decided that this merited a celebration, so what better than a birthday party for María? The plumber agreed heartily and they decided on Saturday afternoon. Petra contacted Irma as they had become fast friends and invited the whole of the butcher's family to the party. Then they told Tacho the plan but suggested that he just bring Marta and the baby on one of their regular visits so that the party would be a surprise for her. They invited some of their neighbours' children too and strung up a *piñata*. Petra and Irma filled the clay pot of the *piñata* with sweets, chewing gum, peanuts still in their shells, tiny bags of popcorn, pieces of sugar cane, small tangerines and apples. It was decorated as a lamb and the men attached it to a rope slung across the patio, then hoisted it up above people's heads.

When Tacho arrived with his family, Marta's delighted surprise was very satisfying for the plotters of the happy event. María was told that the lamb was hers so she wanted to hug it, even though it was the same size as she herself and was swinging about over their heads. Then she was the first to be given a big stick and told to hit the lamb so that it would give the goodies inside to all the children to share. She swung her stick gamely and almost toppled over, but the lamb danced up and down as the men manipulated the rope so it did not break even though she hit it and all the children cheered. The other children were blindfolded when they took their turns wielding the stick. When it came to the older ones, they were twisted round as well before being released to slash the air with the stick in the hope of hitting the elusive lamb. Excitement ran high when one of the girls knocked the lamb's head off. María cried to see her lamb 'hurt', but was comforted when they gave the head to her. The next boy managed a resounding thwack on the body that shattered the clay pot so that the contents came cascading out. At once all the children dived in to retrieve their share. The plumber's big son grabbed little María's hand and pulled her towards the scrum, then filled her lamb's head with most of what he himself picked up. With a satisfied, sunny smile she toddled back to her parents to show off her booty. It was a good party and fun for everyone.

Tired but happy, Tacho took his little family home. They arrived just as the sun was setting and Tacho's heart sank as he saw a familiar figure turning away from their gate.

'Ah, there you are, Tacho!' Chucho greeted him. 'Every time that I come to see you I find the place locked up and yet it looks lived in, so I know that you must be about somewhere nearby. And this is your little daughter? Well, she is certainly a credit to her parents.'

'Hullo, Chucho. Sorry I haven't been here when you came,' Tacho responded, though not very sincerely. He had a sinking feeling of being trapped, but still, he was flattered that Chucho should continue to seek his friendship.

'Come in for a bit, Chucho,' said Marta. 'We have just come from a birthday party given for our little girl as she was one year old this week,' she added proudly.

'One year old and a lovely señorita!' said Chucho gallantly. 'That's cause for a real celebration. I'll be back in a minute,' he added, and he hurried off in the direction of the shop.

'I must get something started for your friend to eat,' Marta said urgently. 'I'm so glad that Petra gave me the extra cake from the party. Could you get me a fresh bucket of water quickly please, Tacho?'

After the meal Marta was occupied with clearing away and then with her daughter, so she left the two men in the kitchen house. When she returned Chucho's hearty voice greeted her: 'Come and join us in a celebratory drink, Marta. You will really enjoy this special stuff,' he said waving a bottle of tequila.

'Just a tiny sip then for the baby's birthday,' she answered carrying a small glass to the table. Then she saw that they were playing cards and Tacho looked up at her rather sheepishly.

'I'll let you continue your game because I can't leave the baby on her own in the other house,' she said, gulping down the tequila hastily.

She went away wondering if it was just a friendly game or if they were really gambling. Chucho had always seemed a nice fellow to her on the few occasions that she had met him, but she knew that he was an old friend from Tacho's days at the building site and Tacho had said that they were a pretty wild lot there. Certainly it was Chucho who had brought the tequila tonight and produced the cards. But, her respectable architect brother-in-law Hector brought tequila home for special celebrations too. Anyway, this was for the men; she would just lie down with María – the party had been such a lovely surprise.

'How very thoughtful dear Petra and Irma are!' she thought happily.

She was unaware how much time had passed when suddenly the door crashed open and she started up as María began to cry.

'You are mine for tonight,' yelled Chucho thickly as he swayed in the doorway.

Then an unsteady Tacho tackled him from behind and sent him sprawling. He dragged Chucho backwards by his feet and his head cracked down on the concrete step.

'Help me!' gasped Tacho. 'Grab his feet!'

Together they dragged the inert form outside the gate. As Chucho stirred, Marta rushed to get water to bathe his head.

'No!' shouted an enraged Tacho. 'Come in and lock the door against that scum! He cheated!'

'But he's hurt, Tacho.'

'No! You are my wife, so do as I say! Now!'

'But we must help him, Tacho!'

'No! He cheated at cards just because he wants you.'

'Do you mean that you actually used me as a stake in your card game?' Marta asked, horrified.

'I lost all my money. Now get back in the house!' Tacho said belligerently.

Marta retreated a little, then with relief she saw Chucho blunder to his feet in the moonlight and stumble away down the street, so she returned to the house. Tacho followed, slamming the door and locking it. This noise frightened María who started to wail again.

'Stop that screeching!' yelled Tacho furiously. Marta was bewildered as she had always known Tacho as a gentle and considerate man. She was thoroughly frightened now, and rushed over to the baby to pick her up and comfort her.

'Leave that brat! I want you in bed! Now!' shouted this threatening, unfamiliar voice as Tacho threw off his clothes.

Marta complied as slowly as she dared, thinking despairingly: 'Do I really know this man at all, even though he is my husband? Has he often been like this before? I never even considered what happens when he meets his friends! And now I am afraid of him, afraid for both María and myself.'

Tacho soon slept drunkenly but Marta lay beside him with questions racing round and round in her mind. How could she cope with this new Tacho? To whom could she talk about it? Who could give her advice? Would such horrible nights be the norm now? What about the church and their friends there? Did this happen to other wives? Was she herself at fault somehow?

Then she began to pray: 'Oh God, what have I done? Help me to know and help me now. Please God, I don't know how to live with this!'

Finally, she fell into an exhausted sleep for a couple of hours, then María woke her and it was another day. She did all the routine things for the beginning of a day and tried to act as normally as possible, but Tacho was irritable when he finally woke up.

'Has that Chucho ever been here when I was away at work?' he asked.

'No,' she replied, startled. 'The only time he came that I know about was at the roof-pouring with everyone else.'

'Well, good!' said Tacho grudgingly. 'If ever he does appear just come indoors and lock the door. Don't even speak to him!'

She looked at him in amazement and said: 'But I thought that he was your friend!'

'I thought so too, but not any more and that's an end to it. Where's my breakfast?'

The confused thoughts started running round in Marta's mind again. She had hoped that he would explain about last night, but he made no reference to it at all. He was usually so loving with María, but this morning he was preoccupied and distant. He did not play with her and made no reference to her party of the day before. The child herself seemed aware of the change in her father and clung to her mother's skirt rather than running to him for a romp as usual.

'Do you have any money left?' Tacho said later.

'Oh yes, you keep me well supplied, so don't worry about the housekeeping.'

'You had better take María to visit her grandmother then, and I will finish that plumbing job for our neighbour.'

'Aren't you coming to church with us then?' María asked in surprise.

'Not today. I have no time and no money. I think you should get back here before dark too.'

'Perhaps I should skip the service for today then and come straight back from my mother's,' Marta said, wondering if that was what he wanted anyway.

'Do as you please, and just leave me a snack in the kitchen,' he said morosely.

Marta left with the baby soon after breakfast. She bought some flowers on the way and told her mother that they were from Tacho with his compliments as he was unavoidably detained today. Her mother was pleased that he had thought of her and asked no more questions.

Tacho seemed like his old self again when they returned home in the afternoon, but he still made no reference to the night before. He had María shrieking with delight as he played with her and Marta happily set about making a good supper for them all. A few weeks later Marta shyly advised Tacho that she was pregnant again.

'Then we must do some more building,' he replied. 'The houses are going up quickly around us here now, and there is talk of them putting in electricity, water and main drainage, and of building that school that they planned from the beginning. Lots of families are moving out here and that will be good for our children. Tito and Chucho both have wives now and seem to have settled down. They are good workers, even if they are rather rough diamonds. They certainly seem to have made quite a reputation for themselves here as reliable builders. Perhaps I'll draw up a contract with them to do my building.'

Marta was very surprised at this suggestion as she had neither seen nor heard anything about Chucho since that dreadful night of the fight.

She said timidly: 'I'm sure my uncle Amadeo would like to help again too, and perhaps the other men from the church.'

She had continued to attend the services regularly, making excuses to their friends for Tacho's absence as he never seemed free to go with her nowadays.

Now he replied: 'Yes, they were all a great help to us last year, but I need to stand on my own feet and not just accept charity. I can pay my workmen now, so I think we will just employ the neighbours. That way they will get to know me better and employ me in their turn.'

Marta was a little hurt at the exclusion of her uncle but, after all, it was Tacho who earned the money so he should be the one to decide how to use it, she reasoned. It certainly would be nice to have a bigger house. Building materials began to pile up inside their fence again and Tacho took to digging trenches for the foundations on free evenings.

One Sunday morning Tino came to visit them. It was a grand reunion and nobody knew quite why they had not seen each other for so long. This tall, well-spoken, serious, but assured young man was very different from the wide-eyed, country boy that Tacho had first met at the orphanage nearly seven years ago. Now he was a graduate from the prepa. school and it seemed that he was doing very well at his studies. His dream was to become a lawyer and he still wanted to go back to the Tutula district to help the people there who had such difficulty with Spanish. He was sure that he did not have a priestly vocation, so he could not continue at the orphanage beyond his graduation. Following the friendly butcher's advice, he also had started a bank account and he had managed to save a little money. He had kept in contact with his family in Mulaca and they were all very proud of him. He had already applied for a place at the university and had high hopes of being granted a scholarship, but for law it was a long training and very expensive. He would have to work hard to earn money to pay all his bills while he continued to study at the same time. He wanted Tacho and Marta to be his guests at the prepa. school graduation ceremony in July.

'Look, Tino, you could come and stay here with us,' Tacho told him. 'You could have the original little kitchen house because by July we hope to have more rooms on our main house. Then the accommodation wouldn't cost you anything. If you did a few jobs around here that would pay for your food too, and then you could take on some other regular job to pay for the college,' he suggested.

'Do you really mean that, Tacho? What do you say, Marta? This would be for several years you know,' Tino said with eagerness lighting up his face.

'Why, of course you must come here, Tino. Isn't Tacho your godfather. And what are godfathers good for if not to help out when necessary?' responded Marta warmly. 'Besides, our little María would love to have an uncle living here, I know!'

'Do you still work for my godfather, the butcher?' Tacho asked then.

'Yes, he is a very good friend. I am very fond of the whole family, but I shall have to get a better-paid job now if I am to make it through college,' sighed Tino in reply.

'Talk it over with him though,' Tacho urged. 'He always has such good ideas and seems to be able to see the whole picture at once.'

'Yes, I will. I'll tell him of your kind suggestion too,' said Tino. 'You haven't seen him yourself

lately, have you, Tacho? I'll tell him how busy you
are with your new building plans now.'

After that Tino found time to come and help quite
often, so they were soon ready for Chucho and
Tito to start building a room for a kitchen. They
planned to add some bedrooms a few months later
so that the original room could become the living
room. With two children they would certainly need
more space, and with an extra bedroom, Marta
thought, they could take in lodgers which would
improve their income.

Marta was a little nervous the first day when
Chucho and Tito turned up to work, but they
greeted her very respectfully and got on with the
building without bothering her. As Tacho had said,
they were hard workers and she could see real
progress on her dream house each day. At the
weekend Tacho took her round to visit Chucho's
and Tito's families along with María. They still had
only the one small hut on their property, but each
was planning his own building after they had
finished work on Tacho's house. The women were
just young girls who turned out to be sisters. They
were rather shy but very pleased to be visited and
to see little María. Tito's girl had given birth to a
baby son just a few months before and the other
sister expected to give birth to Chucho's baby in a
couple of months' time. As they confided to Marta,
they hoped that the men would marry them after
the houses were built. They seemed quite impressed
that Tacho and Marta had been married for more
than a year before María was born.

'Chucho and Tito have often told us about your
wedding,' they said. 'We don't have any fine friends

who could give a fiesta like that for us though!' they added sadly. 'Our father had two families. We were part of the second, so he was never married to our mother, although he spent a lot of time with us till a few years ago. Then he just moved away and abandoned us all without leaving any message or money or anything. We both went to work then, but we didn't earn much and our mother was pleased to get us off her hands when we took up with Chucho and Tito. She had to think of the younger ones.'

'So how old are you?' Marta asked with a sympathetic smile.

'My sister Flora is Chucho's woman and she was fifteen last month. I'm called Elia and I'm Tito's woman. I will be seventeen at the end of this month, and this is my baby son, Gerardo, but we call him Lalo,' the elder sister explained.

María loved baby Lalo and wanted to hug him, so they sat her down on a little palm mat so that she could hold him in her lap with her mother's help. Elia made the most of this opportunity and very soon served them all with coffee and sweet bread rolls.

When they got home Marta said, 'I'm glad we went round there and met those girls, Tacho. I hope that Chucho and Tito are good to them, because they are so eager to please and so proud of their menfolk.'

'Oh, I think those fellows have settled down a bit now. They didn't invite me out to drink with them or even start a game of cards today, and we were visiting them in their own place!'

16

Tacho the plumber

The kitchen was finished, and to Marta's great relief, there had been no big drinking party to celebrate its completion. Tacho had the plumbing all ready, as electricity and water were promised in their street the following month. The people at the corner shop wanted his services in their kitchen too, and in the new bathroom that they were in the process of adding on to their house. Other people had arrived on the plot next to them and were building a very nice house there. They also were eager to employ Tacho as their plumber. He talked it all over with his partner.

'I don't want to leave you in the lurch after all your kindness and help, but it looks as if I could be fully employed locally now,' Tacho told him. 'What do you think? Would you want to work over there with me? How many contracts have we taken on among your neighbours here that are still outstanding?'

'Well, my own son, Selso, finishes secondary school in a few weeks now. As you know he followed your example and learnt plumbing, which is why he has been able to help us a bit lately. If you feel it is time to branch out on your own now, that

will be fine because he can work with me and I am
sure that we two can keep up with the work here. I
could always call on you in an emergency. With
electricity and water coming to your street, you will
probably have a telephone line soon too!'

'Yes, and I could call on you in an emergency as
well,' responded Tacho.

They both laughed and parted very amicably.
When Tacho said goodbye to the family, Petra
repeatedly invited him to bring Marta and their
daughter to visit at the weekends just the same, and
he assured her that they would come often. She
particularly wanted them to be present at her son's
graduation from the secondary school in July when
her brother was to be his nephew's godfather.

'This is going to be a busy summer work-wise
and socially,' Tacho said to Marta that evening. 'First
there's the electricity. Fortunately I know someone
who will wire up the house for us. I'm sure that
Tino will be very glad to have an electric light in his
room to study by in the evenings. As for water, we
have the well, so we can connect into the mains later.
I want to get those bedrooms done during the
canícula when the rains ease up a bit. Then there are
these graduations to attend during July, and your
birthday in August.'

'My birthday?' she exclaimed in surprise. 'But I'm
an old married woman now and no one needs to
worry about *that*. The baby's arrival in November is
much more important, and what about your birthday next month first?'

Tacho laughed and went on to talk about setting
up his own business: 'I think I shall keep my tools
and supplies here in the corner of our main room

for now because it is dry and more secure. I can make the kitchen part of the old house into my workroom and Tino can occupy the other half when he moves in.'

They dressed carefully when it came to Tino's graduation at the end of June as they did not want to be conspicuous. They knew that most of his fellow students came from well-to-do homes and it would be easy to disgrace him if they looked out of place. However, it all went off well and Tacho was very proud to see one of his own people from Mulaca get this qualifying certificate. They went for a quiet celebration supper at a restaurant afterwards and the following day Tino moved in.

July was upon them and Tacho started digging trenches again. He wanted Chucho and Tito to begin work on the planned bedrooms the following week as the ground was fairly dry again now. Tino and little María went with Tacho and Marta to young Selso's graduation at the secondary school, and then on to the plumber's house afterwards where Petra had prepared something special for the occasion. Selso loved playing with María and was very deferential to Tacho. He was determined to work very hard to fill Tacho's place so that he could become a partner with his father in the business and not disappoint his mother. This was a great relief to Tacho as he had felt a bit guilty at leaving this kind friend who had helped him so much and advised him so well. 'But it is much better for the plumber's own son to work with him and carry on in his father's footsteps, if he is willing to do that,' Tacho told himself. When they got home Tacho had a proposition to put to Tino right away.

'Have you found a job yet?' he asked him.

'No, I haven't. Several promising leads have led to nothing,' replied Tino anxiously.

'Well look, I've been thinking,' Tacho said. 'I'm just starting out on my own here, but already I am up to my eyes in offers of work and I don't know how I can make all these contracts and honour them without help. How about if you become my partner? You could do all the necessary office work much better than I can. You could also keep an eye on the supplies as well as doing the buying for me. You could even assist me where two pairs of hands are needed and get some on-the-job experience. I think that our profits should make a decent income for you and if you see something better later on we can change the arrangement. Think about it for a while.'

Tino looked at him with shining eyes.

'That is most generous of you, Tacho, much more than many godfathers would think of doing. I know that you want to do more on this house and improve your property. Are you sure that you really want me as a partner with the new baby coming and everything?'

'Yes, I do,' Tacho responded with emphasis. 'I know you and your family. We share the same background and I can trust you completely. I would have to employ someone anyway, and I would never have the same assurance about someone else. It is a very valuable thing to know all about a prospective partner here in the city where so many people are not what they seem. You understand me and know where I am coming from, and I think that you are fond of my family too.'

'Thank you very much for your confidence in me, Tacho. I don't need to think any more about this. I just accept very gratefully. I only hope that I don't disappoint you. I'm sure that our families back in Mulaca will be happy to know about all this too. Since you have helped me to sort out my immediate future so satisfactorily, I think that I will make a quick trip out there to see everybody, if you don't have any work that is super-urgent for this week?'

'Perhaps you could just help me to plan ahead tomorrow and get some supplies on hand for the jobs that I have taken on already, then you could go for a few days and we would start together in earnest on Monday,' responded Tacho.

'Sounds a good scheme to me,' said Tino gratefully and they parted for the night.

Marta was delighted to hear about this new development. She had been getting a little worried because people kept coming to ask for plumbing work to be done right away, and Tacho never seemed to turn anyone down. It would be so much better with some order and planning, so that they knew how long each job was expected to take and when it should be done by. Then Tacho could make firm contracts with people and do a better job without getting in a muddle. Marta still attended the Baptist church as often as she could, and took little María with her. She wished that Tacho would go too and not work quite so hard. As she boarded the bus to return home that Sunday she saw Tino running to catch the same bus, so they made the rest of the journey together.

Tacho was eager to hear all the news, although Mulaca seemed very distant to him now. It was hard to think of those well-known people these many years older, just as he was himself. The life there seemed very remote from his own daily experiences here in the city.

'Your cousin, Sana, now has three children and the eldest will start "kinder" next school year,' Tino reported.

'I can hardly believe it! Sana the mother of three now! Why, that makes me the uncle of three nephews or nieces since she is my cousin. Do they still live in the old family house?'

'Yes,' Tino answered, 'but there is bad news too. Your grandmother died last January and your father wasn't allowed to get there for the funeral. He and your stepmother are well though and you now have two little sisters and a small brother that you have never met. Your own youngest brother and sister stayed with your father and stepmother as well. Did you realise that your baby sister Rita is now fourteen years old? Both she and Neyo are a great help to the family, but I understand that both Chico and Nino are still as wild as ever. One of them will settle down with a girl for a few months, then break out again and move on. They shoot it out with their opponents as soon as they get into a quarrel, which is often, but they really stick together, though they still seem to be at odds with your father. They even ride into Mulaca sometimes, threatening people that they have a grudge against, and just daring anyone to arrest them or accuse them of any wrongdoing. Beni has a husband and baby, so that's another nephew for you. They live at Red River, down on the coast.'

'Those brothers of mine sound to be completely out of touch!' Tacho burst out. 'But I suppose every-

one has to sort out their own life. I'm sorry that
they are not on good terms with my father though.
I'm sure that he needs their help, but it is good
that he has another wife. Did you say that Beni is
married and has a baby son? Who is my brother-in-
law then? And you say my father's wife's name is
Dora?'

'Hang on, Tacho! I don't know any more details
like the names of the children or anything about
Beni's man. My own family is all right except that
my father is beginning to show his age. My mother
confessed that he gets unmanageably drunk at
every fiesta now and has become a bit of a laughing
stock there in the village. I don't know how it came
about exactly, apart from the village customs and
obligations. He was fine those few days while I was
there, but he kept repeating how sorry he was that
I had decided not to become a priest. He is proud
of what I have achieved, but he has this nagging
suspicion that it would be much more important
to have a son who is in training for the priesthood
than one who is to become a lawyer. I told him
that I plan to return to the area to help people there,
whereas if I became a priest I would probably be
sent to another part of the country, but he wasn't
convinced.'

'Perhaps he will understand better as time
goes on,' suggested Tacho, although he privately
wondered how much truth there might be in his
words.

The next day Chucho and Tito continued work
on the new rooms while Tacho and Tino started
working together on the plumbing obligations for
their neighbours. This meant that they were still near

enough to be called upon if an extra pair of hands was needed briefly for the building work. Tacho and Tino found that they made a good team. They soon became well known locally as reliable workmen and got as much work as they could handle.

'This is marvellous, Tacho! I shall certainly have enough money for the university if we go on like this,' said Tino. 'But when classes start I won't be able to work with you so much because I will be gone every morning, and I will have to take time in the evenings to study too,' he added.

'Yes, I've been thinking about how we can work it out,' responded Tacho. 'For one thing, it is plain that we must build a proper workshop and office, so I'll put Chucho and Tito onto that as soon as they finish these bedrooms. For another, we could take on an apprentice. We could go over to the orphanage and see if there are any other secondary schoolers specialising in plumbing, especially any from the Tutula district. They could get hands-on experience with us. That way we could help them and expand at the same time.'

'That sounds like a good solution, Tacho. But do you mean to offer them a home here apart from the orphanage? We would have to talk it over with Padre Domingo who is in charge now, because the orphanage usually pays all their expenses.'

'Right, well, we'll see about it when their classes start, since yours will begin at about the same time,' said Tacho.

Marta was fully in accord with these plans for expansion as she always hoped to see Tacho take a little more time off work. She planned to make a special meal for everyone on her birthday and to make them all slow down for a few hours. She thought that she would talk to Elia and Flora, Tito's and Chucho's womenfolk, and get them to help her since they were near at hand. They probably had not had the chance to have a family fiesta very often either.

Tacho and Tino helped the builders when it came time to pour the roof of the new bedrooms, and a few days later Tacho and Marta were able to move their bed into one of them, which made their original big room look rather empty. Chucho and Tito were a bit disgruntled that there was to be no celebration for the completion of that phase, but were somewhat mollified when they heard that the new workshop building was needed immediately, so work would continue without a break. They had the foundations completed by the time of Marta's birthday.

They had come to work as usual that morning, and looked up in surprise later on when Elia and Flora turned up with the babies. Tacho and Tino had left early to finish a bathroom in a new house on the next street, but returned at midday with big, self-conscious grins as they presented bouquets to the birthday girl. Marta, who thought that Tacho had forgotten the date, was overwhelmed by the beautiful floral gifts. This made her particularly glad that she and the girls had planned something special for the dinner. When they called the men for the meal, Chucho was not there, but he quickly re-appeared and Marta's heart sank as he waved an all-too-familiar bottle. He and Tito each gave her a jovial birthday hug, then proceeded to spike the soft drinks in the glasses at each place on the table with a dash of tequila. The women served the men first and Tacho was loud in his praise of his lovely wife. Afterwards the men moved outdoors and went over to the porch outside Tino's room to relax while the women and children had their fiesta meal. Chucho left the rest of the bottle of tequila on the table although he did not insist that the women drink it. The men did not seem much affected by what they had drunk, just a little merry, so Marta relaxed and chatted happily with the other young mothers. Elia's baby Lalo was growing fast and crawling every-where when allowed to. Flora's baby girl was now two months old and a delight to María. Flora herself, however, did not look nearly as healthy as her baby, so Marta offered to take her along to the clinic when she went for her next monthly check-up in a few days' time. Both girls were surprised by the suggestion and said that they had never been inside a clinic. Their mother had come and delivered each of their babies and they just followed her advice.

'Isn't that what most girls do?' Elia asked with a puzzled expression.

'I don't know,' Marta replied, 'but they really helped me at the clinic and they are very kind and understanding. Come and see, because that doctor's advice is worth having,' she urged Flora.

They cleared everything away and Marta pressed a pot of leftovers on each girl to take home along with a few tortillas. It all seemed very quiet when they had gone so she wandered over to Tino's room, thinking that all the men must have gone inside. But only Tino answered her call. He was doing some bookwork and said that Chucho and Tito had per-suaded Tacho to accompany them to the cantina to continue the celebration.

Marta returned to the main house thinking disconsolately: 'I planned this as a happy day, but it is all turning out badly now. Where did I go wrong, God? What will Tacho be like when he comes home? Will he and Chucho get into a fight again? Please help me to know what to do!'

As dusk was falling Tino came in and said: 'I'm going over to the cantina, Marta, to see what's happening. I'll try to persuade Tacho to come home, so have some strong coffee ready!'

Marta waited anxiously till finally, by the light of the new streetlamp, she saw Tino half dragging a protesting Tacho towards their gateway. She ran to help and talked soothingly to her husband, but once inside the house he pushed her away and turned on Tino angrily. They urged him into a chair and Marta quickly brought the coffee, but Tacho pettishly knocked the cup out of her hand so that it crashed on the concrete floor. Then he slumped sideways and almost fell to the floor himself.

'If we just get him to bed, perhaps he will sleep,' whispered Marta, and together they managed to half carry him to the bed in the other room. Marta was glad to see that María was still fast asleep, so she hurried to clear up the spilt coffee and to get something for Tino's supper before retiring herself.

'You must call me if there is any trouble later, Marta,' Tino said anxiously as he was saying goodnight.

Marta slid into bed between her husband and little María and was just drifting off to sleep when he rolled over and jabbed her hard with his fist. She let out an involuntary cry, which awakened the child who set up a wail. Tacho growled drunkenly and began to hit out with his fists. Marta tried to move out of reach of the punishing blows while comforting and protecting María at the same time, but he grabbed her and slammed her back down on the bed. Then she pushed the child onto the corner of the bed urgently telling her to get down onto the ground. The child was screaming with fear now, but suddenly the light came on and there was Tino in the doorway. He scooped up María in a blanket and deposited her in the main room, then ran back and pinned Tacho down to let Marta escape.

'Take María to my bed and I'll stay here and keep him quiet,' said Tino through clenched teeth. Sad and afraid, Marta complied. It took a long time to quieten the child, but eventually she slept while her mother lay beside her, bruised and exhausted. She was shocked by this attack from her usually gentle husband and humiliated that it had needed Tino to rescue her. Nonetheless, she was glad that he had been nearby to save her little daughter. She was still shaking uncontrollably, but the house was quiet now with the light out. Finally she dozed off till dawn.

When Tacho awoke and Tino told him what had happened he burst into tears of remorse. Little María only had a very confused impression of the frightening events of the night, so when she saw her beloved father crying she ran over to hug and comfort him. Tino led the sorry figure off for a bath while Marta got some food ready for them all. During a subdued breakfast, Tino reminded him of their commitments for that day, so they soon left to fix up yet another kitchen with running water.

Chucho and Tito put in a very belated appearance but were able to do a bit more work on the new building. They looked sheepishly at Marta but made no reference to the previous evening and did not ask about Tacho. She was glad that they had gone before Tacho and Tino got home that evening, but she was also glad that there was evidence that they had been working. She prepared a welcoming, tasty supper as the best way she knew to show Tacho that she had forgiven him.

Tacho talked to her quietly and earnestly that evening and vowed that it would never happen again. He was horrified when he saw the bruises that he had caused and worriedly inquired about their unborn baby. A few days later, after her checkup at the clinic, he asked again and was relieved when she told him how reassuring the doctor had been that all was well. On Sunday he accompanied his wife and daughter to visit his mother-in-law, armed with a basket of fruit, and then they went on to the service at the church. Everyone gave him a hearty welcome back there, particularly Ana's father and Marta's uncle Amadeo. The latter had been very worried about them but had sensed that it might not be a propitious time to visit. Now, seeing Tacho and hearing of all the work that they had been doing to the house, he smiled and said: 'I must come and see all these improvements and developments for myself. To think that you now have streetlamps – and electricity in the house, as well as these new rooms! That's marvellous! How about if I come over next Saturday?'

'We will be looking out for you, uncle,' they told him happily as they left for home.

When Amadeo arrived he was duly impressed and kept congratulating Tacho on what he had achieved. He was loud in his praise for the way Tacho and Tino were managing their plumbing business, and for the way Tacho was putting his profits into his property.

As he left he said: 'I know someone who wants to sell his old living-room furniture. Would you be interested? I'm sure it won't be very expensive, but I know that it is still in good condition. We could go and see it next Saturday if you like. Just come round to my place about mid-afternoon and I'll take you along there.'

Marta was quite excited by the prospect of furniture, so it was agreed. María was also excited that they would see this nice uncle again quite soon: he had introduced her to lollipops. He had been giving them to her at church for weeks, but to get them on Saturdays as well she recognised as a bonus!

The sofa and armchairs gave their big room a much more lived-in look, and Marta was determined to put pretty curtains everywhere as soon as the bedrooms were plastered and the floors had been put in. The workshop and office were soon finished and the bedroom walls and floors were to be the next project. Chucho and Tito had got into debt, so Tacho had given them all of their contract money in advance to help them settle the debt. On their final day he gave them a bonus in the morning and then rushed off with Tino on an urgent plumbing job to avoid any more 'celebrations'. This unexpected generosity really pleased the men in spite of the lack of a fiesta, so they cleaned up very carefully at the end and were very affable to Marta and the little girl as they left.

'Greetings to Flora, Elia and the babies too,' Marta called. 'Tell them that I will be calling round again soon.'

In short order Tacho and Tino had their tools and plumbing supplies arranged on shelves in the workshop and a big table for Tino to work on in the office. There was just room for a bed as well, so he decided to move over to the more permanent building. They went back to the orphanage one evening and were introduced to Silvano who had taken the plumbing course but had decided to continue on to the prepa. school as he was very keen on mathematics. He jumped at the chance of a steady job and they worked out an arrangement with Padre Domingo whereby Silvano would stay some nights each week at the orphanage and some at Tacho's house. Then Padre Domingo remembered another boy, Abram, who had recently left them to work on a building site.

'He comes back every weekend, so he can't have many friends,' the Padre told them. 'He doesn't seem very happy at all, although he won't admit it. And yes, he must be from the Tutula area as well, because he came with Padre Hilario. I will talk to him next time and find out if he is under contract. If not, I could send him out to see you if you have work for yet another hand. I'm sure he would be much better off with you.'

'That would be good,' said Tacho enthusiastically. 'Yes, we have plenty of work for another apprentice and he would be full-time too. Thank you, Padre. We look forward to meeting Abram, and Silvano here can start work after school tomorrow afternoon.'

The following weekend Abram came to see Tacho and was eager to join them; at the beginning of October he moved in to share the original hut with Silvano. He was indeed from the Tutula district but from another village, San Isidro. He was extremely glad to meet others from the same area and he felt comfortable with them straight away as he knew that they were familiar with his background.

Marta had made the extra bedroom look very attractive and they had advertised its availability at the shop. One day a young man from the electricity commission inquired about lodging there, since he could only get home to his wife and family at weekends. This meant a private income for Marta, but it also meant that she had five men to feed most of the time. They decided that she should employ Elia and Flora to help her, which in turn gave them a small private income too. They were very grateful for the opportunity.

They had just got into a good routine when Marta had to go into the clinic for the birth of baby Antonio. Tacho was inordinately proud of his small son, but had reluctantly agreed to let his mother-in-law take charge again and look after Marta and the children when they left the clinic. Marta refused to stay with her mother more than three weeks this time. She had planned things carefully with Elia and Flora so that they could manage all the meals during her absence. Irma accompanied them at the clinic again and said that she would go and check personally every few days to see that the girls were coping all right with the shopping and money. Once

more Tacho was reminded how fortunate he was
that the butcher had become his godfather and
that he and Irma had remained such good friends
ever since.

Tino and Silvano were studying hard at nights,
the lodger kept to himself, and Abram always
seemed to be worn out by suppertime and ready
for bed. With his family away, Tacho found the
evenings that he was not visiting them very long
and lonely. He took to escorting Elia and Flora home
after supper and staying on there for a game of cards
with Chucho and Tito along with a few drinks. They
did not get wildly drunk nor play for high stakes
during the week, as they were concerned about the
next day's work, but it became a habit. When the
three weeks were up he warmly welcomed his
family home again, but he continued to visit Chucho
and Tito two or three nights a week.

When they heard that main drainage was to be
put in down their street, Tacho decided that it was
time to build a proper bathroom in their own house
and to add one more large bedroom to accommodate his growing family. The small bedroom that
they now occupied could then be let to another
lodger, since the letting was working out very
well with the electrician. Marta was sure that one
more mouth to feed would be no problem with
all the help that she was getting from the girls.
'Also, it's about time that I built a wall round this
property to replace that old, rickety fence,' Tacho
told himself.

With the men's meals to be made regularly
Marta was not free to go visiting so often nowadays,
or even to church. She was proud, however, of

her husband's good reputation and prosperity. Sometimes her uncle Amadeo would visit them on a Saturday and she enjoyed boasting to him about it. He was glad to see them happy and prospering but he noticed that Tacho was frequently out with his friends now and did not spend so much of his free time with his family. He reminded Marta of her blessings and warned her to be careful not to let all these good things in her life become more important to her than God was.

She looked surprised and said: 'But Tacho worked hard for all that we have! I am very grateful to God for my husband and my lovely children, but both Tacho and I work hard and we are trying to help these boys that work for Tacho as well. Surely God should be satisfied with us, even if we can't always get to church?'

Amadeo smiled gently as he replied. 'Who are you working for, my dear? Are you just making a living for yourselves or are you working at this as God's servant? He is the One who gave you the opportunity and the health and the strength.'

'I never thought about it like that, uncle,' she admitted. 'I am sure that God loves me and I am sure of His forgiveness, so I really thank Him for that. I love to attend church and praise Him along with other Christians, but I must admit that I don't think about Him much during the week. He doesn't seem to fit in with our ordinary home routine somehow. With all the work that we do it is hard to think of these things that we buy with our own money as given to us by God.'

'You are right, Marta. Many people find this concept hard to accept,' continued Amadeo. 'We talk glibly about the Señor Jesus Christ, but do we really mean that? "Señor" means "boss", you know.'

'Does it really?' exclaimed Marta in surprise. 'I thought it just meant "mister" and showed our respect.'

'It means both, my dear, but when we use it of Jesus we should be thinking of Him as the Almighty King and Boss who graciously allows us to be His servants. It's a very satisfying thing to work for God, you know, and really gives you happiness. Try it!'

Amadeo left Marta with a lot to think about. 'I really want to be a Christian and belong to God. That's why I kept on going to church with Ana in the first place, even though my mother wasn't very pleased about it. But Tacho doesn't want to talk about these things any more, and I love him and want to please him too because I promised before God to be a good wife. We said that we were going to read the Bible together when we moved out here, but we never have. There doesn't seem to be any time for it now, with Tacho's other friends and interests,' she pondered sadly.

17

Disaster

The years rolled by and two more children were born to Tacho and Marta: another boy, Cándido, and then a little girl, Rosa. Regretfully Silvano left them when he graduated from the prepa. school and another student took his job. Young Abram had become a very skilful and responsible assistant and he had copied Tacho in everything. He followed him to the cantina, he smoked and gambled. He also invested his money in a radio, then a good cassette recorder, later a television set and always plenty of expensive clothes. He spent time with various girls but he could not decide on one that he wanted for a wife.

Tino would have a drink with the other men on special occasions, but never to excess; he also played the occasional game of cards with them, but not for money. His foremost interest was in his studies. He was very kind and considerate to Marta and an ever-present uncle and playmate for the children, who adored him. Marta wondered sometimes how they would manage when he became an independent lawyer and moved away; she recognised that their thriving business owed as much to his office

management and calming influence on Tacho
himself as to the older man's practical skill. With
María at the 'kinder' pre-school nearby, Marta was
fully occupied looking after the two younger ones
and the new baby. In spite of their prosperity and
various useful aids in the house, there did not seem
to be much extra cash and it appeared that Tacho
rarely added to their bank account nowadays. This
made Marta very glad of her independent income
from the lodgers, although she knew that they
would need more bedrooms for their own family
soon.

Tino continued to keep a friendly eye on Tacho
and to help him home when he got drunk. A few
times he became fighting drunk as before, but Tino
managed to protect Marta and the children from the
worst of it. However, one Saturday evening Tacho
picked a fight at the cantina, convinced that his
companions were cheating at cards. Abram ran
home to tell Tino, but by the time they arrived on
the scene the cantina was a wreck and the proprietor
had called the police. Tino tried to reason with Tacho
and was assaulted for his pains. Then he approached
the proprietor but damage had been done to his
property and the man was determined for the matter
to be settled at the Town Hall. Tacho was dragged
away to jail and Tino returned home to tell Marta
the sad news.

Next day he went to the Town Hall to meet the
authorities and see about getting Tacho out. The
fine was a stiff one and then reparation to the cantina
added substantially to the bill. A sober and apparently repentant Tacho went quietly home with Tino,
but that afternoon Tino saw him drinking alone

from his own supply of whisky. Marta and the children returned from church in a taxi as it was the only way that she could manage all four at once and Tacho was furious. He was drunk again now and shouted abuse at her. The children began to cry, so he herded them into the bedroom and slammed the door on them. Then he staggered into the kitchen and started throwing things from the sink and draining board onto the concrete floor. He tried to grab Marta and knocked the radio onto the floor as he lunged at her.

Tino appeared and told Marta to take the children outside and he would get Tacho to bed. He persuaded Tacho to have another drink with him, and the wild mood passed. When Tacho was asleep, Tino helped Marta to move the children's mattress from their bed into a corner of the living room and then she went to clear up the mess in the kitchen so that she could make the supper. She was very thankful to see that she still had enough plates and cups for everyone in spite of the breakages. Nervously, she began her preparations. She was very afraid that the lodgers would complain about all the disturbance and might want to leave, but to her great relief no one mentioned it.

After the meal she settled the little boys down on the mattress and let María lie on the sofa with the baby while she finished her work in the kitchen and prepared for the next morning.

'I'll stay with Tacho, Marta. You sleep in here with the children,' Tino advised.

He carried the sleeping María over to the mattress with her little brothers and Marta took her place on the sofa. She was exhausted and quickly fell asleep, feeling that at least all her children were safe as long as Tino was looking after things.

The children remained asleep in the morning while she tidied the room and got coffee ready for all the men. The lodgers left for work and Tino sent Abram to deal with the most pressing calls for a plumber's attention. The student went to classes and Tino himself offered to take María to her school on his way to his current work experience with a law firm in the city. Marta remembered that Flora would be coming shortly and she decided to have her do the laundry out by the well rather than work in the house, so she quickly gathered up some dirty clothes. Flora could keep an eye on the little boys as she worked, since they were always happy playing with her own two children. Marta had just managed to get them all organised and was feeding the baby when she heard stirrings in the bedroom and then splashing in the bathroom. She made some fresh coffee, reheated the beans, and had eggs ready in case Tacho should want those as well. Flora had brought the day's supply of fresh tortillas with her, so Tacho's breakfast was all ready. He did look rather the worse for wear when he appeared, but he had made an effort to spruce himself up, and Marta made no reference to his looks.

'I really slept late, but I am certainly glad to see some coffee,' he said, reaching for his cup.

'Don't worry about the work. Tino sent Abram to do those plumbing jobs that you promised for today,' Marta hastened to reassure him.

'That Tino seems to look after me all the way around, yet *I'm* supposed to be *his* godfather!' Tacho commented regretfully. 'He helped to pay that dreadful bill at the *cantina* so now we are in debt to him. All that we had in the bank went for the fine at the Town Hall. You do know that I don't *mean* to get into these ghastly situations, don't you? Did I hurt anybody this time? I can't remember a thing!'

'Not here at the house, but it all might have been much worse without Tino,' Marta told him honestly. 'I wonder what we will do when he moves on, Tacho? He still wants to practise law back in Tutula, he says.'

'Yes, I know,' said Tacho glumly. 'He and Abram have faithfully kept up with their families in Mulaca and San Isidro all through the years, and Tino has plenty of contacts in Tutula as well. In spite of his humble background I think they may respect him professionally. I think he may have his eye on a young lady out there too, and it really is time that he was thinking of getting married. He will need all his money when he makes the move though, so I must make sure that he is paid back very soon. Can you manage on just what you get from the lodgers for a few weeks?' he asked anxiously.

'Oh yes, including anything that I need for the children, but I won't have enough to get the radio mended or to replace the dishes,' Marta said worriedly.

'What happened then?' Tacho asked, startled.

'The radio got knocked off the kitchen table in the fracas last night and you pitched several cups and plates onto the floor, so they broke. Look, here are all the pieces and the damaged radio.'

'Oh no, how could I? What else did I do?' groaned Tacho glancing at what she held out and then putting his head in his hands.

'Nothing, because Tino put you to bed and we all slept out here,' she replied.

'I really do owe that young man a lot, much more than just the money,' Tacho said. 'I don't like to be dependent on him like this, but after I have been drinking for a bit I can't stop. I became totally unaware of what I do or say! It is hard to admit that I completely lose control of myself, especially as I can't remember any of it afterwards, but you have shown me enough evidence, so I know it is true that I did all this damage. I believe you, but I hate the truth!'

That evening Tacho and Tino were closeted together in the office for a long time, working out just how to proceed. Tacho was determined to straighten up and shoulder his responsibilities and he knew that he was very lucky to have someone like Tino still willing to help him.

'I must get out and do more of the actual rough work with Abram from now on,' he said. 'Perhaps we should let that student go at the end of this month. If I put my back into it Abram and I can manage it all with your help, Tino.'

'I think you are right,' Tino said thoughtfully. 'That would be one less to pay and one less mouth for Marta to feed.'

'I heard that the local school is expanding and building new classrooms, so they will want more toilets and washrooms probably,' said Tacho. 'If I could get that contract it would be a good lump sum to help me to get on my feet again. It is conveniently near home too. I was working at that nice two-storey house next to the school last week, so I must go and finish the work there tomorrow. At the same time I can find out which building firm is to work at the school and see about that contract.'

They settled down into a strict routine for a few weeks with Tacho and the willing Abram working from early morning till dusk, sometimes doing an evening job too. The student was not unhappy to leave, with all this extra work going on: he had never been as work-sharp as his predecessor. When it came to María's 'graduation' from the 'kinder' school, they all stopped for the day. Everyone was proud and impressed to see the procession of little six-year-olds receiving their documents from the hands of the director of the primary school. He smiled and said something encouraging to each one so that several of the little girls giggled, including María. Then he gave a short speech, welcoming them all as the incoming class to his primary school for the next academic year. Tino was María's godfather for this happy occasion and he gave her a beautiful pair of black, shiny shoes, which delighted her because they looked so grown up. Marta looked forward to receiving the prints of the photographs so that she had a visible reminder of this proud day. She planned to frame the best photo and put it up on the living-room wall beside her wedding photo. The rest would go into a big family album that they had bought and which the children never tired of perusing. They had to identify each separate occasion and everyone in the picture every time.

María's school uniform for the primary school and a few other expenses slowed Tacho down in his repayments to Tino. By Christmas, however, he had managed it, so in the new year he relaxed a bit more. Tino was making regular trips to Tutula now, and one day he shyly told Marta about this wonderful girl from the prestigious Nuñez family. She was two years younger than he, but he had noticed her when she started at the same prepa. school that he had attended years before. Since both came from the Tutula area, it had given them something in common, and now as a promising young lawyer Tino had become acceptable to her family. The wedding was set for the first Saturday after Easter. Tino had made another good friend, who was the eldest son in another important Tutula family. He had promised to stand up with Tino at the wedding and his parents had offered to be the wedding godparents.

'You will all come to my wedding, won't you?' Tino begged Marta. 'My family from Mulaca will be there of course, but so few of them speak much Spanish, even though the children are getting the full six years of primary school right there in the village now. I really do need some relatives who can converse with my future in-laws, and that means you, as I have been part of your family for so long. After all, it is not so isolated out there now: several buses go to Tutula from Oaxaca each day and the road is greatly improved. The journey only takes seven hours, if there are no problems along the way.'

'It might be possible,' Marta replied with a smile. 'You are certainly very persuasive.'

'My godfather for the wedding is giving us a dance all night on the Friday, then we will be off to the Town Hall early on Saturday morning for the civil ceremony. Afterwards we will go to Alicia's house for the wedding breakfast and then to midday

Mass at the parish church for the wedding service. After that it's back to my godfather's for the wedding dinner and another night of dancing. We will be living in one of the houses that belong to Alicia's father. In fact, it is the one right next door to her parents, which pleases her mother very much. My godfather has let me have a room for an office on the high street, just off the main square where the church and the Town Hall are, but I would like to bring Alicia back here for a few weeks at first while I tie up final details at this end.'

'It sounds as if you have fallen on your feet, Tino, and I am very happy for you,' said Marta. 'Of course you must bring Alicia here. One of my lodgers is leaving at Easter, so you two can have that bedroom rather than cram yourselves into the office where you are sleeping now. You have helped us so much and you really deserve this good fortune,' she added with feeling, privately wondering how she could ever have coped without him, and what might happen to her husband when the steadying influence of this resourceful young man had gone from their home.

Tacho seemed to have turned over a new leaf. He had managed to land the school contract and he was putting money away in the bank again regularly. He was determined for all of them to attend Tino's wedding and to be a credit to him. As soon as the lodger moved out just before Easter, Tino moved his belongings into the second bedroom and Abram in his turn moved into the office. The old, original plank building was quite dilapidated now and Tacho planned to pull it down. For the present they would just use their second plot as arable land

and develop it later. Their house was detached and had its own wall round it now for security, like all the other permanent houses that had been built on their street.

Tino left for Tutula and his wedding with Tacho and Marta assuring him that they would be there on the great day with their family. Marta arranged for Abram and the remaining lodger to eat their meals with Elia and Flora while she was away. Tito and Chucho seemed very happy with the idea of their wives doing this and earning a little extra cash.

Tacho and his family travelled to Tutula overnight and arrived rather dishevelled at dawn on the wedding morning. He hardly recognised the town for its many improvements. Now that the road was so much better, it had made access easier and brought lots of visitors. There were a couple of hotels and Tino had reserved rooms for them in the one right on the square. They quickly found their way there after a reviving cup of coffee along with some sweet rolls. Marta unpacked their wedding clothes to be ready for them after a hot shower, while Tacho marvelled at all the conveniences now available. Later María sat primly on her bed and preened herself in her pretty new dress. Antonio was very pleased with his new jeans, which were too long and had to be turned up several times, and with his new belt, which was really useful to keep them properly in place. Young Cándido kept sitting down to show off his new shoes to everybody because they were shiny, and even baby Rosa kept smoothing the frills of her new dress as her father admired it.

When they were all ready they went down to the square again to look around and were just in time to see the wedding party leaving the Town Hall after their civil ceremony. Tino called out a welcome and they went over to be introduced to Alicia and her parents and to congratulate the bride and groom. Tino's parents were there so Tacho had a grand reunion with Rolando and a busy time proudly introducing all his family. Eventually they moved off towards Alicia's home where a sumptuous breakfast and lots more of the family and other guests were waiting.

It was a happy but tiring day. Tacho met several people that he knew, but had trouble conversing freely with them because he had all but forgotten his original language. He and his family were made very welcome by Tino's in-laws who were amazed that Tacho had originated in Mulaca. Tacho was careful to accept only beer or soft drinks so as not to risk getting drunk and disgracing Tino. They left the dance early and picked up Cándido and Rosa who were both fast asleep on someone's bed along with several other small children in their rumpled finery. They slept at the hotel for the rest of the night and caught the early bus back to Oaxaca in the morning. The seven-hour bus ride by day was especially hard on the children. On the outward journey by night they had been able to sleep quite a lot of the time, but now María and Toño were constantly wanting to know how many more mountains they had to cross and *where* was Oaxaca City? They all got very hot and wanted drinks and snacks continually. At last they arrived at the central bus station and got a taxi out to their home. Tacho and Marta were very glad to have arrived in the city while it was still daylight, but now it was dusk as they let themselves in and Marta busied herself getting coffee ready and something substantial for them all to eat.

'Marta, did you move the television?' called Tacho.

'No, of course not! Why?' she countered in surprise.

'Well, it's not here!' said Tacho. 'I knocked on our lodger's door, but he isn't here, it seems. I'll go out to the office and see if Abram knows anything about this, although there is no light on out there so perhaps he isn't in either. It's all very strange.'

Tacho found the doors of the office and his workshop both wide open. All of Abram's belongings were gone and so were all of Tacho's tools. He ran back into the house to tell Marta. As they looked round more carefully they found that several blankets were missing, as well as Marta's electric iron and her blender. Their cassette recorder together with a number of their cassettes were gone too, as well as some of the children's things.

'After all these years living here as part of the family and working with you, how could Abram do this when you have been so generous to him?' said Marta almost in tears.

'I suppose we just made it too easy for him by all going away for a couple of days like that,' Tacho replied sadly. 'He was a really good plumber too. It will make quite a hole in our bank balance to replace those tools, but I shall have to do it right away to finish off that job at the school and fulfil the contract. It will be pretty hard to get it done on time without his assistance now.'

The lodger arrived home at that point and was very glad to see them, but he knew nothing of Abram's movements. They had gone over to Elia and Flora for breakfast that morning together, but he had seen nothing of Abram since then. When they finally got to bed they were glad that it was the hot time of year so that they did not need the blankets immediately. Tino and Alicia arrived a few days later and were appalled to hear the tale of woe. Tino was quite distraught that he could not help Tacho out with the plumbing job in this emergency: the dates were already set for what he needed to get done, and it would be a tight squeeze to get it all accomplished before the deadline for their move to Tutula to start work there as he had promised.

Three weeks later they were saying goodbye to Tino and Alicia. Her brother had driven into the city in his pick-up and came round to collect them along with Tino's belongings. The young couple promised to return often to visit but it was a big adjustment for everyone. Added to all these changes Marta had found that she was pregnant again, but this time she was not feeling well at all.

Tacho's thirty-second birthday was looming, and with so many changes and disappointments Marta wanted to make it a special event this year. She let Elia and Flora in on the secret and also enlisted the aid of her friend Ana and her own younger sister Estela, both of whom were now married. Tacho came home that day to find the room decorated and his favourite dinner cooked and ready. While he was eating with his little sons, a car drove up to the gate. It was Ana and Estela with a magnificent birthday cake. They had brought presents too, but just stayed long enough to accept a piece of the cake along with the family.

Soon after they left, Chucho and Tito turned up. They had obviously learnt of the occasion from their wives and were suitably dressed up. They brought fruit for Marta, sweets for the children and cigarettes and tequila for Tacho. Their own children were trailing them and peeped shyly in the door behind them so, when the men had been served a birthday meal, Marta pulled down some of the balloon decorations for the children to play with. The lodger came in and was served along with the other men, then Tacho sent Marta for some bottles of beer from the corner shop. The man there carried the crate of bottles back for her and was promptly invited to join the party.

The meal was finished and cleared away but the beer continued to circulate. Then Chucho produced a deck of cards. As darkness closed in, the neighbour from the shop noticed the time and tore himself away with regret. A few minutes later his teenage son appeared with another crate of beer and birthday greetings along with his father's compliments, so the beer continued to go round freely.

Marta was afraid now, particularly as a bottle of tequila had also appeared and their lodger was drinking and gambling along with the rest. She told little María to keep the other children playing outside, then slipped out and ran round to tell Elia and Flora. She wanted them to come and somehow persuade their husbands to go home while everyone was still happy. Knowing their men, they were afraid too. They came quickly, ostensibly to collect their children. The little ones were having such fun together that they did not want to leave, so the girls appealed to their husbands for help and eventually they all left in a reasonably good-natured fashion.

Tacho and the lodger continued playing, although both were a bit sluggish now from the effects of the beer and tequila. The table was full of empty bottles. Marta cleared them off and returned them to the crates, then started herding the children towards the bedroom. Toño was still very excited. He grabbed a beer bottle that had a little remaining in it and quickly drank from it. Marta called to him sharply, but he defied her and started to drain the dregs from another bottle. She pushed the others into the bedroom telling María to see to her little sister, then shut the door and came back for Toño. He grabbed yet another bottle and ran to the far corner of the room where his mother caught him and slapped his hand, as her patience was wearing thin in her high state of anxiety. He was unhurt, but this unexpected behaviour from his sweet and gentle mother made him let out a surprised wail.

'How dare you touch my son?' demanded Tacho staggering to his feet. She picked up Toño and tried to hurry to the bedroom with him, but the boy was outraged and started pummelling his mother with his little fists and kicking her in the stomach. She doubled up with pain and dropped the child who started howling in earnest. Then Tacho turned on her and hit her several times before knocking her down. At this the lodger joined in the fray and the two men started a fierce fight.

Toño was wailing in fear now and shaking his mother's inert form to try to wake her up. María peeped out of the bedroom, closed the door again and escaped by the outside door. She was afraid to leave the younger ones, but more afraid to see her mother lying on the floor unconscious while things in the room were getting broken in the fight. She flew down the street to the shop and the kindly owner and his son ran back with her. Drunken yells could be heard dimly from their house, so his wife phoned the police. They came and dragged Tacho and the lodger away, and the shop-owner's son ran back to report to his mother. When she heard about Marta, she phoned for the Red Cross ambulance, then went to Tacho's house to reassure the children. She found her husband trying to straighten up the living room, having put a pillow under Marta's head and thrown a blanket over her where she lay. Soon they heard an ambulance siren coming towards them. Marta was only semi-conscious as they took her away to the hospital. The wailing of the siren had alerted Elia and Flora who came running to the scene. They assured the shopkeeper and his wife that one of them would stay with the children and look after the house. Finally, the night was quiet again.

Next morning the girls persuaded Chucho to go and see what was happening to Tacho and the other man at the Town Hall. He was allowed to see Tacho and reported regretfully to him how things had ended at his house the night before, and how Marta was in hospital. Tacho became sober in an instant and was frantic to know more details, but he had to wait until his case was called. The local authorities were in no hurry, but finally summoned him before them, then fined and cautioned him. 'You know,

Anastasio,' they said to him, 'you have been in this jail several times now for disorderly conduct while drunk. Well, each time the fine will be heavier, and then there is the cost of the damages for you to make good as well. Remember that.'

Their lodger was fined and released at the same time and did not seem to hold any grudge against Tacho for the outcome of their revelry. He was only anxious not to lose his job, so he rushed off to work straight away without returning to the house. Tacho went home to reassure the children as much as he could. The younger ones welcomed him happily, but María was rather afraid of him and kept asking worried questions about her mother. He begged Flora to stay with them all that day, and asked Elia to explain to María's teacher that her mother was ill. Then he went to the shop and apologised to the couple there for the trouble that he had caused them and insisted on paying for the phone calls. The wife was not at all friendly to him: she was rather shocked that the skilled man who had done such a good plumbing job for them, and had seemed so helpful, could have turned into the monster of the previous night.

Tacho was relieved to see that she seemed very concerned about Marta, so he boldly asked if he could trouble her to make one more phone call to the Red Cross hospital to try to get some news about Marta's condition. She phoned and found out that Marta had lost the baby and had been transferred to the civil hospital. She phoned the civil hospital without being asked. They wanted to talk to Tacho because Marta needed a blood transfusion, and they were very glad of this contact with the family. Tacho agreed to go to the hospital immediately and hurriedly paid for all the phone calls.

He found Marta very weak and still haemorrhaging a little, in spite of all their efforts. They were already giving her blood and Tacho went off to replace the half-litre used by donating his own blood to their blood bank. She was fully conscious when he returned to the ward and asked lots of questions about the children and the house. She was relieved to hear that their lodger had been released without too much trouble, but Tacho was very concerned to see how weak and ill she looked. She wept when she told him about the baby and he was full of contrition, realising that the whole fault was his, but he tried not to get too emotional there in the public ward. He went to see the doctor to find out how long she might need to stay in the hospital. He was told that she would need more blood and probably would have to remain four or five days at least.

'And señor, your wife will never be able to have another child now. She may yet need an operation if the repair work we have done is not sufficient,' the doctor added.

Tacho was dazed and went outside to think things through before he returned to his wife to say goodbye for that day. He concluded finally that he had better go and talk to her uncle Amadeo about it all. He could not face his mother-in-law directly with this sad news.

18

Changed

Amadeo was just as welcoming as ever, even though he had seen nothing of Tacho for a long time. He made coffee and they sat down and talked. Naturally he asked after his niece and was told that she was in the hospital. Tacho went on to tell him about the baby and Marta's need for further blood transfusions, then suddenly he broke down and told the whole sordid story. Amadeo did not show any surprise, but gently asked probing questions to get the whole matter straight in his mind. He had not known of Tino's marriage and his move to Tutula, nor of Abram's perfidy and the burglary.

'I will go and see my sister-in-law for you, but I think that she and Honoria will want to look after the children in this emergency,' Amadeo assured him gravely. 'I expect that she will want Marta to go there from the hospital for a few weeks to recuperate too. A miscarriage like that really takes it out of a woman, you know. I am very sorry that things have turned out like this for you, Tacho. You were such a promising young couple.'

'I really want to make it up to Marta because I love her dearly, but I just don't know what

I am doing when I am drunk!' said Tacho miserably.

'Are you just sorry that you have failed Marta, or have you thought that you have failed God too? You made various promises to Him as well when you two got married, you know. We men are a weak lot, Tacho, and yet amazingly God loves us and is concerned about us just the same. We like to think that we are strong, honourable creatures worthy of responsibility and leadership, but we make God very sad when we don't believe Him or take advantage of all that He offers us freely, including forgiveness.'

'I know that I have failed God, Amadeo, but I really did try to be a Christian when I was attending the church regularly. Then later it all seemed too much. Daily life is so different from Sunday at church and you have to act and react in the ways that people around you understand.'

'What makes you think that God doesn't know about everyday life, Tacho? Jesus was here on earth living an ordinary, obscure working man's life for thirty years and then travelled about as a misunderstood teacher for another three years. They tried to make Him fit into the local mould but He kept His integrity.'

'I always forget that he was just a carpenter in a village, but He was God of course,' responded Tacho.

'Yes, He was and is God, but He was human too, an ordinary human baby born to Mary, an obscure, Jewish country girl. He grew up like anyone else, so He knows all about ordinary life for struggling tradespeople. He is concerned about you, Tacho, and really wants to help you. He wants you to enjoy all the good things that He has made available to you.'

'I want that too,' said Tacho determinedly.

'Then perhaps you should talk to Him now,' replied Amadeo. 'You need to tell Jesus of your decision, Tacho.'

So Tacho started praying: 'Lord Jesus, I know there is nothing good left in me, but I know that I am Your creation and that You made everything good to start with. Please forgive me for not taking any notice of You and just going my own way with such disastrous consequences. Amadeo says that You can change me and keep me changed the way that You want me to be. I believe that now, Lord, because I know that You died for me. I know that You are Amadeo's Boss and I want You to be my Boss too, please Lord. Thank You, my God. Amen.'

Tacho turned to Amadeo with a smile.

'It's true that I do feel more peaceful now and ready to face the consequences, which is wonderful, but what should I do next? There seems to be so much to put right.'

'Go home and reassure your children. They are shocked and afraid, I expect, and need to see their normal, loving papa. Tell them that they will be going to stay with their grandmother. Perhaps you should explain to María's teacher at the school too, as she won't be able to attend there for a few weeks. Then catch up on your own work and try reading the Bible in your spare time. Also, you need to tell your friends of your new decision to follow Christ as your Boss. Just telling them about it will help you to hold out against the bad habits that you have let yourself fall into. Meanwhile, I will go and see the children's grandmother and then go on to the hospital to see if they will accept blood from me for the blood bank. I know that there is an age limit, but I may still be acceptable. I want to visit my niece Marta too.'

'I don't know how to thank you, Amadeo, but I certainly thank God for you and for the loving concern that you have always shown me,' said Tacho.

'Yes, brother Tacho. We are doubly in the same family now. You are not only married to my niece, but my brother in God's family as well. When you feel a bit lonely, just think of all your new relatives – they love you too because their Father God does.'

Tacho went home and tried to be as normal as he could with the children. He reminded them of Sunday school and then prayed with them for Jesus to look after their mother in the hospital and bring her home soon. In the afternoon Honoria arrived in a taxi and took the children to stay with their grandmother with the promise that they would see their mother again soon. Amadeo had explained to her and her mother about Marta's miscarriage, but from her pleasant and sympathetic manner with Tacho it was plain that he had not felt the need to tell them the whole, sad story. Tacho went to see Marta every day in between finishing the most urgent plumbing jobs, and tried to call in at his mother-in-law's house as well to romp with the children for a few minutes.

After five days in hospital and two more blood transfusions Marta was discharged. Tacho took her to her mother's house and left her with her mother and the children. She was still very weak and it was plain that she would need several weeks of care and cossetting to recuperate. Tacho had told her of his time with Amadeo and of his new-found faith and suggested that they pray together. Marta was overjoyed and began to sense a new calm and peace in her heart as she also recommitted herself to God. She had always been a little timid and anxious, but now found a new state of joyful serenity which puzzled her mother and sister since she had just lost a child.

'What do you have to be always smiling about in the middle of all these calamities?' Honoria asked sharply.

Marta quietly told her that from now on she and Tacho were going to establish a real Christian home where Jesus Christ was honoured as the most important of all. It would be a far more secure place for the children and, hopefully, other people would find peace and tranquillity there too. Honoria was surprised. What was more Christian about Marta and Tacho now than before all this trouble? She could see that both of them were much happier these days, in spite of losing the baby, and that their faith seemed to be stronger, but she could not understand it.

On Sundays now Tacho took his children with him to church so that they could join the Sunday school. He often called in to see Amadeo on his way to visit Marta, and Amadeo encouraged him to read a bit from the Bible each day and to talk to God about everything that was happening in his life. Tacho often came with questions for Amadeo which had arisen out of what he had been reading, and

Marta's uncle was delighted that his earlier present
had come into its own now and was being well used.
Tacho excitedly reported all these developments to
Marta and told her about some of the new things
that he was learning from the Bible.

'I never really listened before in the church when
the Bible was read,' he confessed, 'because I was
sure that no ordinary people understood it anyway,
and that it was old-fashioned and irrelevant to
everyday life and to me in particular. After all, it
was written so long ago! Then I realised that people
now are just the same inside as they were then, and
that God Himself doesn't change at all. So if the Bible
is God's Word, and I believe that it is now, then
what He has to say in it must still be relevant today.
And it is: the people acted and reacted then just like
people do today. I keep reading things that just stop
me in my tracks and so I know that it is something
that God wants to say to me personally. Just to know
that God sent His Holy Spirit to live in me and to be
with me wherever I am is an amazing comfort, and
so humbling. Why should He care about me so
much when I did nothing but let Him down or
ignore Him altogether? Yet He does care enough
to have forgiven me – He even died for me, and
helped you to forgive me too, Marta. That makes
me feel very humble and so happy!'

On the third Sunday Marta was well enough to
accompany her family to church. They invited Estela
and her husband Enrique to go with them as well,
since Ana and her husband would be there and the
two couples had become good friends. Estela and
Enrique knew several others in the congregation too,
so they would not feel like strangers there. Tacho

and Marta had asked the pastor for their little girl Rosa to be dedicated to the Lord. They also wanted it to be a time of rededication for their entire family, and they wanted their relatives to witness that.

The pastor called Tacho to the front with his family, then gave heartfelt thanks to God for Marta's recovery and for each of the children, mentioning Rosa especially. Then he asked Tacho if he had anything that he wanted to say to the congregation. Tacho was rather diffident but he was determined to tell all these good friends, who had helped him so much, about his change of heart. He asked their forgiveness for his insincerity in the past and thanked them all for their welcoming love to him, their patience with him and their prayers for him. Then he told them of his sad life because he had left God out and of how Amadeo had helped him to realise that Jesus Christ was close by all that time, waiting to receive and forgive and change him for ever.

'Now I want to follow Jesus and I want Him to be the most important person in our home,' Tacho finished.

A radiant Marta stood beside him and added: 'I join my husband in this desire because I really want to follow Jesus wholeheartedly too.'

After the service they asked the pastor if they could be baptised and truly become part of the fellowship there. He told them when the next series of preparation classes would begin and they assured him that they would attend. Estela and Enrique were waiting outside for them and said that they had been quite impressed by the service. They had been very moved by what Tacho and Marta had

said and by how the whole family had been dedicated to God.

'What does it all mean?' Estela asked. 'You even
look different, and you seem much more at peace
with the world.'

They went and sat down in a nearby park to
chat while the children played. Finally Estela and
Enrique agreed to meet Tacho the following evening
and to go with him to visit Amadeo. They also
wanted to come back to the church the following
Sunday and to hear more of what the pastor had to
say, as they had found it very thought-provoking.
All the people there had been so welcoming that
they had not felt strange at all, even though everything about the service was unfamiliar.

As Tacho left her that evening Marta assured him
that she was much stronger now, and that she was
very eager to get back to her own home and to him.
Perhaps by the end of the week she could prove to
everyone that she was fit enough again now. He
hugged her delightedly, but was concerned that she
did not take on too much too soon.

Tacho brought flowers for his mother-in-law on
the following afternoon and apologised for a brief
visit. After a quick game with his boisterous children
and with an encouraging nod from Marta, he left to
meet Estela and Enrique. Amadeo was surprised to
see them all but delighted at this new awakening of
interest on the part of his niece. He had prayed
fervently for his sister-in-law and his four nieces for
many years, but only Marta had ever shown any
inclination to want to know the truth about Jesus
Christ. He did not mind what group of Christians
they might become associated with, just so long as

they responded to the truth in the Bible. He prayed silently as they were settling down, thanking God for opening up this opportunity, and asking for wisdom to help each of these young people to understand clearly God's Way. Tacho animatedly opened his Bible and started asking questions about what he had been reading. Estela and Enrique were soon drawn into the discussion as Amadeo pointed out the practical, present-day application of it all. Together they reread some of the part that had excited Tacho, and very soon the young couple were asking their own thoughtful questions. The evening soon passed and they all agreed to come back again on Thursday. Estela and Enrique wanted to read the same section that Tacho was studying, so Amadeo loaned them a Spanish Good News version of the Bible to take home with them.

'I must see if Marta is strong enough to come then too,' Tacho said as they left for their homes.

It seemed that Estela and Enrique were rather dissatisfied with their life and had been wondering why things had not turned out differently. They had been married only a year but found themselves quarrelling often. Enrique had found that his office colleagues were not particularly scrupulous in dealing with their clients, and not very honest with each other either, but making money had become very important to him, so he was just following the crowd although he hated the hypocrisy. Estela thought only of clothes and was working in an exclusive boutique part-time, but she found that she was never thoroughly happy, never satisfied, however much she owned. They felt that perhaps their moods and feelings would change when they had children, because surely life was supposed to have more meaning than they had found so far?

The next session found them full of questions that they could air at last in a sympathetic atmosphere, and they eagerly lapped up Amadeo's lucid and patient answers. They were very impressed by the way that he kept referring them back to the Bible: 'Don't just listen to me,' he would say, 'but read it for yourselves. Let's look at God's Word and see what He has to say to us.'

'You really seem to know what you are talking about, uncle,' Estela said as they were leaving. 'I am almost convinced that I too need to accept all this and really commit myself to following Jesus Christ as you do. Can we come again next Monday?'

'Of course, my dear. You don't know what a delight it is to me to see your eagerness now after all these years of indifference. Tacho and Marta have become my brother and sister as well as being my niece and nephew, so I am looking forward to having that relationship with you two as well. I'm praying for you every day, you know,' he added, beaming.

'Dear uncle, thank you for that. We'll see you at the church on Sunday and come here again on Monday, then.'

'We will see you at church too,' Tacho said, and added with a bright smile: 'And I am very thankful to say that I'm to be taking Marta and the children home with me again after the service, so I won't manage to get over here to your house again very soon, Amadeo, but we will be praying too.'

Estela and Enrique very soon became believers and joined Tacho and Marta when the classes began in preparation for their baptism. This was a great encouragement to Amadeo, Tacho and Marta, but incomprehensible to Estela's mother and sister who felt that Amadeo had been a bad influence on the younger generation.

Honoria had been tutoring her niece María in reading and her other schoolwork, so when she returned to school with just one week left of the school year, her teacher found that she could manage the end-of-year tests quite easily. This meant that she could continue on to the second grade with her classmates in September which was very satisfactory for all concerned. Toño had been attending the 'kinder' and his teacher said that he was ready to enter the primary school, even though he was a bit young. He was very proud to hear this and uncle Amadeo offered to be his godfather for his graduation from the 'kinder' school. Soon Cándido was heard to say: 'I'm going to school next. When the "kinder" opens again, I shall go to school.'

His parents had a hard time explaining that he had to wait another year as he was not quite old enough yet. There were a few tearful sessions as a result, especially when 1 September arrived and both María and Toño set off for the primary school in their new school uniforms and with snacks in their lunch boxes.

Greatly daring, Marta and Estela invited their mother and sister Honoria to their baptismal service in October.

'This is ridiculous!' snapped their irate mother. 'I remember perfectly well the Masses when each of you were baptised and became members of the Church. Each of you looked like a little angel and I

can't think what has happened to change your
loyalty now. I suppose that interfering Amadeo
persuaded you, but what your husbands are
thinking of to allow this farce, I can't imagine! No
one can be baptised twice!'

Their mother swept out of the room and Honoria
whispered timidly: 'I would like to come, although
I too don't agree with what you are doing, but you
see that I can't upset Mother,' and she crept away
apologetically.

19

Jesus is Boss

The baptismal service was well attended. María, Toño, Cándido and Rosa were all in their best clothes and seated in the front row with their great-uncle Amadeo. As they were singing the first song two more families slid in and people found chairs for them at the back. Chucho and Tito had been amazed at the change in Tacho lately. When he first told them why his outlook and interests were now different, they just laughed. Then in the days following they mocked him unmercifully. To their surprise he did not react violently, and they noticed that he really was different in his speech, his actions, his thoughts and genuine concern for them, as well as in his treatment of his own family. They had talked it over with their womenfolk at home and both Flora and Elia agreed.

'We've noticed a difference in Marta too,' Elia had said. 'She seems so happy, and is always singing about the house now.'

'Yes, she told us that they are going to be baptised soon as a public testimony of their resolve to follow Jesus Christ and to live as He wants people to live,' added Flora. 'I don't understand that. I thought that it was only babies that got baptised in church. She said that they are so thankful for all that God has done for them that they want to take this way to tell everyone about it.'

'Yes, Tacho mentioned that,' said Chucho, 'although why they think God is so good and helping them when Marta lost the baby, I can't imagine. Still, he said it would be a special service at that church where they were married and invited us all to go. What do you think, Tito? It's next Sunday afternoon.'

'Well, you and I went to Tacho's wedding not knowing anything about that church, so we might as well go back there and support him again, especially as he seems to think that this is an important occasion as well,' Tito responded.

'All right, we'll all go,' Chucho decided. 'At least we know where the place is this time.'

So here they all were to find out what a baptismal service for adults was all about. Someone lent them a song-book and showed them the song that everyone was singing. The children stared at everything and were glad when they caught sight of their playmates down at the front of the church. Later, when they were sitting down, Toño was squirming about in his place excitedly. When he turned round and saw them, he waved and then passed on the news to his sisters and little brother who all promptly turned round and waved a welcome too. Their Sunday school friends noticed this, so they turned round as well to smile and wave a welcome, which amazed Tito, Chucho and their families. They listened with interest as the pastor explained about the baptismal service.

Their attention was really caught as first Tacho told how Jesus Christ had changed his life, then Marta told her personal story, followed by Enrique and, finally, Estela. Tito and Chucho remembered many of the unsavoury incidents that Tacho mentioned and were fascinated by his willingness to recount them publicly and to take the blame for such shameful events. Enrique's tale kept their attention riveted too. He was an accountant working for the government and had managed to manipulate the funds to his own advantage several times. Recently he had confessed this to his superiors and, to their amazement, set the record straight. Tito and Chucho exchanged wide-eyed glances when they heard this. Whoever would think of repaying the government any money that he had managed to scrounge? Surely some of his superiors were involved in the same kind of thing and would feel vulnerable now? This Enrique would lose his soft job after this, wouldn't he? They were very impressed that, with his new-found faith, he seemed ready to face the consequences whatever they were, and his wife was backing him up.

One by one the four walked down the steps into the water where the pastor was waiting for them. After the ducking they climbed out the other side smiling radiantly, while the congregation sang a chorus of praise to God for these changed lives. Afterwards, the ladies of the church served coffee and *tamales* and all the church members gave the two newly baptised couples a joyful hug. They chatted to Chucho and Tito and their families in a warm and genuinely interested fashion, so they felt quite at home too. Then María and Toño appeared beside them and excitedly greeted their playmates.

'Do you like our church?' they asked them. 'Come on! Let us show you the rooms where we have Sunday school. We do all kinds of interesting things during our classes. If you like, we could ask your parents if you could come here with us.'

The other children were fascinated by the cheerful Sunday school rooms decorated with illustrations from the Bible and the children's own drawings.

'Yes, we would like to come if we can,' they responded.

María immediately ran back to find Chucho and Tito to ask their permission. They saw no harm in their children getting a little religious education among these friendly people so they willingly agreed. The youngsters certainly had nothing better to do on Sundays, they thought. Elia and Flora agreed it was a very good idea. They secretly hoped that their children's attendance at the Sunday school would give them the opportunity to accompany Marta to the church themselves sometimes, as they were very intrigued by these 'believers'. They wanted their own lives to be different, and had become both wistful and envious as they noted the changes for good in Tacho's household lately. Privately they had each asked Marta a few questions about it, but they did not really understand her answers yet.

The following Sunday, Chucho's and Tito's children were ready and waiting at the gate long before it was time to go. They stood there quietly, bright-eyed with anticipation; their usual boisterous shouts and horse-play were strangely missing as they were all but holding their breath in case someone denied them this new experience at the last minute. They really enjoyed the Sunday school class and were content to sit quietly through the service that followed.

'Do you think that we could come again?' they asked on the way home.

María and Toño were elated that their playmates were so enthusiastic, while Tacho and Marta were delighted that their children wanted others to learn about Jesus Christ. Soon the children were practising for the special Christmas programme and they reported it all in detail to their parents each week. When the invitation came for them to attend the Christmas service, Chucho and Flora as well as Tito and Elia were agog to see what their children had been learning. Again they all received a friendly welcome. To their surprise a number of people recognised them from the time before and came over to chat to them, which gave them a warm feeling of being welcome. There were refreshments afterwards and then three *piñatas* for the children.

It was Christmas Eve and the children were still very excited and wide awake, so Tacho, Tito and Chucho decided to take their families on to the central square in the city (called the *zócalo)* to see the Christmas decorations and lights. They knew that there would be plenty of taxis about all night, so getting home was no problem. They joined the milling crowds celebrating in the *zócalo* and bought funny-face balloons for each of the children. They admired the elaborate nativity scene in front of the government palace, but several times people bumped into them who had had too much to drink, so Tacho quietly spoke to the other men.

'Let's keep away from the drinking tonight and just concentrate on giving our families a happy time to remember,' he said.

Tito and Chucho were finding this novel experience quite enjoyable so they did not argue. They were quite unused to spending time walking around looking at things along with their women and children, and were surprised to see how many other men were doing the same thing. Suddenly, they all became aware of the sound of crashing crockery and moved in the direction of the noise to see what was happening.

'Look, it's the bunuelos!' Marta exclaimed.

'I remember!' Tacho broke in animatedly. 'This is when you eat those special crisply fried pancake things smothered with molasses. Then you make a wish for the New Year and hurl your dish to the ground. If it smashes, they say that your wish will come true.'

'I want to wish, papa! Come on!' Toño exclaimed, dragging at his hand.

'Do bunuelos taste nice, mama?' Cándido asked Marta.

'They are delicious,' his mother replied.

'Can we have a taste, papa?' the children clamoured as they besieged their respective fathers.

So they made their crunching way over the crockery shards to the long tables and found places there. The men ordered bunuelos and shared them out so that there were enough bowls for each of the older children to have one to smash.

'I wish I had a puppy,' said Toño loudly as he flung down his bowl with a mighty crash.

'Oh dear, you are not supposed to say your wish out loud, Toño, or to let anyone know about it until it comes true,' Marta told him with a sympathetic smile.

'I didn't know that, mama,' replied the crestfallen little boy.

The others smashed their bowls with earnest concentration, then walked over the pieces to make sure that they were well broken.

'I think it's about time to go now,' said Tacho.

'We'll have to take a couple of taxis to all fit. How about if I ride with you and your family, Tacho, and the rest go in the second car?' Chucho suggested.

'Sounds fine,' Tacho agreed. 'I think there is a taxi rank on the other street.'

Tacho smartly led them away from the *zócalo*, but the children straggled along, still staring at the coloured lights and decorated Christmas trees in all the windows. There was so much to see! Their fathers found two taxis and they all piled in on top of each other. Tacho and Chucho sat in the back with children on each knee, but they managed to chat just the same.

'Chucho, in spite of what you used to think, you have quite enjoyed the times when you have come to our church, haven't you?' Tacho said.

'Well, yes, and I'm surprised!' responded Chucho. 'I'm even more surprised at the change in you. How did you do it? I have tried to straighten myself out once or twice when I see how hard it is for Flora and the kids sometimes, because I know that they deserve better, but my good intentions never last more than a few days. I'm not even a real fighter-drunk like you that ends up in jail, so why can't I do better the way I want to?'

Tacho decided to take the plunge and be positive.

'Why don't you and Tito and your wives come along to our house this Friday evening and we will all read the Bible together and see what God has to say to us?'

'Now wait a minute, Tacho. We can't understand the Bible! You need to be a priest for that, and they can't seem to explain it in words that ordinary men like me can understand either!'

'No,' Tacho told him earnestly, 'Marta's uncle Amadeo gave us a Good News version of the Bible and it is really clear. It's a bit *too* clear for comfort where it talks about God's opinion of our bad habits! You already know uncle Amadeo. I could ask him to come too, because he knows the Bible really well and he has been a great help to Marta and me. I know you respect him as a reliable, hard worker and so it would be worth listening to what he has to say.'

'Is Amadeo some kind of priest then?' Chucho asked with a puzzled look.

'Oh no! But he knows God pretty well, so he can introduce other people to the Lord as well. Will you come then? See if you can persuade Tito to come with you. My little María can look after the younger children in the bedroom or they can play outside together, then all our wives can join in too.'

'All right, we'll try it, if only to save a bit of money,' said Chucho, laughing. 'Reading the Bible is a lot cheaper than a night on the town! Tito and I can always go out on Saturday and Sunday.'

So it was arranged and Amadeo was delighted to assist when he heard about it. Tito and Chucho arrived with their families soon after dark on Friday. The children were very pleased with this extra opportunity to play together, and they happily went off with María. Then the adults settled down and Amadeo took charge. He had brought a couple of extra Bibles so that each family had one to look at, and he suggested that they start with the Gospel of Luke because it tells what really happened that first Christmas.

They read the first chapter, then Tacho and Marta started making comments and asking questions of Amadeo. Soon the others were joining in the discussion; even the girls ventured some shy questions. Amadeo treated even the most naïve comment seriously, so they were encouraged to air all their thoughts. An hour flew by, and then the children were called in to share the coffee and sweet rolls that Marta had prepared. Flora and Elia were enthusiastic about continuing the following Friday, and without reluctance their menfolk agreed.

'I had never heard all that about holy Mary,' Tito said in wonder. 'Yes, I would definitely like to learn some more.'

So the weekly studies became routine. On Carnival weekend just before Lent, Tito and Chucho decided to celebrate like every other year. They did not bother to ask Tacho to join them as they now knew all about his new determination to avoid drunkenness and they grudgingly respected him for it. They both got hopelessly drunk. Elia helped Tito stagger across the floor and collapse onto their bed, where he fell asleep and began to snore. But Chucho was wild and abusive, so Flora sent her eldest child running to Tacho and Marta for help. They came immediately and Marta took the children home with her along with a dishevelled Flora. Her dress was torn and a large bruise was developing on her face from Chucho's attentions. Tacho wrestled Chucho into bed and stayed the night with him to see that no further commotion ensued. He remembered the times that young Tino had done the same for him and was humbly grateful.

The next morning Chucho was by turns very dismissive of the uproar of the previous night, and then very contrite about the trouble that he had caused. Tacho did not say much, but left him to a cup of strong coffee as soon as Flora and the children reappeared. They made no reference to the night before either.

Friday evening came and Chucho and Tito arrived at the door rather hesitantly. Their wives and children had come ahead and Tacho greeted them with a welcoming smile, so they just came in and took their usual seats. Everyone was surprised to see the pastor from the church arrive with Amadeo. He told them about the local Baptist church that had started some years before quite near to where they lived, along with a Bible college right next door to it.

'I don't want to lose any of you from my church,' he said, 'but it would be much nearer and easier for you to attend there. They have children's activities just the same as we do and, Tacho, perhaps you could enrol in some of the evening classes that the Bible college runs, so that you would be better prepared to run these studies in your home. Think about it.'

This was a brand new idea to Tacho and Marta and they exchanged startled glances, but they were soon immersed in the study of that week's chapter from Luke's Gospel. At the end Chucho was very quiet and thoughtful, then suddenly spoke up as the pastor and Amadeo were leaving.

'May I come and see you tomorrow evening at your church, sir? I would like to talk to you before we consider changing to this nearer church.'

'Yes, I will be at the church tomorrow evening, Chucho. I look forward to a chat with you,' the pastor said with a reassuring smile.

'I think our family will come to your church at least once more while we think about your suggestion, Pastor,' Tacho said in his turn.

Later Tacho and Marta changed to the local church, as the pastor had suggested, and became members there, but continued the Bible studies in their home. Other neighbours joined them. Chucho, Flora and Elia all committed their lives to follow Jesus Christ, so things changed dramatically in Chucho's home. Tito still quite often came to the studies and occasionally attended church services with his family, but was not prepared to make a personal commitment. Chucho and Flora were talking about getting married and being baptised, but Elia felt that she should wait until Tito became a believer too. She was very pleased when later Tito consented to attend the triumphant baptismal service. Along with other neighbours, both Chucho and Flora made a public declaration of their faith in Christ and were baptised in a lake on the outskirts of the city. Everyone joined in a happy picnic lunch together afterwards. Those with food shared with those who had not brought any, and there was plenty for everyone.

In September Tacho started part-time classes at the Bible college. He found the classes stimulating and thought-provoking; but taking notes and coping with the homework was really hard work for him, having been away from school and any need to write much for so many years. He doggedly persevered and began to battle privately with a new challenge: should he become a pastor? What did God really want him to do now?

20

Tacho returns

The Bible college assigned Tacho to help at yet
another local Baptist church, started just a few years
earlier in a nearby *colonia*. He found himself more
and more involved with the congregation there,
so his family went along to support him. Marta had
the new and stretching experience of starting a
Sunday school class for the children. At home she
continued to take in lodgers and Tacho still did some
plumbing jobs, but time for this was greatly reduced
and it was hard to make ends meet sometimes. As
the children got older they had more demands from
school and occasionally Toño was heard to complain
bitterly when funds would not stretch for him to
have exactly what the other boys at school had.
María sunnily reminded him of some of the other
children round about who could not go to school at
all because there was no money for clothes or shoes.
Their fathers were only around part of the time and
often mistreated them. But Toño only took notice of
his richer friends.

One day the following summer Tacho said to
Marta: 'I've been thinking and praying about Bible
college and the pastorate, and I am more and more

convinced that God wants me to be a pastor and evangelist. I see so many other people like I was. They are caught in a trap and they don't know the truth. They don't know that God wants to set them free from their bad habits, their debt and despair, or that He really loves them and cares about what happens to them. If Jesus Christ can change someone like me, then He can certainly change these others if they are introduced to Him. What do you think?'

'Yes, Tacho. I have seen your great concern for others and I am sure that God gave it to you. I have been praying too and even if it is a bit hard for us as a family, I think that you should get more training and become a full-time pastor. If this is our Master's leading, then He will look after us.'

'Thank you for your support, Marta. You are certainly God's gift to me. Now let's pray about it together so that we share in God's peace.'

The following September Tacho became a full-time student and continued to help with the same little church. Cándido now joined María and Toño at the primary school and little Rosa started at the 'kinder' school, so it was arranged that Marta would work in the kitchen at the Bible college to help pay Tacho's fees. In the lull before lunch she would collect Rosa from the 'kinder' and the others would come later straight from school. Then they all could have lunch with their mother in the kitchen after the students had been served. Afterwards María would supervise the younger ones while her mother helped with the washing up.

They soon slipped into this routine but Tacho found it hard to keep up with his studies, although he doggedly spent long hours at his books. Marta also needed to be very disciplined to keep up with the family and her job in the college kitchen, but María was a tremendous help at home, young though she was. Only nine years old when her father started his full-time studies, she seemed as committed as her parents to the project. Those three years sped past with many joys and sorrows. Chucho and Flora continued to be a great encouragement to Tacho and Marta, but Tito still made Elia's life a misery and spent less and less time with his old friends. He would have liked to move his family away from Chucho, but he never had any money to spare, so they continued living in their old, but now very dilapidated, hut, while Chucho had built a snug, solid little house for his family. Chucho found himself increasingly taking on responsibility for his sister-in-law, Elia, as Tito spent more time away.

Then one Saturday he saw Tito in the city market with a strange young woman carrying a baby. Tito grinned self-consciously when he saw who it was.

'Hallo Chucho. I won't need that dog kennel on our land any more! Meet my new wife and baby,' he said brazenly.

'Does that mean that you won't be supporting Elia and your children any more?' asked Chucho, fervently praying that he would manage to keep his temper.

'Oh well, she never expected anything else, did she? After all, we weren't married, so that's the end of it. Micaela's parents live up there on the hillside and she and I have the downstairs flat in their house. We plan to marry before the baby is baptised in the parish church.'

'Thank you for telling me your plans, Tito. But now I never expect to see you on my land again or worrying Elia in any way. I know that you put some money into it at the beginning, but you certainly owe Elia at least that much. So just leave us all alone from now on.'

'Fair enough. I have a good job on this side of the city and I need no reminders of the past!' Tito countered boastfully and guided a smug Micaela away.

Chucho returned home sadly, but was honest enough to realise that, but for his Christian faith, and all the changes that following Christ had brought to his life, he would probably have been in the same position as Tito. He called in to see Tacho and Marta on the way, to tell them this sad news. They took time to pray together before Marta accompanied Chucho to his house to tell Flora and her sister Elia. The latter confessed that she had suspected this for a long time and was glad that it was out in the open. The others reassured her that the church community would help her.

'As you know, you and Flora have helped me a lot already,' she said to Chucho. 'My little job cleaning and cooking for your neighbours, Marta, has meant that we have food and clothes, but there will be extra expenses when Lalo goes to school next year. One good thing to come out of all this is that now I can join the next lot of preparation classes and be baptised. I have wanted to do that for a long time, so that I can be a real member of the church and a better example to my children.'

In his final student year Tacho met Teyo, a young pilot from the north of Mexico who flew with *Alas de Socorro* (Wings of Help), the Mexican arm of the Mission Aviation Fellowship. This organisation made mercy flights to isolated villages as well as ferrying schoolteachers, evangelists and government officials in and out of these 'bush' airstrips. Teyo told Tacho of the people that he had met in these villages and rural towns throughout the state who had never heard the good news about Jesus Christ. He had ferried a young evangelist out to one place where there was as yet no road and they were keen to return there to show the *Jesus* film to local people. They took Tacho with them and all three men were very excited by the enthusiastic response to the film. After that experience Tacho told Teyo about his home village in that same mountainous hinterland, and that he was a Chatino by birth.

'How often do you go home to visit your relatives?' Teyo asked.

'Oh, I haven't been back there for many years,' responded Tacho.

'Then they don't know that you are a real follower of Jesus Christ now? You need to share some of your Christian experience with them,' Teyo urged.

Tacho was very impressed by Teyo's words and in the following weeks the conviction began to grow that he should go back to see his family and share the story of his changed life with them. He talked it over with Marta and they prayed about it often. His first preoccupation, however, was the graduation ceremony at the end of May and he was studying hard for his final exams. At last the great day came and his proud family clapped and clapped as he stepped forward to receive his diploma. There was further excitement a few weeks later when María stepped forward to receive her certificate at her graduation from primary school. She had done very well and received an added award from the school for exceptional work in some subjects. She would have no trouble finding a place in one of the secondary schools, her teachers assured her parents, and they felt like bursting with pride at her accomplishments.

Tacho continued as assistant pastor of the struggling little mission church in the fast-growing development at the edge of the city as well as being an itinerant evangelist. He accompanied Teyo on evangelistic trips more often now. In the intervening years the area where Tacho and his family lived had been built up so that they now had paved streets, shops round the corner and buses passing the house every half hour. Marta's mother no longer enjoyed good health, so she and Honoria sold the family house in the centre of the city and moved out to a very nice bungalow only a few hundred yards away from Tacho and Marta. The children visited their grandmother often and Marta called in briefly every day, even though her mother was querulous and often complained about the cruel blows that fate had dealt her. Isabel and Hector rarely made the effort to visit her, but she always held them up as paragons before the rest of the family.

'No one could have a better daughter and son-in-law,' she would often say in a contented voice. 'Their lives are so full and dedicated to serving society, so they can't be expected to visit a dreadful area like this very much!'

It was hard for Marta to fit in such a discouraging visit daily with all her other responsibilities, but she

persevered and was consistently caring and cheerful.

María started at her new school. Toño started his
final year at the primary school, while Cándido and
Rosa were in earlier years at the same school. Marta
continued working in the Bible college kitchen to
augment their income as Tacho's small and struggling congregation could offer their pastors very
little as a salary. They continued to take in lodgers,
but these were now usually students from the Bible
college. With everybody so fully occupied, the days
flew past and Tacho realised with surprise that it
was already November.

'I must go to Jaguar Mountain and talk to my
brothers before this year ends!' he resolved.

So, with Marta, he made a definite plan and set
off for the coast one day to find his way back inland
to Jaguar Mountain. The bus took all day to reach
the coast and Tacho thought wistfully of how easy it
was to travel with Teyo in the little Wings of Help
plane. They had simply sailed over all these mountain ridges in a matter of minutes instead of these
many weary hours of climbs and descents! Tacho
knew the pastor in the coastal town from their Bible
college training days, and had his address. However, when the bus arrived he wandered along the
seafront first, enjoying the breeze after the long, hot
journey. He soon spotted some Chatinos from the
Tutula area and got into conversation with them. He
asked them if they knew the best way to get to Jaguar
Mountain. No, not through Tutula, they said as the
route through Mulaca was the long way round.

'You go along this coastal road to Red River.
There you change to another bus or some other kind

of public transport to Dry Pond and they will show you the trail to take from there.'

He was given a warm welcome at the local pastor's house and a bed for the night. They were eager for all the news from the city but understood that he would need to leave early the next morning when they heard of his errand. They prayed with him as he left before dawn and urged him to come again on his way home if he should return by the same route. Then he set off into the unknown.

It was easy to get a bus to Red River, and there he found a vehicle about to leave for Dry Pond. It was mid-morning when they got to Dry Pond, but it was already very hot. He was glad that it was the cool season as he was unused to the tropical lowland temperatures and it seemed terribly hot to him. He bought a bottled *refresco* to quench his thirst and enquired of the vendor about the trail to Jaguar Mountain.

'There were some people here just half an hour ago going that way,' the vendor told him. 'They stopped for breakfast here because it is several hours' journey. If you hurry along that trail there you should catch them up. They had children and pack animals with them, so they won't move very fast.'

Tacho wasted no more time but set out at a brisk pace along the trail indicated. He was very glad for the lush vegetation which shaded the path as he climbed through the foothills. After a time he came to the bottom of the escarpment and the beginning of the coffee plantations with enormous trees shading the coffee bushes. Then he saw movement ahead and soon caught up with the family that he had been told about. They greeted him politely and he asked if they were going to the settlement on Jaguar Mountain. The young man and his wife glanced at each other quickly, then the man replied.

'We know the way. Who is it that you want to see there? We might know them.'

'Is Demetrio Ruíz still living there?' Tacho asked. 'I used to know him very well.'

'No, he died two years ago,' was the reply. 'His widow and other members of the family are still there though.'

Tacho winced at the news, only too aware that he had never shared the good news about Jesus Christ with his father. Why had he waited so long to come here? He decided to be direct.

'Do you know the family well, because I am Demetrio's eldest son who went away to Oaxaca.'

Incredulity spread over the young man's face and he burst out: 'But you can't be! You speak only Spanish and you look and act just like any other city person! But what is your name?'

This was an uncharacteristic and very daring question as the Chatinos rarely ask someone's name directly. However, since this conversation was so outrageous and in Spanish, the young man did not feel quite so bound by Chatino tradition. Tacho smiled, recognising the problem, so he decided to volunteer enough information to establish his identity.

'I am Anastasio Ruíz, called Tacho, and my brothers are Francisco (called Chico), Benigno (called Nino) and Ireneo (called Neyo). I have two sisters as well, named Benita (called Beni) and Rita. I left home when I was fifteen years old, just after my mother died. I have heard that my father, Demetrio, married again (a woman called Dora I believe) but I have never met her or their children. Oh yes, I also have an orphaned cousin Susana (called Sana) who returned to our home village of Mulaca along with my grandmother when my father got his new wife to look after him and the other children.'

The young man had been getting more and more excited, and when Tacho finished speaking he grabbed his hand and shook it vigorously.

'You are my lost brother, Tacho!' he exclaimed. 'I am your little brother Nino, and this is my wife Marsé. Her father is Rolando. Remember him?'

'You mean Tino's father? Your godfather, since you are Nino? I'm glad to meet you little sister,' said Tacho, smiling in his turn as he nodded to the young woman.

Nino then relapsed into his own language and chattered on excitedly. Tacho could follow some of it, but he had to respond in Spanish as he had been away too long and discovered, to his chagrin, that he had really forgotten a lot of his native tongue.

After a steep climb and a few more ups and downs they reached a small settlement of good adobe houses. There was a small school, but electricity had not yet arrived as there was still no road to this settlement.

'So this is Jaguar Mountain!' exclaimed Tacho as he stopped to look around him. There were plenty of clumps of banana plants and other lush vegetation, as well as the inevitable coffee bushes.

'Come on, Tacho. The houses of all our family are just up here close together,' called Nino, as he gave the leading mule's bridle a tug and started off again.

They arrived outside an adobe house with a wide porch running the length of it and a padlock on the door. Nino produced a key and unlocked it as well as the door of the kitchen house alongside. They urged Tacho to sit down on the porch bench for a few minutes while they unloaded the mules. Marsé had been carrying a baby on her back the whole way from the coast and now unslung him from her black shawl and put him in the hammock. With a few swings he was fast asleep again which freed her to help with the unloading. A little girl was lifted down first from on top of one mule's load. She just stood where she landed and directed an unblinking stare at this new-found uncle who could not speak her language, while her parents together expertly lowered the cargo from both sides of each pack animal.

Then Marsé retired to the kitchen house and Nino said to Tacho: 'Come with me to Chico's house. I'll leave you there with him while I go and cut some fodder for the animals. Everybody will want to see you, but as Chico is the eldest, you had better go to his house first. We would really like you to stay here with us, but I'm sure that Chico won't allow that arrangement.'

He led the way along the grassy track past their brother Neyo's house and into a big yard with several houses round it.

'Our stepmother lives on that side with her son and younger daughter, while Chico and his family occupy the houses on this side,' explained Nino.

Then a man nearly as old as Tacho came to the kitchen door and called out a greeting to Nino.

'How did you get on in Red River, Nino? Will they be ready for our first consignment of coffee-beans next month?' he asked.

'All that news can wait,' responded Nino. 'Do you know who I've found? Look, do you know who this is? He's not the city gent that he looks!' he said excitedly as he indicated Tacho. 'It's our long-lost brother, Tacho, come back to see us!'

Other people came out of the surrounding houses as they recognised Nino's excited voice, while others had followed them in the gate from the houses that they had passed. Everybody started talking at once, and after he had explained how Tacho had caught up with them on the trail from Dry Pond, Nino disappeared to cut some of the local 'para' grass for his mules.

Tacho had to be introduced to all his younger, previously unknown relatives, as well as try to recognise the older ones. Several neighbours had joined the crowd now and that made it even more confusing. They included some old friends and schoolmates, but they all looked so different now! It took a little while to get used to the idea that Chico, Nino, Neyo and Beni all had families of their own. Little Rita lived with her husband and children in Oaxaca, they informed him.

'And I never knew!' Tacho exclaimed ruefully. 'When did she go there? Do you have her address? I must go and visit my little sister.'

'You have yet another married sister just down in Red River,' cut in Neyo. 'That's Isabel and here is her mother, Dora,' he added as he pushed forward an older woman with a timid smile.

'I am really glad to meet you at last, stepmother,' said Tacho warmly. 'I want to thank you for looking after my father and these brothers and sisters of mine because I know that it was hard work. It was difficult being outlaws from our home village too.'

'I have heard a lot about you, Tacho,' Dora responded. 'Your father often spoke longingly of when you would come back to visit him. He even dreamed of visiting you in Oaxaca, but the idea of searching a city for you was too intimidating. He was sure that you had made good there though, and he was very proud of that. He often pulled out those old photos of your graduation from school and the one of you as Tino's godfather. He kept your letters too and treasured them all.'

'Yes, he often had me reread them to him,' broke in Chico.

'Your youngest brother and sister are here too, Tacho,' continued Dora. 'This is Lencho, who is sixteen now and the man of our household, and this is his wife, Li. And this is Queta, your youngest sister, who is fourteen. She too will be going to Oaxaca soon to help your sister Rita, who has three little ones and none of them at school yet. She and I haven't been back here many weeks since we went to Red River to help your sister, my Isabel. She gave birth to my own first grandchild just three months ago.'

'What a beautiful big family I have, yet I was so lonely in Oaxaca sometimes,' Tacho thought wryly as he smiled contentedly at them all.

21

Beni's story

Very soon Chico's wife called Tacho and her family in for a meal of crisp slices of grilled beef that had been salted and dried to preserve it, along with piping hot fresh tortillas, black beans, chilli sauce and coffee. It turned out that Chico had six children and Tacho wondered when he would get everyone sorted out and learn all their names. He learnt that the other three children that were milling about (and seemed very much at home) belonged to his sister Beni. She had married a good-looking young man from the town above Tutula called San Felipe. He had come to join the outlaws on Jaguar Mountain as he had found himself on the 'hit list' of a notorious family in San Felipe. Demetrio took him in and he turned out to be as wild as Chico and the others. Then he married Beni and seemed to settle down a bit. He worked alongside her father but he continued drinking heavily whenever he had the chance and was very hard to control when drunk. When their first child was a year old he heard that the man who had wanted to kill him had himself been shot, so he decided that it was time to return to San Felipe. His decision was strengthened as relations with his father-in-law, Demetrio, had deteriorated.

So one day he saddled up his own beautiful mule, loaded his belongings onto a pack animal and started out for San Felipe, with Beni leading the pack animal and carrying the baby on her back. They arrived at what he told her was the old family homestead and Beni soon had it habitable and set up housekeeping there. She met his relatives one by one in the succeeding days but there was no rush to welcome her and they did not seem pleased to see her at all. Just one young woman was friendly, the wife of a younger brother who lived fairly close by. This was Nata and she showed her round the town and then introduced her to her own family and friends, so that Beni began to feel less strange in this unfamiliar, cold, high-altitude place.

She soon began to notice that her husband spent less time with them now. She assumed that he was glad to be back with his relatives, but wondered why he often stayed away all night. She cautiously questioned her new friends about her in-laws and soon discovered that she was not really his wife at all as he already had a wife and two children before he fled from San Felipe. Beni was devastated. Should she return home? But how could she, with her little daughter still so young and expecting another child in a few months' time. She decided that she would choose a favourable time when the man seemed most amiable, and then broach the sad subject to him. The time came and Beni screwed up her resolve to bring the matter into the open.

'I know about Emelia and your other children,' she blurted out.

He looked up in surprise and said: 'So what? Why should you be the only one?'

'But I'm not your wife at all if you were married to her before you even came to Jaguar Mountain! What can I say to the priest when our baby is born?'

'No problem. Of course you are my wife and don't you forget it! That other priest married us down in Dry Pond.'

'But it doesn't count since you already had a wife, because you married her with a proper wedding which was registered at the Town Hall here.'

The man began to look ugly and approached her threateningly.

'How do you know all this? Who has been talking to you behind my back? Don't go around discussing me with just anybody in this town, do you hear? You are my wife and just make sure that your children are my children too. Now forget it and come to bed.'

After that Beni was never really comfortable with any of his family except Nata, who continued to be a real friend. After a few years he began to be very abusive when drunk and was soon mistreating Beni. She had two miscarriages, which made him very angry. Finally, she became pregnant again. He was quite kind to her for a few months and seemed delighted when a baby boy was born. He spent more time with them and would often play with the baby, but soon he became drunk and abusive again, and would beat Beni and the two older children. One day he returned home early to find no hot fire so no hot food, and the baby crying. He flew into a rage and started hitting the older children with a leather strap. Beni had left them to look after the baby while she washed clothes for their neighbours to earn a little money: there were always small items that the children needed for school and their father never gave her any ready cash. From where she was working at the spring below their house she heard the children screaming. In panic she abandoned the laundry and ran up the hill to rescue them. She understood the situation at a glance and attacked their father with her fists as she shouted to the children to run away and hide. He soon pinned her down and lashed her unmercifully with the strap, then his fist crashed into her face and she lost consciousness.

When she came to, she found Nata bending over her anxiously with the children sobbing in the background.

'Can you move to the bed if I help you?' Nata inquired. 'You can rest there for now because he has gone and I don't suppose he will come back tonight. I heard the commotion and then your children came running into my house wild-eyed and screaming. I finally got them calmed down enough to tell me what it was all about. You just rest here now and I will go down to the spring and collect up the clothes. Who were you washing for today?'

'They belong to old Tila next door,' replied Beni, groaning as she tried to sit up.

With little Gloria's help, Nata managed to get Beni to the bed and tucked the blanket round her.

'You stay with your mother while I go and get those clothes,' Nata instructed eight-year-old Gloria, 'and keep an eye on your little sister. You can both bring some firewood into the kitchen and I will help you to make a fire when I get back.'

A few minutes later Beni called to Gloria to bring her a drink of water.

'Is the baby sleeping now?' she asked.

'The baby isn't here, mama, and I don't know where he is,' replied her daughter. 'He wasn't in the hammock any more when we came back with Nata.'

'What's happened to him then? I must find my baby!' said Beni urgently, groaning as she struggled to get up. 'Help me, Gloria! Find me a stick to lean on. We must find your brother!'

'Nata will be back in a minute, mama. Let's wait and see if she knows anything.'

Beni was too battered and bruised to move far, so she just sat on the side of the bed shivering. As soon as Nata appeared in the doorway, Beni burst out: 'He must have taken my baby! Did you see him, Nata? Whatever can he have done with his baby son? I must find my baby!'

'I was so concerned about you that I didn't remember the baby,' Nata said with consternation. 'He must have taken him to his other home or else to his mother. Don't worry, I'll soon find out if the child is with my mother-in-law or where else he might be. I took the clothes back to old Tila and here is the money. Now I'll just get that fire going, then Gloria can manage to reheat the beans, tortillas and coffee for you all because you must try to eat. I'll go and find out what's happening. I can leave my daughter to get supper for my family and to tell her father that I am visiting his mother. That woman often sends me on errands at this inconvenient time of day so he won't think anything of it.'

She whisked into the kitchen, got the fire going with a piece of pitchpine, lit the simple oil lamp there and then she was gone. Gloria had helped her mother enough times to be quite efficient at heating things up, so she soon had her little sister seated on a stool near the fire with a bowl of hot coffee in her hand. Then she carefully carried some coffee to her mother before heating the tortillas and serving the beans. Beni was glad of the hot coffee as she was shivering uncontrollably now, but she refused to eat anything although her little daughters tucked in hungrily. Where was her baby son? What if her man returned still angry? All kinds of dark thoughts swept through her mind.

Gloria was worried too and crept back to her mother's bedside to ask: 'Mama, my aunt Nata said that you must eat something or you will be really ill. You need your strength, she said. I'm sorry that I didn't look after the baby very well, but my father really hurt us with that strap. Do you think aunt Nata will find him?'

'I'm too worried to eat, dear. I would like another bowl of coffee though. It's lovely and hot. You are going to be a very good housewife and I'm proud of you. Your aunt Nata will bring us some news after she has seen your grandmother.'

'Yes, mama. I'm looking after Pola, so don't worry about us, and I'm sure aunt Nata will be back soon,' the little girl responded gravely and returned to the kitchen house.

She found that her little sister had not lost her appetite, so she was a bit comforted and had something to eat herself too. And then Nata was back again looking a trifle more cheerful.

'Yes, Beni, your baby is with my mother-in-law and she is really looking after him. After all, she is his grandmother, but she has hardly ever seen him before, with her son keeping you apart as he has. He himself isn't there though and his mother was quite vague about his whereabouts when I enquired.'

'I must get my baby back and leave here,' said Beni determinedly. 'I'm not his wife and he doesn't really want me anyway. I'm very afraid of him now and of what he might do to my children.'

'I will help you all I can, Beni, but I don't want to antagonise my own husband by being at odds with his family, even though I am not very fond of them. Ours is a very happy little family when they don't interfere. My brother would probably help us though, because he has always mistrusted my in-laws. I will go and talk to him later, but now I must go home and see to my own family. Rest tonight, Beni, and we'll see what happens tomorrow.'

Next day Beni's bruises were very sore but she was able to get about a bit and take charge of the family. News soon came that the children's father was now in jail because he had got roaring drunk at the cantina and picked a fight with the town secretary. His family would have to produce money for the fine before he could be released, so this gained a little respite from fear for Beni. Nata and her brother, Simón, concocted a plan to spirit the baby away from his grandmother and to get Beni and all three of her children out of the town before dark. Simón would go with them. It would be assumed that they had fled down the mountain to nearby Tutula, but Simón secretly planned to take them up over the pass and down to the village of San Isidro. He and Nata had lots of relatives there, so he knew every inch of the trail and could manage it even at night.

Beni was afraid that Nata's husband would punish her for helping but Simón reassured her: 'No, Beni, Nata just has a little part in all this and will be ostentatiously at home all day or on legitimate errands with plenty of witnesses, so she won't get blamed. I don't think anyone will miss me either as I am not married or anything and I often go off on trips for my father. I sometimes stay down at the coast working for months at a time and everyone knows that.'

So Beni and her children escaped with Simón's help. She had to rest for a couple of days in San Isidro and then Simón escorted them all the way to Jaguar Mountain. That had been two years ago and Beni still looked haggard. Simón had enjoyed the company of the outlaws, so he returned often to visit Jaguar Mountain after he got himself a job in Red River on the coast. He soon spied young Isabel and asked for her hand in marriage, as he got rather lonely living alone in the Spanish-speaking town, but he was not at all keen to return to his native San Felipe or even to his own relatives in San Isidro.

Tacho was saddened by this recital of his sister Beni's bleak history. He realised that she now lived in constant fear, but he was glad to hear of the bravery and initiative of his new young brother-in-law Simón who had helped her to escape from such an intolerable situation.

The next morning everyone was up early and Chico had a mule saddled ready for Tacho to accom-

pany them to their coffee plantation. They were
going to the most distant point of their groves to
start the first picking of the coffee berries. Only Dora
would stay at home with the school-age children
and the little ones; the babies were going on their
mothers' backs. Dora would look after the young
ones from Nino's household too, as the brothers
continued to work together just as they had with
their father. It turned out that Neyo and María had
no children as yet although they had been together
for several years. Tacho was glad that it would not
be a very long ride as he was unused to the saddle,
but then he was no longer used to tramping these
mountain trails either and his legs were definitely
feeling the effects of yesterday's journey. He was
rather startled to see how well-armed the men were,
even though he had known that the land problem
between Mulaca itself and the community on Jaguar
Mountain was still unresolved.

'All of my family are still outlaws,' he reminded
himself, 'and they desperately need to hear what
Jesus Christ has done in my life and how He cares
about them as well and wants to change their lives
for the better too.'

Tacho enjoyed the day. He found that he quickly
slipped back into his old efficient way of picking
coffee berries and knew instinctively which ones
were ready for plucking. At midday they returned
with their sacks of berries. Dora had a good meal
ready for everyone and afterwards the men took
turns at the handles of the dehulling machines to
get the soft pulp of the berries away and leave the
green coffee beans ready for drying. It was quite
tiring work to keep those handles turning at a steady

pace. After being washed, the beans were all spread out to dry on a large slab of concrete in the main yard. All this work needed to be accomplished speedily so that no bean would still be damp at sunset when they were all raked up again and put into sacks to avoid the dew. They would be spread out again over several succeeding days. They needed to be in the hot sun to dry out thoroughly and to mature before being transported to the coast for sale. The family had quickly worked through the plantation as this was the preliminary picking and only a few berries were ripe on each bush as yet. Next month it would be heavier work and again in January.

As dusk fell Tacho said, 'I must go home to my family tomorrow but I would like you all to gather here at Chico's house this evening because I have something that I want to tell you.'

'We'll see you later then,' they all responded cheerily as they scattered to their own homes.

22

'Why I came'

They slipped into the lamplit house one by one. Palm mats were unrolled on the floor and soon several little children were asleep there, all sharing one blanket. The mothers sat on the mats nursing their babies, and Tacho's brothers joined him at the table.

Chico said to Tacho: 'Now tell us everything – we are all listening.'

Tacho began at the time that he left Mulaca with the priest as a youngster of fifteen and told them all about his experiences in the city: school, the dormitory, work in the market and his employer's kindness; work on the building sites, the good and the bad of the city. He spoke about meeting Marta and Amadeo at the Baptist church, about marriage, and the bad influence of his old friends and the desperation that followed. Then he told them about his liberation when he finally understood the truth about Jesus Christ and put his faith in Him, and about the dramatic change in his own life and at home. Finally, he came to God's reminder to him about his brothers and sisters, still outlaws on Jaguar Mountain with no hope of forgiveness or change.

'I was sure that God wanted me to come and tell you the Good News that He cares about you and that you don't have to die unforgiven. Jesus died instead. He changed me from someone who was no good to anyone – not to myself, nor to my family, nor to anyone else in the world. He took me into His family and assured me that I too am one of God's children now. If He accepted even me, He certainly wants all of you to be His children as well. Jesus is my Boss now and He sent His Holy Spirit to live in me and make me new and different. Yes, I look the same and my body will die like anyone else's, but the real me, I will live for ever in Christ's kingdom.'

There was silence for a moment at the end of Tacho's long story. He prayed fervently in his heart that God would make these rough relatives of his receptive to the truth and not angered by his recital.

Then Chico burst out: 'Tacho, I'm tired of being an outlaw and having to shoot to kill people so that they don't kill me! I'm tired of being afraid all the time. I want to know more of this truth about Jesus Christ because I want to be changed and at peace in my heart like you are.'

Tacho explained more about the need to be truly sorry for all that had been done wrong, and the need for a desire to put those wrongs right if possible, and to try to do what God considers right regardless of other people's opinion. Humanly speaking, this is impossible, he said, but Jesus can change anyone and keep them changed by the power of His Holy Spirit if they really want to be His followers. Tacho then read some of Jesus Christ's words to them from the Bible to show them what it means to be a real Christian.

'I believe what Jesus says, Tacho. Is it really possible for Him to forgive me and change me?' Chico responded.

'Yes, Chico. I'm going to talk to Him now – that's what prayer really is, you know. You heard Him talk to us when I read from the Bible just now, so we need to reply. I'll pray first, then you, Chico. You tell Him how sorry you are and that you want to follow Him. Then thank Him for dying in your place and for giving you new life. Offer Him your own life as His follower.'

Tacho prayed and thanked God for each of these dear relatives that had been preserved to hear the Good News. He prayed for their enlightenment and that they would fully understand the truth. Afterwards Chico prayed brokenly and poured out his heart to God, asking forgiveness and pledging his allegiance to Jesus Christ in the future. At the end Chico himself was in tears and a very emotional Tacho could only hug him warmly and say: 'Now you are my brother twice over. We had the same father, but he died, and now we both have the same heavenly Father who is alive and really cares about us.'

The others carefully picked up the sleeping children, then quietly and pensively dispersed to their own homes, but Tacho and Chico stayed up talking together, enjoying their new-found fellowship. Finally, Chico's wife reminded them that Tacho must leave early in the morning and already it was after midnight. Tacho gave Chico his Bible and suggested that he read the Gospel of John first.

He showed him where to find it and promised to return for another visit before the year ended.

'Our brothers were really listening too, Tacho, even though they don't understand much Spanish. Perhaps they will become real Christians as well when they understand better.'

'We must pray for them, Chico, and for all your wives and children, that God will help them to understand so that they recognise the truth and believe,' responded Tacho.

They slept, and a few hours later Tacho was on his way home. Chico accompanied him to Dry Pond, and by the afternoon he was back in the coastal town telling the joyful news to his friend the pastor there.

'I won't stay the night this time though,' he said in response to a repeated invitation. 'I'll take the night bus back to Oaxaca so that I can share the news quickly with Marta and the others who have been praying anxiously about this trip.'

Everyone who heard Tacho's report was amazed. They could only thank God that Tacho's brother's life had been transformed. Tacho told them of Chico's wild youth when he had certainly killed some people, but now he just wanted to follow Jesus Christ and to live as God wanted him to. His small, city congregation kept Tacho busy and he enlisted their interest and prayer support for his 'missionary' journeys to his family on Jaguar Mountain. He set about making arrangements to be away again for several days the following month.

The weeks quickly passed and soon he found himself on the night bus to the coast again. He was more prepared this time and went straight on to Red River and so to Dry Pond, where he had a good breakfast before starting the hard slog up the mountainside to the Jaguar Mountain community.

This time they all gathered together on the night of his arrival, eager to hear more. Chico greeted him with a radiant smile: 'Tacho, I know for sure that God has forgiven me, even though I have done many terrible things. Jesus is my Boss now and with His help I won't do anything like that ever again,' he said humbly but determinedly.

He had been reading John's Gospel avidly and had lots of questions for Tacho. One thing caused him sadness though: 'I want to share all this with my wife and talk over with our brothers the wonderful things that I am reading, but I don't know how to express it in our own language and they understand so little Spanish. I too would learn much faster if I heard it in Chatino, Tacho.'

Tacho resolved to re-learn the language of his childhood so that he could be a more effective witness to his own people. Meanwhile he tried to speak clearly, and to say the same thing in several different ways each time to help his relatives to understand. He begged God earnestly for help with his teaching and explanation of the truth so that his hearers could understand, and particularly that they would be able to understand when he read from God's Word, the Bible. He had brought more Bibles with him this time and gave one each to Nino, Beni and Neyo and to Lencho for Dora's household.

Lencho looked wistfully at the book in his hands and said, 'Well, if it is so important, someone will have to help me to read it, because you know that Isabel, Queta and I were all born out here and had no chance to go to school at all and neither did my wife Li. I can sound words out a bit, but I don't understand enough Spanish to know what they mean.'

Chico responded immediately. 'I will help you as much as I can, little brother, if you come over here to my house regularly in the evenings.'

Tacho talked to them until almost midnight. Then both Nino and Beni tearfully asked him to help them ask God's forgiveness because they both wanted to commit their lives to following Jesus Christ. Tacho was overjoyed.

'That makes four of us in one family that are really God's children now!' he exclaimed.

The next morning Dora said that Lencho would accompany him to Red River. Since he would have a few hours before the night bus was due, Lencho would take him to his sister Isabel's house so that he could meet her and Simón.

Soon they were on their way and Tacho discovered that his young brother's command of Spanish was indeed limited, so he concentrated on dredging up some of his very rusty Chatino. Lencho proved a willing, cheerful and patient teacher and, as the words were recalled to his mind, Tacho found to his delight that the correct pronunciation came back almost automatically. However, he was going to have to work hard to remember the words, and that was quite difficult as none of it was written down.

When they arrived at Isabel's house at the edge of the town Lencho burst into a long explanation of Tacho's presence to his sister. She was very pleased to see them both, and especially to meet this eldest brother who had been only a legend to her up till then. Having lived in Red River for a year she had learnt more of the national language than young Lencho and so was able to converse more easily with Tacho. He enjoyed making the acquaintance of her solemn, chubby little son too, but he had lost count of how many nephews, nieces and other relatives he now had! He soon discovered that the family called Isabel 'Sabay', and as she busied herself getting them something to eat he looked around at her little house.

'Simón will be home at six o' clock, so I need to make a meal anyway,' she said. 'You will stay and have something to eat with us, won't you? There is a bus to Oaxaca that goes direct from here at nine o'clock, so surely you can stay with us till then.'

'Yes, thank you, little sister. That would be very convenient and I definitely want to meet Simón, especially after hearing Beni's story,' Tacho responded.

'My husband is a very brave and good man,' rejoined Sabay proudly.

Suddenly Tacho's idle gaze was caught by a book up on a little shelf by the mirror. Perhaps it was a Roman Catholic missal, but it certainly looked like a Bible. He looked round with more attention and realised that there was no altar table in Sabay's little house. Could it be a Bible? Tacho's curiosity was really aroused now.

'Is that a Bible that you have there, little sister?' he enquired.

'Yes, it is,' Sabay replied quietly.

'Do you read it?'

'I can't very well, because I never learnt to read properly, but Simón reads it to me. It is God's Word, you know.'

'Yes, I do know,' said Tacho. 'And do you believe it?'

'Oh yes. We meet together with a group of people here in Red River and they have introduced us to the real Jesus Christ who is alive and loves us.'

'That's marvellous, little sister. I am a Christian too along with my wife, and I have become a pastor in the city. I came back to Jaguar Mountain to tell the family about the wonderful way in which Jesus Christ has changed my life, and now Chico, Nino and Beni all believe too. It is truly wonderful to find that you and your husband belong to Christ's family as well.'

'Oh Tacho, we have been praying so earnestly for wisdom to recognise the right opportunity to talk to our families about Jesus Christ and to tell them of our new faith and changed lives. God is so good to bring you to talk to our relatives ahead of me like this. What an encouragement it is! Simón will be so pleased. Praise God! Praise God!'

Sabay hugged Tacho and then skipped back to the stove while Lencho looked on in amazement. His quiet, reserved, undemonstrative elder sister was certainly acting out of character! This proved that something really had happened to change her. She and Simón worked very hard to make ends meet and on his few previous visits Lencho had been sorry to see his sister so tired and dragging about. She had seemed rather depressed, he thought, but that was obviously a thing of the past. Here she was talking animatedly to Tacho as if he had always been around, sharing details of their family life with confidence, apparently assuming that he would understand all that was going on.

'This being a Christian seems to give people instant rapport,' he thought in amazement.

In between the earnest chatter and paying attention to the baby, Sabay had somehow managed to get the meal ready by the time that Simón arrived. As he threw down his rope bag and went to wash at the tap out in their yard, Sabay dashed out to tell him the exciting news about their visitor. Simón came in with a broad grin on his face.

'It is good to meet you at last, Tacho, and to find that you belong to God's family too. Isn't it wonderful to be sure of His forgiveness and to be free of that dead weight of wrongdoing? And to never be lonely any more is marvellous! How very gracious of our Boss to send His Spirit to live in our hearts and to accompany us always!'

'Yes, little brother, I agree. I am so happy to meet you both and to find that you are believers too. It is lovely to know that my new little nephew here will grow up in a home where Jesus Christ is in charge,' Tacho said as he looked fondly at the sleeping baby.

The time flew past as they ate together and shared experiences.

'It is almost time for my bus!' exclaimed Tacho suddenly. 'Let's just thank God that He gave us this happy time together and for all that He has done for each of us. We must continue to pray for our relatives too.'

So they prayed together and then Simón and Lencho ran with Tacho to the bus stop. Tacho promised to return in a month's time, but now it was back again to Oaxaca City with even better news for Marta and the others than from his previous trip. The pilot Teyo was especially glad to hear the news.

Another month passed rapidly and, with eager anticipation, Tacho boarded the night bus for the coast once again. On his arrival in Red River at dawn, he went directly to Sabay and Simón's house so he was able to see Simón before he left for work at 7 a.m. Sabay produced a tasty breakfast.

'I won't leave Jaguar Mountain till after midday tomorrow, so I won't be able to stop here again this time, little sister, because I'll only be just in time to catch the night bus. I hope to come again next month though.'

'Perhaps I could go out there with you next time you come, and talk to my mother about Jesus Christ,' Sabay said thoughtfully. 'Simón and I will pray about it and tell you when you come.'

Tacho's face lit up as he responded: 'In that case I will try to come the evening before and stay the night with you here. Then we can start out early in the morning and it will be easier travelling for the baby.'

'God bless you on the road, Tacho,' she said with a smile as he left the house bound for Jaguar Mountain.

Again the family gathered to hear what Tacho had to tell them and to ask him questions about living as a Christian. A few of the neighbours were there too this time and Tacho began to find out which other Mulaca families were among the outlaws. They included Frero, a former friend from his village schooldays, along with his two teenage sons. They wanted to know why Tacho had told his brothers not to join in the local festivities at

Christmas and New Year. Each year the Jaguar
Mountain community put on a mini-event modelled
on the one held in the main village of Mulaca, except
that a priest never came to them. The drunkenness
was more pronounced than ever and fights were the
norm, often with shooting.

'We are real men out here, not like those poor
specimens in the main village,' they boasted.

Tacho told them that he had not forbidden
anyone to take part in the fiesta. He told them also,
however, of his own deliverance from alcoholism
and of the happiness and peace in his life now that
he was free from it and without fear.

'I let drink rule me before, but now Jesus is my
Boss and it makes all the difference,' he said. 'Jesus
cares about you too, you know. Yes, He was born into
the world at Christmas in the same way as any other
human baby. The Virgin Mary was His mother, but
it wasn't a sex act that made her pregnant; it was the
work of the Holy Spirit of God and He chose Joseph
to marry her and to be the stepfather of Jesus. The
Lord Jesus didn't stay a baby either. He grew up in
the normal way, which is why He knows all about
life on this earth. Joseph was a country carpenter, so
Jesus grew up in that ordinary carpenter's home in
a country village. Then He allowed Himself to be
killed on the cross so that God could forgive us for
all the bad things that we have done.

'Jesus really died and He died instead of us, but
the great news is that He came to life again and is
alive now. He saves us when we believe in Him,
and changes our hearts and minds when we allow
Him to take charge of our lives. My brothers Chico
and Nino believe this now, and so does my sister

Beni, so they are not afraid any more. Jesus is our Boss and we don't want to disappoint Him. We know that He doesn't like drunkenness and fighting, so we don't want to be a part of that kind of behaviour any more. He has promised that we will go to be with Him when we die, so we are not afraid of death any more either.'

'But the fiesta is the custom and we must keep our village traditions, even if we are outlaws,' expostulated his old friend. 'Anyway, your brothers have killed people, Tacho. We all have since we have been at odds with the main village. We have done many other harmful things to the people there, and will again if necessary. Not even the priest will come out here on this mountain, so we know that there is no forgiveness for us! God doesn't care about people like us, if there is a God!'

'God will forgive even murder if you are really sorry that you did it and are willing to let Him change your life completely,' Tacho responded.

Then Neyo broke in urgently, regardless of the audience. 'Tacho, Mariana and I have talked all this over and we want to be Christians too. We are tired of this constant fear which never lessens however faithfully we keep the customs.'

So Tacho explained things to them once again and both Neyo and Mariana prayed there in front of everyone else. Neyo broke down as he confessed to killing two Mulaca men who had been planting a cornfield that encroached on Jaguar Mountain, and of how he had deliberately broken down the fences round other Mulaca men's fields and driven cattle into them to destroy the crops. Many times he had been angry with Mariana and had beaten her

savagely because they still had no children even
after five years of marriage. He had hidden close to
the edge of the village and molested young women
out gathering firewood in the hope of making one
pregnant to prove that their family problem was
Mariana's fault. Once started, his confession went
on for a long time. Even his own brothers and sisters
were shaken by the long recital, although they had
thought that they knew all about him. Finally, he
looked up at Tacho and a happy smile spread over
his face.

'It really is true. I feel clean inside now – God
really has forgiven me and I begin to feel different
already. I knew that I was bad inside, but I just urged
myself on to even worse behaviour to show that I
didn't care. But now Jesus is my Boss and I want to
live differently, so that He won't need to be ashamed
of me. I loved being popular in the *cantina* just
because I could strum the guitar a little bit and sing
those lurid songs, but now I want to sing for Jesus.
Is that possible, Tacho?'

'Oh yes. There are lots of songs of praise and
worship that we can sing to God. We must all learn
to sing them together and you can lead us with your
guitar.'

Then Frero said thoughtfully: 'I'm glad that you
came back and found us here, Tacho. I'm glad that I
was here tonight. This is all new to me, but it sounds
like the truth and I want to hear more. I see a real
difference in you. Did you say that you are going
back to Oaxaca tomorrow? When will we see you
again?'

Tacho promised to return the following month.
However, as he was not leaving till the next after-

noon, perhaps they could all meet in the morning
for a Bible study. They began in John's Gospel and,
from the thoughtful comments and questions that
came from both Chico and Nino, Tacho knew that
they had taken his suggestion from his previous visit
seriously and had been reading it for themselves in
the intervening weeks. At the end he gave a Bible to
Frero, and further suggested that they all meet
regularly to read the Bible and talk it over together
and to pray for one another. Neyo had a battery tape
recorder with several cassettes of favourite *cantina*
songs. Tacho said that he would bring a cassette of
Christian songs next time so that they could learn
to sing songs that please God.

'Could you buy me a tape recorder in the city,
Tacho?' Chico asked. 'Perhaps you could buy
several Christian cassettes for us as well. I'll give
you some money because I know that these things
cost quite a bit. What about your bus fare too? You
keep coming here for our benefit and it must cost a
lot. Perhaps we can make a little collection to help
you with that, and anyone who would like to help
can.'

Tacho was amazed that already God was putting
such thoughtfulness and concern into the heart of
his rough brother. The return journey to the city
went very quickly as he thanked God and prayed
for each one of his relatives and his old friend, Frero.
He could hardly wait to share all his excitement at
what he was seeing God do.

He burst into his home calling urgently: 'Marta,
Marta, my young brother Neyo and his wife
Mariana have become believers too! Cándido, you
just have time before you go to school to run round

to Chucho and Flora and see if they can spare an hour this morning to hear my good news. Marta, I'm going to phone your uncle Amadeo and your sister Estela and her husband as well as Teyo to see when they are all free to hear all the exciting things that have been happening out there.'

'Yes, it would be lovely to see them all. Invite them over for the evening if they can come tonight. Don't stay on the phone too long though because I have the breakfast all ready and I want to hear all about the trip before I go to the Bible school this morning,' said Marta.

Chucho and Flora had arrived before Tacho finished his phone calls so Marta sat them down with cups of coffee.

'They will all be coming this evening, Marta,' Tacho said with satisfaction as he came back into the room.

He came to the table beaming and led them all in a prayer of thanksgiving for the food, for a safe journey and for all that God was doing to convince his brothers of the truth about Jesus Christ. Everyone listened with rapt attention to his account of this latest journey. They all shared his joy and thanked God for Neyo's and Mariana's change of heart.

'I must go and visit my little sister Rita this afternoon and tell her about all this. If she becomes a Christian too, then all of us that are my mother's children will be united in God's family,' Tacho said happily.

Later that day he set out to find Rita's address. She lived in a part of the city that was rapidly expanding up the mountainside, having outgrown the valley floor. After various enquiries and taking two buses, he found the house on a side-street. It was inside a high wall with a big gate made of flattened tin cans nailed to wooden bars. He knocked vigorously, and after a lull the gate was opened a crack by a young woman carrying a baby.

'Yes?' she enquired.

Tacho greeted her pleasantly and explained who he was. Clearly surprised, she invited him into the patio. He could see that this was not considered a very safe part of the city, so he continued his explanation identifying himself beyond all doubt to allay her fears.

With an incredulous smile of welcome she replied, 'You had better come in, because I am Rita. I hardly remember you at all, Tacho, except that many times I have looked at those photos that you sent to our father so long ago. I met my husband in Red River six years ago and we moved here to Oaxaca straight away.'

Tacho told her of his recent visits to Jaguar Mountain and gave news of all the family. When her eager questions about them were all answered, Rita asked: 'Forgive me for asking, Tacho, but after all these years of silence, why did you suddenly feel this need to re-establish contact with our family?'

It was the opening that Tacho had prayed for. He told her all about his own change of heart and allegiance to Jesus Christ and of how he had felt compelled to go and tell the family what had happened to him and how he had changed. He told her also of his hope and prayer for all the family.

'How wonderful, Tacho,' exclaimed Rita delightedly as she reached out to hug him. 'My husband

Pablo and I are Christians too. We were baptised last year and joined the Pentecostal church just two streets away from here. It was through the brothers there that we came to know the truth about Jesus.'

'This really is the goodness of God! So I have another Christian brother-in-law! I really look forward to meeting Pablo,' Tacho exclaimed excitedly.

It was another emotional moment for him and he smiled through tears of joy.

'And to think that I had no idea of all that God has been doing to extend His Kingdom in the hearts of members of my family!' he said shaking his head in amazement.

Pablo worked in a bicycle shop so he did not get home till eight at night, but Rita promised that they would go over to visit Tacho and Marta on Sunday afternoon, now that she knew the address and how to get there. Tacho suddenly became aware that the afternoon had gone, so he hastily said goodbye to Rita for the present and made his way home.

It was a grand reunion when Amadeo, Teyo, Estela and Enrique arrived that evening. Several hours flew past as they listened to Tacho's recital and then shared some of their own good experiences of the Christian way of life.

As they were leaving Teyo said: 'Listen, Tacho. I will be making another evangelistic flight out to the Mixtec area in four weeks' time. I will be picking up a Christian dentist on the coast first. Would you like to come too? You could talk to the people while he attends to their teeth. Afterwards I could drop you at his town there on the coast and it would be much easier for you to get to Jaguar Mountain. In fact, I am supposed to stay the weekend with the dentist and speak in his church on the Sunday, so I could wait for you on Monday morning and bring you back in the plane with me. Would that be convenient?'

'It would beat that all-night bus journey, certainly!' replied Tacho with enthusiasm. 'I will check with the pastor that I work with to see if it is all right to be away over the weekend like that, and I'll let you know. I do hope it works out!'

On Sunday Rita arrived with her family soon after breakfast. They wanted to go to church with Tacho and Marta that day and show a united family front to the believers there. It was a very special day for them all as they got to know each other both as blood family and as Christian family. There was so much for the adults to share and the cousins were delighted with each other too. María took charge of the baby and Rosa looked after the toddler while the boys tirelessly played with the four-year-old boy. When the day came to an end they vowed to keep in touch more closely. Rita and Pablo were especially eager to keep up with the developments in the Jaguar Mountain community, and Rita could not thank God enough for what He was doing in the hearts and lives of her brothers.

The pastor had no objection to Tacho going with Teyo on an evangelistic trip and so it was arranged. They started off in the little plane early on a Thursday morning, had breakfast with the dentist, then arrived in the Mixtec village by mid-morning. The dental patients were already awaiting their arrival, so the dentist quickly set to work and carried on as long as the light lasted, while Teyo and Tacho chatted quietly with anyone who understood Spanish. That evening they showed a biblical film which fascinated the local people, although few of them understood everything that was said in it. On Friday they were up before dawn for some breakfast and then the dentist worked until the last possible minute before scrambling his equipment together and hurrying to the airstrip with Tacho. Teyo had gone ahead to check over the plane so that they could take off immediately and arrive at the coast before sunset. From the dentist's home it was easy for Tacho to get a bus for Red River where he received a warm welcome from Simón and Sabay. In short order she had supper ready and everything organised to accompany Tacho the following day. Simón assured him that he could manage very well for the days that his wife would be away, and that he would be praying for them both on the road.

Everyone at Jaguar Mountain was glad to see Tacho again and Dora's face lit up when she saw that her daughter and baby grandson were with him. They all met together in Chico's house that same evening along with several of the neighbours. Frero, Tacho's old school friend, and his sons were present again, together with one of his brothers and a cousin.

'We have heard from your brothers how your life has changed, Tacho, and that you no longer get drunk or beat your wife and children. They say that you are not afraid of anything now, but we want to hear you tell us how it all happened,' they said earnestly.

So Tacho told his story once more and they all listened attentively.

'But it's not just me,' he finished. 'Hear this testimony from my brothers who have been with you all these years.'

Then Chico, Nino and Neyo all told of the new sense of peace in their hearts, their assurance of God's forgiveness and their desire to live for Him in the future. They rejoiced in their new freedom from the crushing fear of impending retribution, although they now wanted to make things right.

'You all know my little sister, Sabay, too and her man, Simón,' said Tacho. 'Well, they are happily married now and they also have entered Jesus Christ's way. He is their Boss now. So tell us about it, Sabay.'

She had thought to quietly talk to her mother about all the changes that had come into her life, but now Sabay bravely grasped this opportunity to recount to the whole group all that had happened to Simón and herself down in Red River.

When she had finished, she spoke directly to her brothers: 'It is really good to be properly married so that your children have legal names. Also, God is happy to see united families. I'm sure our pastor would be glad to bless your marriages in our church if you came to the judge in Red River for the legal ceremony. At the same time you could publicly ask God to bless your children and help you to teach them about him.'

'We never even thought about weddings,' responded Chico. 'We couldn't have gone to the church in Mulaca anyway and it seemed too difficult and unnecessary to try elsewhere. Our children haven't been baptised either, which has always worried their mothers, so perhaps that's a good idea, Sabay. If it is what God wants, then we want to do it if the mothers of our children are happy to take part in this kind of wedding. We must talk it all over and make some arrangements. There are other things that we need to put right too.'

Tacho agreed that something must be done to put things right with the people of Mulaca. They could not bring back the dead, but they could do something for the widows. Also they could submit themselves to the village authorities, take whatever punishment was meted out to them, and pay without argument any fines exacted. They needed to discuss the vexed question of the use of Jaguar Mountain land too.

'The authorities will all be there tomorrow as usual since it is Sunday,' Tacho said at last. 'If you really want to do something about this, let's go down there and see them. You can put yourselves into their hands and see what happens. But you each need to talk it all over with your wives, because they will suffer too if the authorities put you in jail or if they demand all your coffee in fines, or some other punishment like that. Let's pray about it now, and if you feel that God really wants you to do this, then we must start out before dawn tomorrow.'

'Before we pray I want to say that I believe as well now and so does my son Po,' Frero broke in. 'I have been reading that Bible that you gave me and Chico helped me to understand some things better, so I asked Christ's forgiveness and committed my life to His Way. I have entered His road and I want to follow Him always. So I want to come with you to Mulaca tomorrow because I am just as guilty as your brothers, Tacho, and I am truly ashamed now.'

They prayed fervently together, then scattered to their homes. Nino's wife Marsé lingered a moment to say: 'Nino and I have been talking over all that you have told us. Together we have been reading that Bible that you gave us too. I had more chance to go to school in Mulaca because my family is still there, so I learnt to read Spanish quite well. We believe all that we understand and I wanted you to know that I have entered Jesus' road too. Nino and I pray together and we are teaching our children what we have learnt. Thank you for coming to show us the way, Tacho. It is wonderful not to be afraid any longer and it will be good to get things straightened out in Mulaca, even if it means heavy punishment.' She left Tacho overwhelmed with gratitude to God for the privilege of seeing the Holy Spirit at work in the lives of his family and friends.

Everyone was up again before dawn, as the men were firmly resolved to go to the authorities in Mulaca and turn themselves in. They wanted to get things straightened out while Tacho was still there with them. The womenfolk were prepared for the consequences as they were sick and tired of the estrangement from the village and the rest of their relatives there. Young Lencho was determined to accompany his brothers and so prove himself a man ready to take any punishment necessary. Frero and his son were there too.

When they rode into Mulaca the streets emptied as if by magic. Frantic mothers grabbed up their little children in spite of indignant cries and resistance to such an unexpected interruption to their play. They

rushed indoors with them, calling wildly to the
older ones to come in, then closed and barred all
their windows and doors. Everyone knew that the
appearance of the men from Jaguar Mountain meant
gunfire and probably more deaths. The village
seemed to be holding its collective breath as Tacho
and the others made their way to the council's office
in the central square. None of them was armed, but
the people of Mulaca did not take time to notice this
most unusual fact. They filed into the mayor's office
and all identified themselves. Then Chico explained
their errand at length. Only the mayor, his assistant
and the council's secretary had been in the office
when they arrived, but word of their presence
spread like wildfire and more council members kept
slipping in and taking their places round the walls,
while the duty policemen crowded the doorway to
listen too.

After his initial shock, the mayor gradually
relaxed as he gave his full attention to what Chico
was saying. Soon he began asking incredulous questions. Then he turned to the others and questioned
them all in turn. It took a lot to convince him
that the Ruíz family to a man had indeed had this
tremendous change of heart. He got Tacho to explain
again the reasons for his advice to his brothers to
turn themselves in, and their desire to set things
straight where they could.

Finally he said: 'Well, you must all stay here in
jail until tomorrow so that the council can deliberate
on this matter. You are free to go, Tacho, as you
were not involved in all the trouble, but I would
like you to come back next weekend so that we can
sort out some of the details of this affair. We will

give our preliminary decision to your brothers and
Frero tomorrow though.'

The astonished police took charge of the unresisting prisoners. Before committing them to the
village's one-room jail they searched them as they
simply could not believe that they had come
unarmed. Tacho took their horses to Rolando's
house where he was greeted enthusiastically and
plied with questions as to what was going on. He
told them the whole story, as inquisitive neighbours
and friends also came in to hear all about it as well.
They had heard all sorts of wild rumours, and now
crowded round the door and open window. Sana
and her husband arrived and pushed through the
crowd into the house. She and Tacho had trouble
recognising one another and wished that they had
some privacy to catch up on each other's lives, but
Rolando's questions took precedence as it was his
house. Finally, Rolando's wife announced that it was
time to eat and the crowd reluctantly melted away,
since it is the height of bad manners for a Chatino
to watch people eating, especially in their own
home. Sana and her husband were invited to stay
and eat, so she promptly gave her baby to her
husband and went to help Rolando's wife to serve
the men first. Tacho noticed some signs of Rolando's
prosperity, not least the well-built concrete and brick
house with its flat roof for drying coffee, and its
internal plumbing to kitchen and bathroom. He
enquired about Tino and Alicia in Tutula. Rolando
was very proud of his son's achievements.

'He helped us with all this so that we really live
comfortably now. He and Alicia are not stuck up at
all – they come to visit us regularly and bring our

lovely grandchildren to see us. Of course, it is much easier now with the road to Tutula. The bus comes in every day and several shop-owners have small lorries. The village council here owns a lorry too. It carries people and cargo and makes at least one journey to Tutula every day. During the coffee season it was very busy and made repeated trips every day. Tino helped me to start a coffee plantation and we had a very good crop this year. He has his own small lorry as well as a car, so I don't have to rely on the village truck for my cargo to be shifted, which is a great help. You see that small room on the end? He got his mother set up with a general shop there and his lorry brings in the supplies that she orders regularly.'

'Wow, Tino really is helping the whole village by helping you like this. I am impressed,' Tacho said beaming.

'Yes, he helps us all in many ways,' continued Tino's enthusiastic father. 'Anyone from here can get help from him with legal problems too, or with filling in government forms. We are no longer at the mercy of fast-talking Spanish-speakers because Tino understands them and knows all the legal angles too, so we don't get cheated by outsiders as much as we used to.'

'That's really good news,' Tacho responded, then added with a sly grin: 'I bet you are not sorry any more that Tino became a lawyer rather than a priest! Perhaps I will be able to visit him next weekend – the mayor said that I must return here then with my brothers. It will be easier to come direct via Tutula now that there is a road and a bus all the way. But I must get back out to Jaguar Mountain quickly today because I will never be able to find the trail after dark, and I need to let the women there know what is happening.'

'Come direct here next weekend then, Tacho. You must stay with us,' said Rolando jovially as Tacho left them.

Sana's husband accompanied him part of the way, to be sure that he kept to the right trail, and he arrived back at the Jaguar Mountain community just at dusk. He reported everything to the anxious women waiting there.

'We were praying for you all, and that God would help the village council to believe you and to be fair in their judgement,' said Sabay.

'And God really has changed our hearts and thoughts,' added Marsé, 'because Mariana and I were not afraid at all. Jesus really is with us all the time, just as He promised.'

Sabay and Tacho were on the trail down to Dry Pond before dawn the next morning. They arrived in Red River and Tacho caught a bus along the coastal highway almost immediately. He reached the dentist's house to find that he and Teyo were enjoying a leisurely breakfast. As Tacho was invited to join them, he recounted all the exciting developments that he had been involved in over the weekend. The three men prayed humbly together and committed themselves and all their activities to God's direction and control once more.

'It is a very good thing that the outcome does not depend on us. God really is the sovereign ruler and He knows what He is doing,' Teyo remarked on their way to the airstrip.

As they flew along above the familiar mountains Tacho sighed.

'How I wish that I had continued practising my language. How could I have forgotten my own language like this? There are so many of my people that don't understand Spanish and I can't really talk to them any more. I can't tell them how much God cares about them and that He wants to free them from their terrible fears.'

Teyo broke in and said: 'Did you know that there is an English couple who speak your language? They have been out to Tutula and Mulaca many times and they are translating God's Word into Chatino.'

'Did you say there are English people who speak Chatino? That's incredible! How would they learn it when there are no books?'

'They have been writing it down as they go along,' Teyo told him. 'They worked out an alphabet first and then started to make books and to translate the Bible. They live and work in Mitla a lot of the time. Would you like to meet them?'

'Do you know these people then, Captain Teyo?' responded Tacho with surprise. 'Of course I would like to meet them and find out more about this. I can't believe that anyone could make books in my language, especially God's Word! That's fantastic!'

They agreed that, once the matter between Tacho's brothers and the Mulaca village council was settled, Tacho would contact Teyo again about meeting these foreign translators.

23

Triple approach to Mulaca

Early on Saturday morning Tacho boarded the bus in Oaxaca City for Tutula. He was amazed to see how much the road had improved since he had last travelled this way to Tino's wedding, and immeasurably since he travelled it in the jeep with the priest. The county town had changed and developed too. The building trade was booming and there were more hotels in the town now. Some of the streets were concrete; the big church was refurbished and the central square paved. There were also rumours that soon the road into Tutula would be tarmacked, as well as the main road to the coast.

Tacho went straight to Tino's house where he received a warm welcome. He explained about his need to go to Mulaca.

'You must stay with us tonight, Tacho, and I will take you to Mulaca myself early tomorrow,' Tino said. 'Perhaps I can be of some help too. This evangelical teaching must be really powerful for your brothers to have such a change of heart though. It should make a lot of difference to their sentence that they gave themselves up freely like this, but it is rather unprecedented.'

He looked very thoughtful and rather puzzled, but then his three little girls demanded Tacho's attention. The eldest was attending the local 'kinder' school now and was intrigued by the idea that this was her father's godfather who had come to see them. She wanted to know if Tacho had any little girls at home in Oaxaca, and did they go to the 'kinder' there.

The adults stayed up late, catching up with each other's news. Tino was amazed at the change for the good in Tacho. He asked several probing questions about his faith as he could see that the change was not just a passing phase. Just as Tacho said, it had to be God's work that had changed his outlook so much. As for the change in his brothers, that was phenomenal. Apparently Tino's own sister Marsé and his brother-in-law Nino had become 'believers' too. 'Well, if this means a permanent solution to the Mulaca–versus–Jaguar Mountain problem, that would be a miracle indeed,' Tino thought.

Next day Tino drove Tacho to Mulaca as promised. They found Tacho's brothers already at the council office. Only Neyo and Lencho had been allowed out of jail the previous Monday so that they could return home to Jaguar Mountain for some sacks of coffee and money to pay their fines. The village secretary had prepared a list of all the widows and families where someone had been injured because of the Ruíz brothers or Frero Santiago. Now all of them were going as a body to visit each one officially, to deed them a part of the Jaguar Mountain coffee plantation, to pay them each some money, and to apologise as best they could. They were also to give them valuable stock such as cattle, mules, donkeys, other domestic animals or trees.

The little procession started out with the secretary and another member of the council accompanying them to record each transaction as they visited each house. One or two of the widows had only young children, so they did not feel able to cope with a large sum of money in the house or a plantation to look after. Instead they gratefully accepted a sack of coffee and pigs or poultry that they could keep near their houses, plus the promise of sacks of maize corn and beans to come regularly in the months ahead.

The Mulaca residents were amazed to see all this. However, it would take more time for them to be convinced of the genuine change for good in the situation on Jaguar Mountain and in the people there. The village council outlined some projects that they wanted help with. They needed both money and days of work for these, and also named the final figure of each man's fine and the date by which they should all comply with these conditions. The council decided that there was no point in taking the matter to higher authority since the guilty ones had come forward of their own free will and had agreed without argument to all the fines and conditions that had been stipulated. They felt that they could manage their own affairs better than the county or state authorities, as they were convinced that outsiders did not understand the Chatino way of thinking.

While there Tacho respectfully asked for permission to visit the homes of the people in Mulaca

to tell them of his new faith and of all the good that
God had done in his life. He also wanted permission
to preach and teach if a group met together to listen.
He was readily given permission to visit and to chat,
but the mayor wanted to see his credentials for
preaching and teaching. He was impressed when
Tacho promised that he would bring his certificate
of graduation from the Bible school and his official
registration as a Baptist pastor for their official
authorisation the next time that he came.

They all parted amicably and a new era began
for Mulaca as the news got round. Several men came
to apply to the village authorities for reinstatement
to land on Jaguar Mountain that they had cultivated
before the reign of the outlaws. They were given
permission to reclaim that land and awarded
damages from the Jaguar Mountain community. It
took many months to sort out the whole affair to
everyone's satisfaction, but finally it was done.

Then one day in Oaxaca Tacho reminded Teyo of
his promise concerning the English couple. So Teyo
took him to Mitla and introduced him to the
translators. They urged Tacho to tell them of what
God had been doing among his family members.
They had known about the riot long ago and about
the Jaguar Mountain community of outlaws. They
had known Padre Juan as well and had met several
of the widows in Mulaca, so they were fascinated
and delighted by all that Tacho had to tell them.
Tacho in his turn was amazed to find that they could
indeed speak Chatino and had been working with a
committee of Chatino people from the highland area
to translate the New Testament into their language.
They were currently doing the final preparation of

the manuscript for printing and also were working on a bilingual dictionary between highland Chatino and Spanish. They showed him the Gospels of Luke and John that were in print already as separate books, and some other Chatino books for learning to read. It was almost too much for Tacho to take in so suddenly.

'This is what my people need,' he said stroking one of the Gospel books in his hand, 'God's Word in our own language. Even my family, especially my sisters-in-law, don't really understand Spanish. They need the Scriptures in Chatino and they need to hear the message in Chatino so that it enters their hearts. They need to know all of the Good News of Jesus Christ!'

The Englishman showed him some cassettes of Chatino Scripture read by people from Mulaca and San Antonio. As he listened to one, his expression changed and he turned to Teyo in excitement: 'That's Chatino! They really are reading God's Word in my language!'

After that happy meeting the English couple kept in touch with Tacho as he continued to visit Mulaca and Jaguar Mountain.

The next time that they saw him he had another remarkable report to make. Back in Mulaca again, he was talking to an old acquaintance when the man looked along the street beyond him and said: 'Look, here comes Esteban. He believes like you do and is telling everybody that he meets here how Jesus Christ has changed his life. He grew up in another place but his father was a Mulaca man so he and his brother came back here as arrogant young men. They had money to throw about and they were hard drinkers, reckless gamblers, womanisers and trigger-happy. They caused trouble wherever they went and spent many nights in jail. Finally, the village barred Esteban from ever returning here because of his atrocious behaviour and he ran off with someone else's wife. He had already deserted his own woman in Tutula. That all happened many years ago and now he has come back as an evangelist. He made a public apology to the village council and he really is different.'

Tacho moved forward to meet Esteban and soon discovered that he was indeed a fellow believer. Each of them was delighted by the encounter. They found that they both were more at home speaking in Spanish, having both been away from the area for so long. It turned out that Esteban had run away to the same coastal town where the pilot's friend, the dentist, lived. With his wild living he had no reserves when he became very ill; there was no money for doctors' bills or expensive medicine and he was almost at the end of his tether when he encountered God in reality and his life was transformed. Slowly he regained his strength. He was so grateful to God for the assurance of forgiveness and salvation and for the fact that he was healed, that he felt that he could do nothing else but spread the Good News about Jesus Christ. He would work for a few weeks as a day-labourer to provide for his wife and two daughters, then go off on an evangelistic trip. Finally, God reminded him of his own people, of their need to hear the Good News too and of his own need to put right the wrongs from which he had absconded in the past. He had married Gina when they heard that her husband was dead, but he needed to find and help the woman and child that he had deserted in Tutula. He had just returned to Mulaca and was staying with his once equally wild brother. This man was so impressed with the change in Esteban that he had already believed too.

Tacho told his own tale and the two men rejoiced together as they marvelled at God's timing that both should be in Mulaca on the same errand at the same time.

'How loving and caring of our God to encourage us like this, brother,' Tacho said. 'He arranged for us both to meet here and share our histories!'

'Yes. Who could have guessed that He would choose such terribly bad men as we were to save and to change completely? We have a very wonderful, miracle-working God. Praise Him!' responded Esteban.

With renewed enthusiasm they continued their visiting, each in a separate direction. Then Tacho heard that the man who had been the village secretary during the riot twenty years before had finally been released from jail and returned home.

'Armando is different now,' Tacho was told. 'He reads the Bible a lot just like a priest and he will explain it to anyone who goes to his house. He keeps inviting people to go and read it with him. He even thanks God that he had to go to prison because he says that he would never have known the truth about God or believed in Jesus Christ as his Saviour and Boss if he had not gone to prison.'

Tacho vaguely remembered the secretary as a young and very capable Spanish-speaker. His family had come to Mulaca from another county and had been given permission to settle there, even though they spoke no Chatino. His older brother had married a local girl and had a big family, so their children grew up speaking both languages. Armando had married also and his wife had followed him loyally when he was taken to the Tutula jail and later to the state prison in Oaxaca. She had faithfully visited him all through those prison years. Then they had taken him far away to a high-security prison for the last few years of his sentence and she was not allowed to follow. She had been overjoyed by his release, but although released he had to stay near the prison on parole for the final year, and it was during that time that he had met a group of Open Brethren believers and heard the truth about Jesus Christ. He gave his allegiance to Christ and found that all his bitter feelings towards the people of Mulaca were gone, even towards the rest of the council members who had deserted him and left him as scapegoat to serve their corporate prison sentence alone. Neither did he feel any ill will towards his jailers any longer. He forgave all of them as he was sure that God had forgiven him and them, so he wanted them also to know God's wonderful peace in their hearts along with the assurance of God's love and acceptance, whoever they were.

Tacho learnt all this when he visited Armando. Sadly, however, when Armando's wife realised that he was now an evangelical, she deserted him and returned to her own relatives. She took their children with her and none of them would speak to him or allow him to speak to them at all, which caused him great sadness. When he first returned to the area he had gone to Red River to find his mother and younger brother who had fled there because of all the trouble at the time of the riot. It was an especially joyful reunion because he found that they too had become believers there in Red River, but now they were ready to return to Mulaca with him. Perhaps the solidarity of all three had been too much for Armando's wife. He invited Tacho to preach to the little group that met for Bible study in his house whenever Tacho visited Mulaca.

Esteban, Armando and Tacho were utterly astounded by the amazing thing that God had done. They were three very different men from three very different families and with very different experiences of life, but all from the same village. God had met each one in a different way when he was in desperate need and without hope, and had transformed their lives so that their hearts were full of calm joy and confident hope. Now He had brought them all back to their home village at the same time! They could only thank God together and dedicate themselves to His service with new enthusiasm. Each one's knowledge of Christ had come through a different tradition. They agreed, however, that what mattered most was their common allegiance to Jesus Christ and that they should tell all their neighbours the truth about Him rather than urging any denominational doctrines.

With the improved understanding between Mulaca and the Jaguar Mountain community, Nino and Marsé moved back to the village to be near Marsé's family, and so that their children could be in the school there. They joined Armando's Bible-study group, but they were still very sensitive to gibes from the neighbours and very aware of those neighbours' fear of the calamities an evangelical presence in the village was supposed to cause. The meetings were usually in the evenings, so often they would go separately and skulk round by devious routes to get to Armando's back gate and slip in unobtrusively.

Many people began to listen more attentively to the quiet witness of Esteban and Armando, and to Tacho when he visited. As their old friends and neighbours watched them and saw that their lives corroborated what they were saying, they began to take notice of their message. Then Esteban invited an evangelistic medical team of foreigners to visit Mulaca. Members of the local council were eager for the village to receive this free, expert medical aid, and happily gave their permission for the team to come there. Many people listened to and accepted the Christian message preached by members of the team, even though they did not fully understand the implications, since the presentation was entirely in Spanish.

Soon after this, opposition developed as some people began to feel that their old ways were threatened by all these new ideas and teaching. They feared that the local customs might change. They had always lived with suspicion and fear, so these new ideas and the change in the characters of those who embraced them caused fear too.

Then, although the troubles with Jaguar Mountain were a thing of the past, a new threat arose that resulted in more vicious killing. People had become used to their somewhat more affluent lifestyle since they had acquired their coffee plantations and the timber money. Some became greedy and found illegal ways to make even more money, and this resulted in a wild fringe element once more. Murders became frequent again and stark fear was rife. It was easy for the opposition to start rumours that the believers were to blame for the calamities because they did not strictly adhere to all the old traditions. When rocks were hurled onto his roof to break the tiles and disturb the Bible studies, Armando decided to move to the city for a few weeks and let things calm down a bit. He went to see Tacho and warned him not to visit for a while. Nino and Marsé moved their little family into Oaxaca, where they went to stay with Tacho since they wanted to continue learning more about Christ's way.

The growing group of believers in Mulaca had wanted to build a church to meet in, as their numbers had outgrown the largest home there. One of them had given family land for the building and, as things were quieter, the council had given them permission to go ahead and build. Esteban recruited more help from other groups of believers on the coast and brought in men and building materials to help the local group so that they had made a good start on the foundations. They were all encouraged and had worked with a will, but one day a group of hot-headed young men with rifles rode by. They were inflamed by drink and the doubts of the opposition, and when they saw the believers at work they opened fire on them. Esteban was wounded in the thigh, so all the visitors left the village early the following day and took Esteban with them to have the bullet removed. As a result, the building project stopped, and a number of the Chatino believers prudently moved out into the countryside for the time being. Most thinking people in Mulaca, however, greatly respected the integrity of the believers and were impressed by the way that they did not fight back and held no grudge against those that opposed them. So when the time came to elect new village authorities later in the year, several of the well-known believers were elected to responsible positions. Among them, Armando was asked to resume his old role as village secretary. At this turn of events the large group of believers felt reassured enough to start again on their church building.

Meanwhile Neyo and Mariana had joined Nino and Marsé in Oaxaca and Nino had got a permanent job as a night-watchman in a big building supplies warehouse. Eventually he was able to acquire a piece of land at the growing edge of the city and to build a house which Neyo and Mariana shared. Tacho had been inducted as pastor of a new and struggling little Baptist congregation so his brothers and their wives and children all attended these services regularly, even though it was a long bus journey from where they lived.

With Tacho's encouragement Nino, Marsé, Neyo and Mariana all had a growing conviction that they should declare their faith publicly to the congregation and be baptised. So, after some preparation, the great day was fixed. The English couple was invited to this special event and they met the rest of the congregation on a tiny, flat piece of grass beside a stream half-way up a mountain outside the city. A little, rather ancient bus chugged

up the mountain road to bring the majority of the
congregation there from the church. It was the rainy
season again so the stream had become a raging,
red, muddy torrent. Several of the men, including
Tacho, produced spades, took off their shoes, rolled
up their trouser legs and set to work to dig a quieter
pool at the edge of the stream. This was to serve as
the baptistry. There were three other candidates for
baptism from the congregation and Tacho was quite
overcome with joy. All seven gave personal
testimony to the change in their lives when Jesus
Christ, who called Himself the Light, dispelled the
darkness for them – the darkness of fear, ignorance,
superstition and wickedness. The three city dwellers
spoke first and then Nino stumbled through in
Spanish, but Tacho translated for Neyo who broke
down several times as he confessed to his evil past
once more. Both Marsé and Mariana asked Tacho to
translate for them as well.

While this was happening, another bus full of
people arrived. It transpired that they also had come
for a baptismal service in the same place. They were
very pleased to see that their spades would be
unnecessary as the pool had been dug already. They
had a small group of guitarists with them and they
all joined in the songs of praise. Then Tacho moved
into the muddy pool and two other men stood guard
farther out in the water to catch anyone who might
stumble and be caught in the current. The seven
came forward one by one and were baptised as the
singing continued. Afterwards the pastor from the
other congregation moved forward into the water
with his assistant. Each of their four candidates,
before moving on into the water to be baptised,

stopped at the water's edge to speak of the change that Jesus Christ had made in their lives and to thank Him for His forgiveness.

Hides of plastic sheets had been hastily rigged among the bushes as changing rooms and they bulged and rustled as those who had been in the water changed into dry clothes with nervous excitement amid warm-hearted banter from outside. Then everyone from both congregations gathered together to share what they had brought for a picnic, and praised God for the opportunity to fraternise with fellow-believers on such a happy occasion. Tacho soon discovered that this was the same Pentecostal group to which Pablo and Rita belonged, and their pastor was delighted to make the acquaintance of Rita's brothers and sisters-in-law.

'Only our loving God could have arranged this!' he exclaimed.

They were all sorry that Pablo and Rita themselves had been unable to attend that day, but their pastor promised to visit them and tell them all about it. Suddenly, the fellowship and picnic were interrupted by a crack of thunder. Everyone grabbed their belongings and ran for the shelter of the vehicles as the downpour began. The bus drivers sprinted ahead, afraid that they would not be able to get the buses up the steep slope and back onto the road if all the people were inside: it was fast becoming a mud slide with water running down it. With some potentially dangerous slithering, both drivers managed it and the people all got soaked as they trudged up the slippery trail behind them. Rather bedraggled, they clambered into their respective buses on the road. Their spirits were not affected by all this, however, as it was a normal rainy season afternoon. Both busloads left with their passengers singing songs of praise and thanks to God, and they continued singing all the way back into the city.

Neyo and Mariana sought medical help while they were living in the city concerning their childlessness and the family prayed earnestly with them about the problem. They underwent various tests, but the results were never conclusive. Finally, they were reconciled to being childless and recognised that it was not necessarily a punishment from God, because He had already forgiven them for their past. This freed them to be happy together and to rejoice in their opportunities to praise and serve God. So they contentedly returned to Jaguar Mountain for a time.

In Mulaca also there had been several baptismal services and with the increased number of believers the building of the church walls had been accomplished. They now met inside it for their services even though the roof was still lacking. News came that Esteban was much better, but his leg was permanently affected and his days of tramping the mountain trails were over. Any future evangelistic trips would have to be by bus or other vehicle, so he hardly ever visited Mulaca again.

24

God's Word available

Marta continued working at the Bible school and took in lodgers to help their income. With the children growing up and various school and teenage needs to meet, finances were a constant concern, but God rewarded their trust and there was always just enough.

Nino and Marsé's children settled well in the city schools, so Marsé took a part-time job as a maid in a doctor's house in a more affluent area of the city. Nino continued in his regular night-watchman's job, so with their own house and a regular income they drifted into a comfortable and satisfactory routine. Tacho continued to visit his relatives in the Jaguar Mountain community fairly regularly, and their little fellowship thrived as he became more and more fluent in his native tongue again and was able to explain things better. Both Chico's and Frero's wives 'entered Christ's way'. So too did Dora, Tacho's stepmother, along with her daughter, Queta, and her son Lencho and his wife, Li.

'Now we will all go down to Red River and get married properly,' Chico said to the others. 'We can go to the judge there for the legal ceremony and then arrange with the pastor at Sabay and Simón's church for a multiple wedding blessing service, because we all want God to bless our families. We want other believers to know that we also are followers of Jesus Christ now.'

When Tacho returned and heard what they had done, he was delighted. He was especially pleased that they had taken the initiative, made all these arrangements and carried it through because they wanted to please God.

'We must start talking about the meaning of baptism too,' he said. 'Now that so many of you want to do what God wants you to do, it would be good for you to be baptised as a public testimony to your faith in Jesus Christ.'

'Yes,' said Chico, 'I have thought about that, especially when I heard about my brothers' baptism in Oaxaca and those other believers in Mulaca, but I wanted to wait until my wife entered the way too so that we could be baptised together. Now that we are united in every way, baptism is the next thing to do. So that's what we want.'

They discussed the significance of baptism at length and decided that they all wanted to acknowledge Jesus as their Saviour and Boss in this way. They planned it for Tacho's visit the following month, with a fiesta meal after the ceremony. They would invite Sabay and Simón that weekend too and any Mulaca relatives who might like to be present. Everyone was learning more Spanish songs now as Neyo and Mariana had brought back many new ones with them from Oaxaca, so they sang a lot in their meetings. Tacho offered to deliver an invitation to the baptismal service to Sabay and

Simón on his way home, while Lencho and one of Frero's sons were to go to Mulaca later that week to invite the people from there.

Again Tacho had a glowing report of his visit to give to all the interested parties back in Oaxaca, and he looked forward with great anticipation to his next visit to Jaguar Mountain. There was plenty to keep him busy in the city in the meantime.

Early one morning there was a persistent banging on the gate and an urgent voice calling: 'Anastasio Ruíz, Tacho, Tacho, is this your house?'

He went to the gate and found his sister Beni and her three children looking very frightened. When he got them inside Beni collapsed exhausted and in tears, while her daughter Gloria tried to explain in rather inadequate Spanish: 'When my uncle Lencho went to Mulaca to invite the people to the baptismal service he saw my father. He was very drunk and very angry and friends told Lencho that he was looking for us. Someone had told him that our relatives still lived on Jaguar Mountain, so he was looking for a riding animal to go out there. Lencho just talked to Armando and one or two others, then left Frero's son, Po, to finish inviting people to the baptism while he galloped back to warn us. My mother was very afraid of what he might do if he found us, so that's why we packed a few clothes quickly and fled in the night down to Red River to Sabay's house. We couldn't stay with them for long because their house is so small, so last night we caught the bus to Oaxaca and now we have found you, finally!'

Over the years, Tacho and Marta had managed to build a second storey onto their house and let the rooms out to students at the Bible school while their own growing family occupied the ground floor. Tacho used the old office as his study and the occasional unexpected visitor occupied the bed that was still there. The old tool room next to it had become the laundry room, but they never had sufficient funds to start another building on the adjoining plot. One of the rooms upstairs was free at that time, so they installed Beni and her family there temporarily, although another student had already booked that room and would arrive in two months' time.

At the church on Sunday Tacho briefly told the congregation of his sister's plight. They took up a collection for the refugees then and there, and continued to help them with little gifts of money and food in the weeks and months to come. Marta had inherited a property nearby with a half-finished building on it. There was a big garage area on the ground floor with two flats above. No windows had been put in as yet, and there was no plaster on the brick walls, no floor in the garage and no doors except in the external walls. They had been letting it out as a workshop, but when it became vacant again at the end of the month, Beni and children moved there in spite of the lack of facilities. Tacho's congregation helped, and so did the nearby congregation at the church next to the Bible school. They gave odd bits of furniture and bedding as well as food and money. They found a cleaning job for Beni at a factory and her daughter Gloria was able to get a part-time job as a housemaid while she continued her schooling.

Tacho returned to Jaguar Mountain accompanied by Nino for a very joyful baptismal service, which was a great encouragement to them all and a thought-provoking challenge to some of the visitors. He learnt that Gloria's father had indeed been there in search of his children and their mother. He had issued all kinds of dire threats and it had been very hard to get rid of him without lying. This experience had really tested their new Christian faith: he had been contemptuous and cynical when they told him of their allegiance to Jesus Christ and had cursed them to their faces. He was sure that they were hiding Beni from him and threatened to return regularly till he found her. They decided regretfully that Tacho should not visit them again for a few months in case his presence gave the man a clue as to Beni's whereabouts.

One day that summer the English couple arrived at Tacho's house with the first copy of the West Highland Chatino New Testament. Tacho was ecstatic and immediately ordered a copy for himself.

'I've been practising and I can read Chatino much better now,' he said. 'I remember much more and can speak it much more fluently now as well. My brothers and their families really don't understand Spanish very well at all. Can you bring a boxful of these New Testaments to the church next Sunday? We will have a separate Sunday school class for the Chatino people there and use this New Testament.'

That Sunday service was a most rewarding experience for the translators as Tacho thanked God for the coming of His Word written in the heart language of the Chatino people. Then he asked Marsé to pray and thank God in her own language.

The congregation broke up into classes with Marta teaching the Spanish-speaking adults, their daughter María and her young man teaching the children's classes, while Tacho and the English couple had a Bible study in the Letter to the Ephesians with the Chatinos. Neyo and Mariana had returned for a few weeks and were staying with Nino's family again, so, together with Beni, Gloria and another visiting relative from Mulaca who had recently become a believer, there was a good class. The discovery that they could speak to God in their own language, and that God's Word was now in their mother tongue as well, was exciting for everyone. Discussion of the passage was animated and the application to themselves immediate, but all found that they would need to apply themselves and practise in order to read the Chatino fluently. This was a little hard to take as they had expected instant ability. The English couple pointed out that even Spanish-speakers had to take time to learn to read their own language, but the sharp disappointment remained. Neyo's ability to read Spanish was abysmal, as his opportunity for schooling had been so sketchy, but he had expected to read his own language without effort and was very discouraged that he could not.

The following year when the English couple was available more often, the Chatino class continued regularly and worked through John's Gospel. Much of it was a revelation to the participants even though they had been believers now for several years. Tacho himself asked for private reading tutorials and became animated and enthusiastic as his accuracy and fluency improved by leaps and bounds. Even he marvelled at the new insight that he gained as he read God's Word in Chatino.

Through the gifts and help of relatives and friends, Beni was able to acquire a tiny plot of land next to Nino's to build her own small dwelling. When she had gathered her basic materials together, Tacho's entire congregation went over for the day to help erect the house. Several other Chatinos had fled to the city from Mulaca because of the trouble and murder threats, and they had come to Nino for help as a fellow villager. As a result, a small Chatino enclave had developed in this one area at the edge of the city. With Tacho's encouragement, Nino and Marsé decided to open their home to their neighbours for regular Christian meetings conducted mainly in Chatino. This saved them a long bus journey to Tacho's church on the other side of the city.

One day Nino said to the Englishman: 'You know that I was one of the first to buy a Chatino New Testament, but when I saw that it was hard for me to read it, I put it away on a high shelf in my house. Many months later I saw it up there gathering dust and I thought: "That book is God's Word in my language. How is it that I can't read it? Surely God will help me if I try and ask for His help." So I took it down and carried it to work with me because I have a lot of spare hours as night-watchman in between my regular checks all round the property. I began to study it every night and soon found that I could follow along quite easily at our Sunday classes.'

A few weeks later the Englishman noticed that Nino's Chatino New Testament was now well marked with coloured crayons.

'So you still read your New Testament quite a lot,' he remarked.

'Oh yes,' Nino replied with a happy grin. 'I'm really learning a lot more than I ever understood before. It took a bit of practice and concentration to learn to read the Chatino, but now I read it all the time and it helps me to understand some of the Spanish too. I really enjoy reading it in the night by myself and God has started speaking to me from it. I think He wants me to return to Mulaca with my family as a missionary to my own people, so I am going to study part-time at the Bible school for these next two years in preparation.'

María had continued to be an encouragement to her parents. She started work as a secretary in a small office and soon she and Lucas, the young man who helped to teach the Sunday school children, came to tell Tacho and Marta that they wanted to get married. Lucas was apprenticed to a garage mechanic and knew that he could not yet support a wife, but they were willing to wait for eighteen months for their wedding. Tacho and Marta were very happy at the prospect of welcoming Lucas into the family and advised the young couple to both start bank accounts and save all that they could from their wages. Lucas' mother was a widow and she too was very pleased at her only son's choice of a bride. She greatly enjoyed getting to know María better as the months went by and was especially glad that Lucas had chosen a Christian girl. She herself attended the church next to the Bible school, so she already knew María's whole family. They decided that the wedding should be held at her church, as there was a large hall nearby for the reception. So they started making plans.

The year and a half soon passed and they were down to counting the days. Marta could hardly believe that more than eighteen years had passed since María's birth and yet so much had happened in that time. Some events had been painful or shocking and the pains and shocks had not stopped when they became Christ's followers, but they had been granted unusual strength, courage and wisdom to cope with such trauma since then. With just weeks to go to María's wedding day, a phone call had come from Toño who now lived in another part of the city where he worked for a Oaxaca radio station.

'The girl that I have been living with for the past six months got pregnant,' he told his parents baldly, 'so we went to the registry office this morning and got married. I will bring my wife to meet you next weekend if you like, and yes, we will attend María's wedding. She may be older and cleverer than I am, but I stole the march on her this time and we will be the first to present you with a grandchild, and that before Christmas!'

Marta was severely shocked by the news but managed to rally enough to reply weakly: 'It's good to hear from you at last, Toño. We really look forward to meeting your wife, son, but I have to admit that I am very disappointed not to have had anything to do with your wedding, or even been present for it. Your father will feel that too as you are our eldest son and we wanted to do something special for you. He had hoped to have the honour of performing the ceremony in his church and giving you his blessing publicly, but we will be delighted to welcome our new daughter-in-law.'

'Yes, well, we didn't feel the need of any church ceremony, mama,' Toño replied offhandedly. 'After all, we have established a home already. I'll bring Elena with me next Saturday and we will talk more then. Bye.'

Cándido and Rosa helped to lighten the rather formal atmosphere when Toño brought Elena home the following Saturday. Tacho certainly had been devastated by the news when Marta told him of her phone conversation with Toño. But, after praying about the matter together, both Tacho and Marta had found a new peace in their sore hearts as they faced the fact that their older children were now adults and quite prepared to make their own decisions, whether good or bad.

Then María's wedding day was upon them and the church was filled to capacity. Many could not get in but stood at the open doors and windows. All of the young couple's friends and relatives had been invited as well as the entire congregation from each of the two small churches, and it was a very happy occasion. The radiant bride appeared on the arm of her father and the bridegroom had eyes for no one else. They repeated the solemn vows in clear voices and obviously meant their sincere promises to each other before God.

The Jaguar Mountain contingent had come in force and had picked up Sabay and Simón with their children along the way. Rita and Pablo had brought their children too, so it was a grand reunion for Tacho's family and a time when they could thank God together for His goodness to them all and for

His patience with them. It was wonderful to be united in God's family as believers as well as by blood ties. The children happily set about getting to know each other as cousins and their wild excitement mounted as they pooled ideas for new games.

The young couple had worked hard to finish off and improve the flat above the garage where Beni and her children had taken refuge before they had their own home. Lucas would use the garage space below to house his own old banger and to do any small mechanical jobs that he could for their neighbours in his spare time. María would continue her work in the office for the present as well as be a homemaker, while together they would carry on their work with the children in the church.

After all the excitement Tacho resumed regular visits to Jaguar Mountain. Soon he was asking the English couple: 'Can't we translate some Christian songs into Chatino?'

'Yes. Actually, there are one or two Chatino songs already,' the man replied. 'There is one that we translated from Spanish in the middle of the night! Once when we visited Mulaca we stayed with the leader of the believers there. He and I worked it out from our beds while everyone else was asleep. And then he introduced it to the whole congregation in the service the next day. There is also a short one that Esteban composed which is an original Chatino chorus with its own tune to thank God for His provision for us. We sing it at mealtimes occasionally. There are a couple of other choruses like that, plus one that thanks God for His Word in our own languages.'

Tacho got very excited when he heard this and wanted the Englishman to make a cassette of these songs and to teach them to the people who met together at Nino's house. They were soon singing them lustily, delighted to really understand what they were singing about, and they asked for more. Neyo and Mariana were back in Oaxaca briefly and Tacho told the Englishman that Neyo only wanted to play his guitar and sing to praise God now. The Englishman marvelled at God's arrangements and perfect timing because he knew that a songwriters' workshop was planned for the following month to encourage local believers to produce songs in their own languages. He invited Neyo and Mariana to attend.

The workshop proved to be a stimulating two weeks with participants from ten different language groups. There were combined classes in the mornings conducted in the national language, and in the afternoons each language group worked in its own language. The guitar classes were graded from beginners in grade one to very accomplished guitarists in grade five. Neyo joined the grade three group and Mariana was thrilled to be loaned a guitar and put in the beginners' class, as she had never been allowed to touch her husband's guitar. After an hour of strumming, everyone met together for a very basic music-theory class exploring rhythm and timing as well as different kinds of notes and scales.

Later on that first day they all learnt a new but very simple Spanish chorus with an uncomplicated guitar accompaniment. The homework for that afternoon was for each language group to translate that same chorus into its own language. Each group was assigned one of the guitar teachers to help with the music, while a linguist–translator worked with each group to check on the theological content, the timing and the beat, so that each syllable had a note of the tune and stressed syllables fell on stressed notes. For tone languages there was the added problem of a syllable pronounced on a high tone needing to fall on a higher note than a syllable with a low tone. The next morning excitement and tension were high as each group presented its new song to the whole class. After that first presentation it dawned on everyone that they really could praise God in their own mother tongue and the enthusiasm mounted. Their new assignment for the second day was to translate another Spanish song of their own choosing. In succeeding days they progressed to putting their own words to a known tune, then to making a ballad-type song with an original tune which told a Bible story, and so to setting a Bible verse to original music.

One day they had a class on songs for children and how to teach them, and that day each group produced an original children's chorus. This happened to be the day that Tacho turned up on a surprise visit. He was so intrigued by the whole concept of a songwriters' workshop for indigenous musicians that he just could not keep away! He was truly amazed at what Neyo and Mariana had already produced and was an inspiration to everyone as he enthusiastically joined in with the production of the children's song after listening to the morning lecture with rapt attention. A very jolly little tune resulted, with easily repeated actions and words. This drew prolonged applause from the whole class when it was presented by the Chatino group the following day. Finally, each group's new songs were recorded on a master cassette with high quality equipment and accompanied by their guitar teacher. They produced a booklet of the words to go along with the cassette and there was the opportunity to make copies of both.

About this time they learnt more about the groups of believers in the eastern region of the Chatino area. Their speech was rather different and a separate New Testament translation was being prepared for them. What caught the attention of Tacho and his brothers, however, was that God had given those people a songwriter. Neyo was fascinated by the story of a believer who was blind and whose wife had deserted him and left him helpless. This man did not blame God for his misfortunes but prayed earnestly that he would be helped to praise God whatever his circumstances. Shortly afterwards the blind man awoke one morning humming a tune, and the Chatino words to it popped into his head. So he started to sing them and found that he was praising God. Since then God had given him many Christian songs, all original and with original tunes. A friend in his congregation picked out the tune on his guitar from the man's singing and then accompanied him. The local Bible translator got the songs written down, and made a songbook to go with a cassette of the composer singing his songs accompanied by his friend the guitarist. The blind man then visited other congregations in the area and taught them to sing the new songs. He told the people in other villages: 'Now, if you don't say things in quite the same way that we do, just alter the words to the way that you speak, so that we can all praise God together from our hearts in words that we really understand.'

Hearing all this inspired Neyo to listen carefully to the cassettes of this blind believer singing his songs. He liked the tunes and where he did not understand the words in this other brand of Chatino, he improvised as the man had suggested. Thus, the West Highland Chatino song repertoire grew steadily with this local help.

The group at Nino's house quickly learned Neyo's new songs. Then Neyo himself returned with Mariana to Jaguar Mountain and taught the believers there to sing them as well as the new ones that he culled from the blind composer's cassettes. All this inspired him to practise reading more and, by dint of diligent effort for some months, he became able to read fluently and with real expression as he understood more and more. As a result, both he and his wife grew steadily in their knowledge and understanding of 'Christ's way' and became really good representatives of their Boss, Jesus.

Nino's two years at the Bible school passed rapidly and he was commissioned as a Baptist missionary together with his wife, Marsé. They had been planning ahead and Nino had already made a trip to Mulaca to contact relatives there and some old friends among the believers. He had secured permission to build a permanent house on what was the old family plot and had set about gathering building materials together. Now he finally gave in his notice as night-watchman and went to Mulaca to build his house. He deliberately made the main room extra big so that they could hold meetings there. He also made arrangements for his children to be registered in the local schools for the coming year. Tacho helped him for a day or two and then returned to the city with the news that all was going well. When all was ready, Nino hired a lorry from a Mulaca resident and returned to the city to move his family and belongings out to their new home. Plastering, painting and other jobs continued on the house after the family had moved in, but they were soon happily settled. Even the younger children seemed very aware that they were there as God's messengers.

The family prayed and sang in their own language and Nino read and taught from the Chatino New Testament, so several other people began to ask questions. Tacho visited them frequently and he read and preached in Chatino too. The big group of believers in the village had finally completed the roof of their church. It was a beautiful big building on the river-bank with modern loudspeaker equipment and musical instruments, but they still used the Spanish Bible and usually sang and prayed in Spanish, although much of the preaching was in Chatino.

The autumn rains were very severe that year and as the people were preparing for bed one night they were aware of a terrible storm brewing. The 'rain-wind' began, a downpour of almost horizontal rain slashing into everything because of the mighty wind driving it. The river began to rise, trees were uprooted by the wind and crashed down the mountainsides; with all the noise of the hurricane most people were afraid to go to bed. Many whose homes were on the lower street by the river-bank were evacuated to the homes of relatives higher up in the centre of the village. Suddenly there was an ominous roar in the distance ending in a dull crash. People began to notice that in spite of the continuing heavy rain the muddy water in the river was going down! This seemed inexplicable, but the strange phenomenon thoroughly frightened most of the remaining riverside dwellers, so they frantically started seeking refuge for their families and belongings higher up in the village. Three or four hours later the wind had dropped but the steady rain continued to fall. People became aware of a dreadful noise that grew louder and louder. Suddenly a great wall of water, mud, rocks, trees and other debris swept down the river carrying away everything in its path, including many houses and the big, new, brick and concrete church that Esteban had helped to build. A few elderly people who had refused to panic and move from their homes earlier were swept away, along with one young mother who rushed back to rescue her baby after carrying her small son to safety. From the bank he saw his mother and baby sister knocked over in the flood, so screaming in terror he leapt into the water to follow her and all three were lost.

Another mother from among the believers had left an older child to look after two very sleepy little ones in their home on the other side of the river. She and her husband had taken the rest of their family to visit relatives in the village to help in a work project. When she heard that people were moving up from their riverside houses she was afraid that her own home would be flooded too, so she rushed back there with her baby on her back.

She and the older child feverishly threw their belongings together and carried them to higher ground. Then, seeing that the river was now very shallow, she roused the sleeping children and decided to return to the rest of the family. When they got to the water's edge she could hear the distant roar so she told the older child to run on ahead and get help, then she started across with the three little ones. Before they could climb the bank on the other side the wave caught them and all four were washed away in full view of her husband and older children as they came running down to the riverside to help.

In the morning light the devastation was plain. Hurricane Pauline had wrought havoc throughout the area. Bridges and buildings had been swept away in the floods; avalanches, mud slides and land-slips blocked the roads; millions of trees had been torn up by the roots or their crowns had been snapped off so that only a bare pole of the trunk was left standing. Whole trees and branches littered the mountainsides and the coastal area. In the seaside town, cars and small boats had been picked up like toys and tossed about by the wind so that they landed in the middle of roads, on flat roofs or in people's gardens, damaged beyond repair. Telephone and power cables were down and inextricably tangled up together or festooning those trees that were still standing, so there was no communication with the state capital or anywhere else. It was the same at Tutula, Red River and the other towns in the area. Mulaca, however, was one of a number of isolated villages where a satellite phone had been installed in recent years and these still worked. They

were able therefore to report on the situation to the
state authorities. The Mulaca telephonist was
besieged with calls from frantic relatives living in
Oaxaca City or elsewhere in the country.

The state authorities promptly sent helicopters
to investigate the extent of the damage and to take
emergency aid to the stricken towns and villages.
The army was brought in to help restore communi-
cations by clearing the main roads so that relief aid
could be brought by land. They also helped dig in
the ruins to rescue whomever and whatever they
could. The death toll throughout the area was
comparatively small, but there were many injured
and the problem of supplying the victims with clean
water, food, clothing, medical aid and shelter was
immense. Military helicopters worked from first
light until dusk.

The country's contingency plans were put into
effective operation, including radio and television
appeals for clothing, non-perishable food, bottled
water, blankets, medicines, etc. The response all over
the country was tremendous and supplies were
collected and processed by the Red Cross and other
agencies in the inland cities. Ordinary people and
small businesses were wonderfully generous as
well as all those who could afford to be; the first
big, rough-road lorries were soon loaded up with
individual emergency ration packs that were prepared from the donations. They moved up the
approach roads as far as they could and distribution
began. Able-bodied people from the stricken area
were encouraged to walk out to the lorries if possible
so that the helicopters could serve the most distant
and isolated places, and also ferry in medical

teams. The army engineers worked round the clock
to put in temporary bridges and the roadmen
operating earth-moving equipment were equally
zealous, so the lorry-loads of relief supplies moved
forward many miles through the mountains each
day. In the towns, electricians, firemen and
telephone technicians tackled the horrendous task
of re-establishing power and telephone lines, but
everyone recognised that the top priority was to get
the mains water supply back into operation,
preferably uncontaminated. Constant warnings
about contamination were given by every means
possible, which for a day or two meant chiefly
posters on walls and someone announcing a
warning through a megaphone on street corners:
'Drink only bottled water or boil your water for
several minutes. It is dangerous to drink "raw"
water. Keep a watch on your children so that they
do not drink contaminated water.'

After a few days people began to arrive from
other countries to help too. Skilled medical
personnel and other professionals came, and later
many great lorries of relief aid were driven from
Guatemala, Canada and the United States.

As soon as the road system was cleared enough
for a vehicle to get through, Nino and a friend set
off from Mulaca for Oaxaca City. They went to see
Tacho and then together they went to the Red Cross
depot. They were told that if they could hire a lorry
they would be allocated a load of individual
emergency ration packs called 'dispensers'. Through
Christian contacts they were loaned a lorry and
some city evangelicals gave money for the petrol
too. The trip back to Mulaca over the very rough

road surface took many hours, but with God's help they arrived safely and began distributing their load. They served widows and orphans first, then the rest of the destitute families, without considering any affiliation they might have. The village council was very impressed that they were so impartial and not just looking after their own families and their church group. Some unscrupulous traders were taking advantage of the situation by selling necessary items like soap at very inflated prices, which was causing a lot of hardship. As soon as the distribution was completed Nino and his friend returned to the city with a careful list of the destitute and of those who had received dispensers, and another list of the things that the village particularly lacked. The Red Cross gave Nino a second load immediately, which was gratefully received in the village. They made yet another trip the following week and the Red Cross gave them money to buy building materials for quick, makeshift shelters. Nino knew exactly where to go to buy these materials because of his experience as night-watchman at the big warehouse. When they got back with this load people eagerly set to work because they had been greatly encouraged by all this evidence that people far away cared what happened to them. They started to think positively about the future and remaking their lives.

As the roads became more usable again, more government and other aid arrived to rebuild the damaged primary school and other public buildings and to deliver more long-term supplies. The people remembered, however, how Nino and his friend had taken the initiative and got aid for them at the most difficult time when the journey was still very hazardous. In the past some of them had been quite opposed to him and to his message concerning the Good News of Jesus Christ, but now they were asking thoughtful questions. Why was he willing to risk his own life to help people in need, including even those who had been unkind to him and his family? He replied that he wanted to do what Jesus would do and invited them to study the Bible with him to find out what Jesus had to say to people in this world. So his little congregation grew.

With their church building gone, the bigger group of believers split into three: those who wanted to hear and use only Spanish met with Armando in his house; another group met with the pastor in a different section of the village in the biggest house available there; the third group met with another of their leaders in yet another part of the village where a believer had a large house. The pastor tried to keep in touch with all three groups as they hoped to be together in one building again some day. It took them a long time to recover from the shock of their losses and their sadness, so that they could really praise God wholeheartedly again.

Opposition was always there in one form or another, but gradually the faith of the believers deepened as they increasingly relied on God Himself. Those who listened to the cassettes of readings from the New Testament began to learn more of God's truth along with those who read His Word for themselves. They became strong and serene as they were released from the terrible fears that had hung over them all of their lives.

Nino and Marsé are well integrated into Mulaca society now. Tacho continues to divide his time between his small church in Oaxaca City and missionary visits to Mulaca and Jaguar Mountain. God is at work among these Chatino people and the stark fear that has haunted them for more than two millennia is being dispelled by the knowledge of Jesus Christ who is the Light.

Distinctives

Vaughan Roberts

ISBN 1–85078–331–4

In a fresh and readable style, the author of *Turning Points*, Vaughan Roberts, issues a challenging call to Christians to live out their faith. We should be different from the world around us – Christian distinctives should set us apart in how we live, think, act and speak. Targeting difficult but crucial areas such as our attitude to money and possessions, sexuality, contentment, relativism and service, this is holiness in the tradition of J.C. Ryle for the contemporary generation.

VAUGHAN ROBERTS is rector of St Ebbe's Church, Oxford. He is a popular conference speaker and University Christian Union speaker.

OM
publishing

Out of the Comfort Zone

GEORGE VERWER

ISBN 1–85078–353–5

Reading this book could seriously change your attitude!
George Verwer has managed to write a book that is humble
and hard-hitting at the same time. He doesn't pull any
punches in his heart's cry for a 'grace-awakened' approach
to mission, and wants to cut through superficial
'spirituality' that may be lurking inside you. George Verwer
is known throughout the world as a motivator and
mobiliser. *Out of the Comfort Zone* should only be read by
those who are willing to accept God's grace, catch His
vision and respond with action in the world of mission.

OM
publishing

The George Verwer Collection

ISBN 1–85078–296–2

George Verwer has inspired and encouraged thousands in their Christian discipleship. Now three of his best-loved books, *The Revolution of Love*, *No Turning Back* and *Hunger For Reality* are brought together in this three-in-one collection. The trilogy points us to love as the central theme of Christian life, calls us to effective service and revolutionizes our lives so that they are consistent and productive.

> 'Immensely readable and full of the practical aspects of spiritual principles.'
>
> *Evangelism Today*

> 'A wealth of good material.'
>
> Martin Goldsmith
> *Church of England Newspaper*

Over 100,000 copies sold.

GEORGE VERWER is the founder and International Director of Operation Mobilisation. He has an international preaching ministry based in Britain.

OM
publishing

Future Leader

Viv Thomas

ISBN 0–85364–949–9

Leadership is a key to success in any organisation.

All the more reason to get it right, says Viv Thomas in a book that sets out to discern the kind of leadership that is needed as we enter a new millennium.

Drawing on biblical models and organisational management research, along with personal experience of some of the evangelical world's most influential leaders, the author provides a model of leadership that is:

- Driven by compassion, not obsession.
- Rooted in relationships, not systems.
- Promotes life, not self-image.

If we fail in these areas, he argues, most of what we do in terms of goals, strategies, skills, mission and communication will eventually be blown away.

This stimulating and inspiring book will test all who might aspire to lead.

VIV THOMAS is the International Co-ordinator of Leadership Development with Operation Mobilisation. He has a world-wide preaching and teaching ministry, with an emphasis on developing leaders. He is also a visiting lecturer at All Nations Christian College in Hertfordshire.

paternoster
press

Fire Within

Woo Yung

1-85078-355-1

In this moving autobiography of Wu Yung, leader of the church in Taiwan, his personal experiences of faith in God provide the reader with valuable insights into effective church witness and itinerant world-wide ministry.

OM
publishing